Cabin Crew Conflict

Cabin Crew Conflict

The British Airways Dispute 2009–11

Phil Taylor and Sian Moore
with Robert Byford

Foreword by Len McCluskey
Preface by Duncan Holley

With an Afterword by John Hendy QC

PLUTO PRESS

First published 2019 by Pluto Press
345 Archway Road, London N6 5AA

www.plutobooks.com

British Library Cataloguing in Publication Data
A catalogue record for this book is available from the British Library

ISBN   978 0 7453 3991 7   Hardback
ISBN   978 1 7868 0489 1   PDF eBook
ISBN   978 1 7868 0491 4   Kindle eBook
ISBN   978 1 7868 0490 7   EPUB eBook

Typeset by Stanford DTP Services, Northampton, England

Simultaneously printed in the United Kingdom and United States of America

Sometimes in life you have to stand up and be counted. To stand by others, even when you know there will be cost in doing so. This book is dedicated to those who did exactly that.

Contents

Photographs

Acknowledgements

The authors owe a major debt of gratitude to the cabin crew respondents, who so generously gave their time to be interviewed in the midst of taxing work rosters and, often, demanding domestic commitments. BASSA officers were unanimously supportive of the book project, helping us to gain access to the crew. In this respect, acknowledgement is due also to the moderators of the Cabin Crew Forum who posted our requests for interview volunteers. Given that so many individuals helped to make this book a reality it might seem invidious to single out individuals, but Louise and Duncan Holley deserve special mention. On a flight to Newark in March 2010 Phil met Louise when travelling to the International Labour Process Conference at Rutgers University, and she explained the importance of the threat to cabin crew and to BASSA. Phil initiated the letter to the *Guardian* at that conference that was eventually signed by more than 200 employment relations academics. Through that initiative the path to the book was laid.

Phil and Sian are indebted to Jane Hardy, Geraint Harvey and an anonymous third reviewer for their observations on an advanced draft, and to Andrew Smith, Tracy Walsh and Mike Richardson for their views on an earlier draft. Nicky Marcus, Duncan Holley and Adrian Smith made critical comments that contributed to the final shape of the book. Dave Lyddon made helpful recommendations on relevant literature on strikes and Andy Clark did similarly for work on oral history methods. Finally, thanks are due to Anisha Badshah and Edie Parry for their tremendous work on the index.

Foreword

Len McCluskey

By the time I officially became general secretary of Unite, the BA–BASSA dispute was well into its second year, but I was already very familiar with its origins and dynamics, having sat in on many of the negotiations between the two sides held under the auspices of the TUC and ACAS. Over those early, tempestuous days in 2010 I got to know the BASSA reps and committee well and could see right from the start these people had a genuine grievance towards a company that was not only attempting to ride roughshod over their terms and agreements but was also looking, so it seemed, to try and annihilate the union itself.

Despite the picture British Airways attempted to paint of a group of dysfunctional representatives who were out of control, I found them all to be the exact opposite: very functional, very organised, very determined, intelligent and very much in touch with the membership who reciprocated by placing their utmost trust in them. There is a time to fight, but there is also a time to be pragmatic, and it was reassuring to discover that BASSA were prepared and capable of doing both. They were not militants as BA would have the media believe, they were not rebel rousers or politically motivated but they knew what was right and wrong and were prepared to stand up and be counted.

The BASSA committee in particular were a formidable united force. Lizanne Malone (the chair) and Duncan Holley (the secretary) worked well together and as neither were 'shrinking violets' they provided BASSA with the firm leadership so important in times of siege. The membership were diverse and disparate, but through the tireless work of all the BASSA reps the relationship between them was solid as a rock, an essential ingredient in any dispute. Both Lizanne and Duncan were indebted to Nigel Stott, the worldwide convenor, who they regarded as being the shrewdest tactician and negotiator of any union and I can only agree 100 per cent with their sentiments. Ably supported by Chris Harrison, Nigel was a match for any manager and he also had that priceless knack of being able to articulate complex issues in layman's terms to branch meetings that were attended by literally thousands of members at any one time. Duncan, Lizanne, Nigel and Chris made a strong team – I recognised that and I was happy to join them and give them my support from the outset.

For disputes to be successful – and believe me this dispute was successful – the union must have the trust of its membership and be able to communicate and thanks to the committee and the representatives BASSA had the total trust of the community while totally out-communicating BA.

This dispute of 2009–11 – as acrimonious at it was – has been compared with the miners' dispute, and in its own way I can see why. This was a bloody feud that was about so much more than crewing levels or wage restructuring. This was a conflict that went to the very heart of what industrial relations between workers and managers were becoming. BA were ruthlessly trying to remove the one obstacle they had to achieving a total dominance over its workforce, and the fact that BASSA and its members were able to resist such a sustained assault is an achievement that deserves to be regarded as one of the union movement's finest hours in this country. This has duly been recognised by Sian Moore and Phil Taylor in the fact they have spent the time they have producing the body of work you currently hold in your hands.

The reps will tell you, though, that without the strength and bravery of the membership nothing would have been achieved, and they are correct. At Bedfont in particular, I met and spoke to as many striking crew as I could and to a man and woman they impressed me with their integrity and resolution. Many were enduring financial hardship because of the staff travel ban, plenty had been disciplined and some even sacked, but I was immediately impressed by how determined they all were to see this dispute through to the bitter end. The atmosphere at Bedfont was remarkable and uplifting and to someone who has had a lifetime being involved in all levels of the union movement, a joy to behold. Camaraderie and pride were there in abundance; it warmed the heart, stoked the engines and created faith for the future. Taking industrial action is no laughing matter, but the good humour and dignity displayed by all the crew I met made me wonder on many occasions why this valuable community was under attack by their employer. It really did not make sense, but as I came to learn, not a lot did make sense with BA and its attitude to industrial relations.

Turning the pages of this book and reading the thoughts and opinions from those who spoke to Sian and Phil, it all comes flooding back. I am so pleased it is all down in writing. I am so gratified the crew kept their faith in Unite and I am so elated that they were ultimately rewarded for showing that faith. Nothing is forever, as we trade unionists know only too well, and many of those who took industrial action have since left BA. I have heard so many say that going on strike was one of their proudest ever moments, and one they will hold dear for the rest of their days. This book is a celebration of their achievements and I am just glad I was able to play some sort of role in the story and its outcome. Quite frankly, it was a privilege.

Len McCluskey has been general secretary of Unite the Union since January 2011

Preface

Duncan Holley

In one of the darkest days during the dispute (and there were some very dark days), when it seemed the whole world including the government, the opposition, the courts, the media, elements within the police and even parts of our own union were against us, there suddenly appeared a beacon of light that shone through the gloom.

A letter appeared in *The Guardian* from a bunch of academics that actually stood up for the striking British Airways (BA) cabin crew and outlined why we were right to do what we were doing and how we, as trade unionists, were being victimised by the country at large. Then, I knew none of these academics but I wanted to hug and kiss each one individually because they gave me back my self-belief and confidence that what the British Airlines Stewards and Stewardesses Association (BASSA) and our membership was doing was justified and worthwhile, and that we had support out there.

Anyone who has taken industrial action – or even tried to in modern-day Britain – will know just how heavily the odds are stacked against withdrawing their labour. Yes, maybe the pendulum needed to swing away from excessive union power in the 1970s, but with Mrs Thatcher pulling with all her might the pendulum has swung far too far, and as things stand today union rights lie in comparative tatters, with Tory boot boys – descendants from the Chingford skinhead, Norman Tebbit – polishing their boots, preparing to apply another kicking.

We survived our dispute virtually intact; give or take a few dismissals (of which I was one), we emerged the other side with our terms and conditions protected, our travel concessions restored, but much more importantly with our dignity and honour preserved. That was a massive achievement in itself, but there is no doubt the industrial action, which lasted longer than the miners' dispute, like theirs caused splits and scars that will take years to heal. Non-strikers (and in particular pilots who trained as cabin crew) will never be forgiven, at least not by me!

We know now what some of us feared then: this was not a strike about establishing an alternative workforce or removing a purser[1] from a 747, this was a dispute that was engineered by BA to bring about the end of a trade union that had long been a thorn in its side, a union that had over the years fought tooth and nail to protect the terms and conditions of a workforce that by and large were prepared to stand by their union. British Airways failed in that respect: BASSA is still alive and very much kicking, and – what is most important, and something to be taken on board by our national airline – remains trusted far more by the employees.

One of BA's main objectives over the first decade of this century was to alter its philosophy towards industrial relations. The outbreak of the dispute in 2009 showed we failed in that aim, but I like to think that by 2011, with the members and their union showing no signs of giving in, BA suddenly came to their senses. Aviation is a cut-throat business – the union recognised and recognises this – but BA now know that if the first throat they try and cut is one of its cabin crew then the lambs will not go quietly to the slaughter.

I remain proud of what I did during the dispute, I am proud of what the union did, but most of all I am proud of what the members did.

Duncan Holley was branch secretary of BASSA from May 1998 to June 2012

Timeline

2008

16 May   BA announces profits of £883 million, up 45%.

20 June   Project Columbus announced.

2009

28 January   BA remove crew member from routes entitled to an extra crew member

11 February   Willie Walsh's pay increases by 34% over 2005–8.

24 February   BA announce crew expected to make savings of £82 million.

June   Just over 1,000 BA employees accept voluntary redundancy.

6 October   BA announces 1,700 cabin crew job cuts and pay freeze.

30 October   Unite issues legal challenge to BA over changes to contracts including crewing levels.

2 November   BASSA branch meeting Sandown; Len McCluskey reiterates Unite support for BASSA. Meeting backs call for a ballot for industrial action.

5 November   A High Court Judge rules cabin crew have a legitimate claim against BA for breach of contract and case will be heard in full on 1 February 2010.

7 November   Unite announces ballot to be held between 16 November and 14 December.

16 November   BA impose the removal of a crew member on long-haul flights going against agreed crew complements.

14 December   Branch meeting of 2,000 at Sandown announces ballot result: 92% in favour of strike action on a 93% turnout – 12 days of strikes over the Christmas period announced.

15 December   Unite receive a letter attempting to injunct strike action.

17 December   High Court denies BA cabin crew the right to strike. Unite announce decision to reballot. Duncan Holley refused regular release for union duties and is charged with gross misconduct for refusing to be rostered.

2010

18 January	Unite announces fresh ballot. BA writes to all staff asking for volunteers to cover for cabin crew during any industrial action.
24 January	Unite warn BALPA (the Pilot's union) that it is unacceptable for it to take a neutral stance in the dispute when pilots are being recruited as volunteers to break the strike.
31 January	BA establish graffiti board for employees to write comments backing BA.
11 February	BA lawyers try to force Unite to disclose the names of 32 individuals posting on the BASSA Forum. 15 cabin crew members (the Facebook 15) suspended for 'bullying and harassment' and breaches of data protection.
19 February	High Court rules in BA's favour over changes in contracts including crewing levels.
22 February	Ballot result: 80% in favour of strike action on an 80% turnout.
28 February	BA train volunteers to replace striking crew.
10 March	BA formally reject Unites formal offer following talks. Industrial action now inevitable.
12 March	Strike dates announced: 20–22 and 27–30 March .
15 March	Prime Minister Gordon Brown describes planned strikes as 'deplorable' and says they should be called off.
19 March	Meeting at Sandown; 1,500 members turn up.
20 March	First day of three-day strike – BA fly one-third of normal operation. BA withdraw staff travel concessions.
15 April	50 BASSA members suspended so far.
27 April	Failure of talks over staff travel and disciplinary hearings – union announce ballot on latest offer with recommendation to reject.
6 May	Duncan Holley, BASSA branch secretary, is sacked.
7 May	BASSA overwhelmingly reject BA offer – 81% vote no.
10 May	New strike dates announced: 18–22 May; 24–8 May; 30–31 May; 1–3 June; 5–9 June.
17 May	BA get injunction to halt further industrial action.
19 May	BASSA organise lobby of BA's investors through an open-top bus meeting.
20 May	Unite win appeal against injunction granted to BA. Strike days go ahead.

21–23 May	BA announces significant losses – Unite offer to suspend the strike.
24 May	Strike action begins – cabin crew launch a five-day walkout.
9 June	Strikes end, Unite expects to announce new ballot for further action.
22 June	Unite announce three new areas will be balloted on 29 June: full reinstatement of staff travel; withdrawal of unwarranted disciplinary procedures; companies continued disregard of collective agreement.
24 June	Mixed Fleet a reality.
25 June	Derek Simpson meets BA with ACAS, amended proposal put forward to the union for consideration.
27 June	Unite cannot recommend deal to members as it does not reinstate staff travel.
29 June	Branch meeting cancelled. BA refuse to de-roster reps. Postal vote to be issued on whether to accept or reject deal.
20 July	67% of cabin crew reject offer.
31 July	80 cabin crew suspended and 13 sacked because of incidents related to the dispute.
6 August	BASSA representative Nicky Marcus suspended.
6 September	Quarterly Branch Meeting: 1,500 attend. Everyone dressed in yellow. No progress made in talks. Vote passed to initiate ballot for industrial action.
26 September	BA loses £531 million. Walsh awarded £1 million bonus.
30 September	High Court claim re withdrawal of concessions for 7,000 staff travel issued and served.
20 October	New offer document drawn up between Unite and BA.
27 October	Ballot on offer delayed by legal issues.
9 November	BASSA change mind on recommending a yes vote in ballot, ballot on offer goes ahead.
11 November	In light of BASSA not recommending deal ballot suspended.
21 November	Len McCluskey elected general secretary of Unite.
15 December	Unite give BA seven days' notice of strike ballot.

2011

| 6 January | Nicky Marcus sacked. |
| 10 January | Unite report that nearly three out of four members of BA cabin crew have witnessed or been victims of bullying. |

11 January	Branch meeting addressed by Len McCluskey.
21 January	Ballot result: 79% vote for industrial action on a 75% turnout. BA merges with Iberia to create parent company IAG.
8 February	Unite cancel ballot after ERS qualification to its official report.
28 March	83% vote for industrial action on a 72% turnout in a new ballot.
14 April	BA and Unite agree a 28-day extension before any further strike action is called.
11 May	Working Together – A Joint Settlement agreed by BASSA and BA.
12 May	Branch meeting at Bedfont votes to accept deal.
22 June	92% vote to accept the terms of the agreement on a 72% turnout.

1

Introduction

On 22 days during 2010 and 2011 Heathrow Airport presented an unusual sight – row upon row of stationary aircraft with their union jack emblazoned tail-fins standing to attention. British Airways' Terminal 5 (T5), normally a busy hub of arriving and departing passenger planes, was at a standstill, the most obvious manifestation of acrimonious conflict between British Airways (BA) and its cabin crew, who were members of the British Airlines Stewards and Stewardesses Association (BASSA), part of Unite the Union. Stasis at T5 contrasted sharply with the buzz of activity only a short distance away at Bedfont Football Club, close to Heathrow's perimeter and BASSA's operational headquarters on strike days. Here striking cabin crew, their families and their supporters gathered together in mass rallies which resembled carnivals of protest against the draconian actions of British Airways and its Chief Executive Officer (CEO), Willie Walsh. These strike days were the most dramatic events in a protracted dispute that pitched the cabin crew against one of Britain's most powerful flagship companies in one of the most bitter industrial relations conflicts of recent decades.

The bald statistics are that the dispute involved 22 strike days and cost BA an estimated £150 million in lost revenue.[1] The issues of contestation were hugely important, essentially the imposition of major changes to cabin crew's working conditions which threatened the effectiveness, if not the existence, of BASSA. Indeed, the BA–BASSA dispute and the strikes that were so crucial an element of BASSA's action raised much broader issues regarding the continued relevance of strike action in contemporary employment relations and the conditions under which groups of workers not noted for their militancy engaged in sustained collective action in defence of their conditions. The dispute also focuses attention on the effectiveness of union strategy and tactics in a neo-liberal era in which workers face belligerent employers and how, through both traditional and innovative methods, they are able to develop their own power resources to counter those of the employers.

More than anything this book tells the story of the dispute from the perspective of and in the words of the cabin crew participants. Indeed, the principal aim that motivated the authors was to write a book for BASSA members, activists and representatives which would provide a meaningful account of events and their involvement in them. From the authors' initial interactions with cabin crew it was clear that for very many cabin crew, the dispute was a momentous episode and significant event in their lives. While composing a narrative composed of many voices that would be read and welcomed by the participants, the objective, as explained more fully below, was also to deliver an account and analysis that would appeal to a number of audiences simultaneously. One such purpose was to make a contribution to the academic literature on industrial conflict and strikes.

Strikes in the industrial relations literature

There is not the space here for a critical discussion of the extensive literature on strikes. Readers may wish to consult work by Eldridge, Hyman, Shorter and Tilly, Batstone et al., Franzosi and Kelly.[2] Godard[3] has provided a reflection on the work of Richard Hyman, who has been hugely influential in developing understanding of strikes. For those interested in an overview of the subject excellent chapters can be found in the texts of Williams and of Blyton and Turnbull.[4]

The overall conclusion from this literature is that strikes are multi-causal social phenomena that are not reducible to a single factor, even though the UK government uses single-principle categories in its recording and measurement of working days lost through strikes.[5] The most commonly reported single cause of strikes is pay, yet the issue of pay is often bound up with other conflictual issues integral to the employment relationship, so that union pay claims may be related to the effects of managerial restructuring, to increases in work effort or to changing shift patterns. In the wider literature the distinction is often drawn between the proximate and underlying causes of strikes, a complex interaction to which a single attributed cause cannot do justice. Without pre-empting a full analysis of the roots, sources and immediate triggers of BASSA's action, underlying causes may be identified in the changing political economy of civil aviation, industry-wide deregulation and liberalisation, intensified market competition driving industry-wide cost (particularly labour cost) reduction and the concomitant compulsion to restructure operations and to dilute 'legacy' terms and conditions. If these might be seen as macro-level factors, then operating at another level might be firm level factors, in this case British Airways' market and product strategies and its conflictual tradition of industrial relations and people management, which must be considered alongside numerable factors relating to union capacity, organisation, leadership, resources, orientation and preparedness to act. Then, the proximate or trigger causes intercede, in this case British Airways' determination to impose thoroughgoing change to employment contracts, working conditions, collective bargaining and union influence. The multi-causal and multi-layered nature of the BASSA strike is explored in Chapter 2 and described by cabin crew participants in the following chapters.

In the field of industrial relations it is widely acknowledged that there are three frameworks. The first of these, the unitarist framework, sees strikes as the result of poor communication or the actions of agitators or troublemakers and, as such, can be easily dismissed as lacking explanatory purchase. If the second, the pluralist framework, emphasises the institutions and processes of collective bargaining and recognises conflict as legitimate, it is the Marxist framework that provides the most convincing general theory of strikes. Rooted in the theory that society is divided into antagonistic classes (and thus employment relationships), it provides the most effective analytical framework. Such a verdict is true not just in the narrow sense of explaining why collective bargaining might break down, but also in the broader sense of understanding that the basis of action is the outcome of the existence of distinct worker interests and the impulse to organise collectively.

Two important themes from the literature help locate the BA–BASSA. First, there has been universal acknowledgement that there is a relationship (often highly complex) between the incidence of strikes and broader economic conditions.[6] When unemployment is low, workers tend to be more confident and more likely to pursue their demands through striking but, equally, in these circumstances employers may be more likely to concede to union demands in order to avert strike disruption.[7] Conversely, when unemployment is high, workers may be less confident but, with employers' commitment to cost-cutting, workers may have more reason to believe they have no choice but to withdraw their labour. While macro-economic conditions exercise a *general* influence on strike activity, it is important to acknowledge the possibility of variation, for at the level of sector, company or even plant or region, broadly similar economic conditions may lead to differential outcomes. The BA–BASSA strike took place in the wake of financial crisis and during economic recession, but in a period of high employment and against a general backdrop of depressed strike activity.

The second theme is the attempt to identify strike-prone industries and to explain the reasons for this pattern of behaviour. Kerr and Siegel[8] argued that groups of workers, including miners, dockers, sailors and loggers, who formed powerful localised and/or occupational communities that were strongly unionised, were most strike-prone. This theory that workers at society's margins were most likely to strike was potently challenged by Shorter and Tilly.[9] They argued that the most strike-prone were to be found in the big urban centres with all their occupational diversity, rather than in isolated communities. Acknowledging this debate, how might the BA–BASSA strike be regarded? There is a sense in which the term community is meaningful, for British Airways' crew certainly defined themselves as a community in occupational, social and solidaristic terms (see Chapters 4–6). This powerful notion of community was the wellspring of collectivism which underpinned the strike and which BASSA was able to tap into.[10] For cabin crew, as for other groups of workers, the construction and lived experiences of community were crucial for mobilisation and sustaining collective action.

The strike process

Lyddon has observed that attempts to analyse the strike *process* are relatively uncommon.[11] A classic study by Hiller[12] does provide a valuable account of a 'processual model of strikes'[13] and is based on the collection of data over an extended time frame. Hiller identified several separate processes of a strike; organisation, mobilisation, maintaining group morale, controlling strike-breakers, neutralising employers' manoeuvres, shaping public opinion and demobilisation.[14] The book's introduction suggested that strikes consist of 'a cycle of typical events which take place in a more or less regular and predictable way',[15] observations that must be qualified by the fact that these identifiable processes do not necessarily occur in fixed order and might overlap. For example, the historical shift from continuous to non-consecutive episodes of strike activity (one day or two day strikes) in recent UK industrial relations, in part due to legal constraint, challenges this notion of a regular order to the strike process.

So, notwithstanding similarities in the processes and common characteristics, no two strikes are identical. Gouldner, in his seminal study of a 'wildcat strike' (a strike not called or sanctioned by a union leadership), made a universally valid point: 'A "strike" is a social phenomenon of enormous complexity which, in its totality, is never susceptible to complete description, let alone complete explanation.'[16] An important element in this complexity is what Eldridge[17] described as 'vocabularies of motive', the ways that workers and their union *frame* and rationalise their actions.[18] Chapters 3–6 of the present volume are peppered with these 'vocabularies of motive', particularly the crew's conviction that their actions were justified because British Airways had transgressed what was morally right as much as the fact that company's actions posed a very material threat to their conditions.

It is remarkable that few studies of strike action have placed at their centre the dynamics of strikes and the meanings of action as expressed by those workers directly involved in them.[19] Exceptions include Kars's account of a 4-month strike by women workers for union recognition at a mill in Saylor, near Chicago.[20] He revealed how participants were transformed by the experience, a major theme of this book (Chapter 6). A real strength of Kars's work lies in the systematic interviews conducted in the strike's aftermath with the union leadership and with samples of rank-and-file participants and 'fence-sitters', although those with non-strikers had to be abandoned because of heightened emotions. Consequently, the narrative contains extensive quotes on organising tactics, on songs, on workers' still fresh recollections of the picket lines, their experiences and broader views. A significant general conclusion, of salience to the BA–BASSA dispute, was that 'conflict establishes the identity of groups within a social system by strengthening group consciousness'.[21]

A study of the seven-week unofficial strike by 8,500 glassworkers at Pilkingtons in St Helens (Lancashire) in 1970[22] was (and remains) hugely significant since as the authors, Lane and Roberts, observe until their book 'nobody [had] ever attempted a full-scale study of a strike in the UK'.[23] Key to understanding the strike's dynamics was workers' disillusionment with the General and Municipal Workers Union which prompted them to set up a rank-and-file strike committee. This development contrasts, of course, with the BA–BASSA case which was an official dispute that saw, despite tensions at the outcome (Chapter 6), strong bonds of unity between BASSA leaders and members. Nevertheless, Lane and Roberts emphasise certain outstanding and common features of strikes that do have relevance to the BA–BASSA dispute. Strikes are 'an emotional explosion of discontent', inflamed by the accumulation of grievances. Further, their occurrence reflects the efficiency (or otherwise) of the machinery for the settlement of grievances and they tend to happen when a group of workers hold a strategic position in a system of production and are willing to exploit it, an observation consistent with the distinction between structural and associational power.[24]

The structural dimension derives from 'the location of workers within the economic system', which includes the strategic importance of groups of workers to their respective businesses. In this respect, the 'product' of civil aviation is highly perishable and, if flights are cancelled, airlines cannot easily recover lost traffic in the short term, and strike disruption may cause damage to the brand and even threaten permanent loss of custom. To realise the potential of 'structural power' requires 'associational power', the effectiveness of collective bargaining and the willingness and ability to exercise that power. This was the challenge confronting BASSA in 2009.

Yet perhaps the greatest strength of Lane and Roberts's work lies in the importance placed on testing the theories of strikes within the 'strike situation itself', so that 'it is only against evidence collected about the views and attitudes of people whilst they are actually participating in strikes that theories purporting to explain the incidence of strikes can be properly verified'.[25] Previous studies, they argued, tended to overlook the fact that a strike is a power struggle which affects both the course of the strike itself and the aftermath, and is also a reflection of the state of industrial relations preceding the dispute. All strikes represent a crisis in the established system of authority and discovering exactly what happens during them is central to understanding their significance.

In stressing a strike's uniqueness ('no two of them occur in exactly the same circumstances'[26]), Lane and Roberts distinguish between an official strike (organised and sanctioned by a union) and an unofficial strike (neither organised nor sanctioned). Their explanation of an official strike as 'strategically planned with defences well-dug and deployed in advance ... akin to a military operation'[27] is apposite. The war metaphor describes British Airways senior management's meticulous marshalling of internal and external resources but, given the asymmetrical (unequal) power relations between company and union, Lane and Roberts might overstate the equivalence of resources available to workers and unions. However, in regarding worker participants as the key data source, Lane and Roberts's work further resounds with the BA–BASSA study.[28]

Worker testimony showed that 'participants' aims and attitudes [did] not remain static',[29] changing over the course of the lengthy action, reflecting the dynamic nature of the strike phenomenon – characteristics evident in the dispute (see Chapter 6). Attitudes to work and authority were transformed, not least because the withdrawal of labour necessarily means, even temporarily, the suspension of managerial command.[30] Nevertheless, many Pilkingtons strikers rejected the idea that they were acting in a political manner, a position generally shared by cabin crew, although a minority did see, or came to, see the dispute in explicitly political terms. At Pilkingtons, as with the cabin crew, the strike was for many a transformative experience in which workers discovered capacities they did not know they possessed. Finally, 'a feeling of elation, a feeling of liberation' reported by a Pilkingtons striker[31] was also expressed by BASSA members, notably at the mass rallies and picket lines (see Chapter 5).

Lane and Roberts, finally, amplify Kars's insistence on explaining the complex meanings of a strike through using non-complicated language:

> This book has been written by professional social scientists but not just *for* other social scientists: we have tried … to write in such a way that it can be read by anyone who is interested in strikes in general and this one in particular. On the other hand, we naturally hope that our colleagues will not find it too 'slight'.[32]

This clear formulation, emphasising nuanced explanation of the complicated and multi-layered phenomenon of a strike, but in accessible language, has informed this account of the BA–BASSA dispute.

Many themes from Lane and Roberts recur in Fantasia's classic study of strike action and are centred on his concept of 'cultures of solidarity'.[33] The book articulated 'the lived experience of workers' in three strikes in the United States (and one in Italy), the first a wildcat in a unionised steel mill, the second a fight by workers for unionisation at a small hospital and the third at a grain processing plant. Rare insight into the processes of mobilisation, organisation and especially the 'vocabularies of motive' are delivered in the first case by the author's participant account and in the remaining cases by extensive retrospective interviews. The principal conclusion, similar to that of Lane and Roberts, and anticipating the cabin crew study (see Chapter 6), is that workers' consciousness is not unchanging and a fixed body of ideas, but changes in the course of struggle based on their lived experiences, political influences and varied cultural expressions.

Woolfson and Foster provided an inside view of the 103-day worker occupation against the closure of the Caterpillar plant in Uddingston near Glasgow that began in January 1987.[34] Based on a 'fly-on-the-wall' approach, the authors were permitted access to meetings of the joint occupation committee and taped proceedings and debates. The narrative is laced with worker quotes and chunks of dialogue from meetings. The concluding chapter focuses on the lessons of the occupation, locating the Caterpillar action in the context of working-class movement and traditions in the west of Scotland, drawing comparisons with the Upper Clyde Shipbuilders occupation of 1971, itself the subject of a study by the same authors.[35] The quotes in the Caterpillar book are more objective political commentary, in contrast to this BA–BASSA study, in which the participants provide lengthier, more subjective and experiential testimony.

Lang and Dodkins's account of industrial action and the sacking of 5,500 workers by News International in 1986 focused on 600 workers, half of whom were women.[36] The authors, themselves participants, recorded interviews with SOGAT (Society of Graphical and Allied Trades) members a year after the dispute. The testimony overall tends to be more reflective than Woolfson and Foster's, and the final chapter is concerned with personal consequences of the strike, including financial hardship and the strains on relationships. In these respects, their book bears certain similarities to ours.

An important recent book by Anitha and Pearson titled *Striking Women* gives voices to those involved in two key events in the history of UK industrial relations that were led by South Asian women: the 1976–8 Grunwick strike and the 2005 Gate Gourmet dispute.[37] The latter is particularly pertinent to this book, since (as our Chapter 2 explains) the women prepared in-flight meal trays at Heathrow for the airline catering company bought from British Airways as part of its outsourcing operation. Gate Gourmet is then part of the backdrop to the BA–BASSA dispute. *Striking Women* uses interviews with women participating in Grunwick and Gate Gourmet and challenges to some extent the trade union narrative of fortieth anniversary celebrations of the Grunwick Strike and the role of trade unions in both disputes. Further, it explores how 'the identities of different groups of minority women workers such as their gender, race, ethnicity, diverse class positions, migration histories and family circumstances are mobilised and reproduced in migrant labour markets and shape particular political possibilities in response to exploitation at work.'[38] At the same time it locates the disputes in the imperial, political and industrial history of the countries from where the women came. This book on the BA–BASSA dispute similarly explores the interaction of gender, sexuality and ethnicity with class (Chapter 6).

Finally, an account of the 2002–3 firefighters' strikes, an extended chapter in the official history of the FBU, is based on interviews with 100 full-time and lay officers, activists and members.[39] Combined with industrial relations analysis it provides an intimate analysis of the sources, dynamic, processes and experiences of perhaps the single most important strike occurring under the new Labour governments.

Other work on individual strikes, and particularly those that flourished during and following Thatcher's offensive on the working class, includes accounts of the 1980 steel strike,[40] the 1984–5 miners' strike[41] and the 1995–6 Merseyside dockers' lock-out.[42] In addition, a number of journal articles have focused on strikes or industrial conflict.[43] Two other books that do not fit exactly within the strict categories of specific strikes or worker testimony deserve inclusion in this discussion. Darlington and Lyddon's uplifting account of class struggle in 1972, deriving from multiple documentary sources including quotes from leading participants, delivers compelling insight into the high water mark of strike action in post-Second World War Britain.[44] Further Gall's monograph on the Communication Workers Union (previously the Union of Communication Workers) is constructed initially on interviews with postal workers and lay official interviews in Scotland and then on extensive interviews with full-time officers on the postal side.[45] Combining forensic examination of union, employer and newspaper documentary sources with interview evidence, the book delivers a nuanced account of the meaning of militancy, providing a conceptual underpinning for understanding both national official strikes and the wave of unofficial strikes that occurred in the Royal Mail during the 1990s.

The work of Kars, Lane and Roberts, Fantasia, Wolfson and Foster, Lang and Dodkins, Anitha and Pearson and Moore, Wright and Taylor in particular constitutes a tradition of research and writing that utilises first-hand participant accounts that explore the processes, dynamics, meanings and significance of strikes from the bottom up, but which are located within their institutional, political-economic and social contexts. The narrative now turns to the important issues of how our first-hand accounts were garnered, the profile of the participants and the research methods adopted.

Sources, methods and testimony

The origins of this book lie in the authors' engagement with and support for the cabin crew and BASSA, which preceded the first strike days and continued for the duration of the conflict. Relationships were established with BASSA officers and activists during this period. Out of discussions following the dispute the idea flourished that a documentary account should be written. From the outset, the intention was to compose a narrative of the dispute, but one that would go beyond this and be based in large part on the first hand testimonies of participants.

The authors were permitted to address BASSA branch meetings at Bedfont in early 2012, at which they explained the purpose of the proposed book and their approach to gathering data, specifically through interviews with cabin crew, BASSA representatives and activists. Appeals for volunteers were made at these meetings and BASSA encouraged participation in emails to members. Additional subjects were attained through the personal contacts and recommendations of those interviewed, in what is termed 'snowballing' in the academic research methods literature. Prior to each interview, the principal aim of capturing the participant's experiences and perceptions, 'warts and all', was reiterated.

Face-to-face interviews were conducted between September 2011 and February 2013 on union premises, in hotels and restaurants, and in participants' homes. Interviews lasted a minimum of ninety minutes, but the duration of most was over two hours. Following a pilot study, a draft interview schedule was amended and implemented around distinct themes, including employment histories, changing experiences of work, skill utilisation and customer service, attitudes to the company and management, experiences of BASSA and industrial relations, participation in the 2009–11 dispute and strikes, and reflections on the dispute.[46] More than sixty in-depth interviews were conducted with cabin crew and a further two with Unite officers involved in the dispute (see Appendix for details of participants).

The majority of interviewees were union reps or crew members who were active during the dispute, but the participants included a number of BASSA members who did see themselves as 'activists'. Interviewees were guaranteed anonymity, except where consent to identify individuals was explicitly given. The hostile environment and legacy of victimisation during and after the dispute meant that in most cases pseudonyms have been used to protect cabin crew (seven real names have been used with permission; see Appendix). Participants were split equally between men and women, which did not exactly correspond to the gender composition of the membership overall, which at the start of the dispute was 64 per cent female and 36 per cent male.[47] BASSA's gender composition, however, was consistent with that of the workforce as a whole, a reflection of the very high level of union density. The gender, sexuality, race, ethnic and age profiles of participants were broadly consistent with those of the BASSA reps, if not the more diverse overall membership of the union. Although reps were disproportionately male, several women held leading positions during the dispute, notably Lizanne Malone, who was chair of the BASSA branch.

Roughly two-thirds of interviewees worked long-haul (Worldwide) and one-third short-haul (Eurofleet), while one interviewee from the single fleet at Gatwick was among the handful who struck at that airport. The fifty participants comprised twenty cabin service directors, nine pursers, nineteen cabin crew and two Unite officers. Testimony may thus reflect the BASSA representative/activist base and seniority. Nevertheless, against the potential charge that this sample is skewed, it must be acknowledged that these participants, by dint of their active participation in the dispute, do give privileged insight into the processes of mobilisation and organisation.[48] To reiterate, the study did not involve purposive sampling. Rather, the authors interviewed both those who responded to appeals to take part and those who were recommended by these participants.

Semi-structured interview schedules aimed to structure the interview process and to facilitate comparison of responses for analytical purposes. The authors, who conducted all of the interviews, were keen to avoid inflexible questioning that might inhibit employees from freely volunteering their experiences, perceptions and feelings. It is widely acknowledged, particularly in the use of oral history, that interviewees do not give responses in formal, logical sequence. Narrators explain life events through hierarchies of significance and associated events rather than conforming to the researcher's need to reconstruct chronological sequence.[49] There are inevitably streams of consciousness or leaps between memories, recalled experiences and ideas. As Portelli illustrates, this internal and collective dialogue and reorganisation is a fundamental strength of oral history interviewing, as the participant tells the listener 'not only what they did, but what they wanted to do, what they believed they were doing, and what they now think they did'.[50]

Oral narratives defy neat categorisation, which raises several challenges for presentation and analysis. Should researchers err on the side of caution and extract from a longer quote only those sentences or parts of sentences that pertain to a particular question or specific theme? This approach carries the danger that quotes can be fragments, divorced from the wider contexts and meanings. Or, should researchers present longer, unexpurgated passages that contain multiple themes? The danger here is the quotations might ramble and lack focus. These editorial dilemmas and contradictions are extensively discussed by oral historians. Schopes, for example, emphasises the dilemmas of ethics, authenticity and interpretation involved in the act of translating interviews into publication.[51] Through each stage of transcribing, editing, publishing and revising, the text becomes further removed from the orality of the original source. Such processes are inevitable in print publication, but they do need to be acknowledged. To clarify, the authors have attempted to steer a course between these polarities, deliberating on what to include or exclude and in what order the quotes should be positioned. In places the testimonies have been 'crafted', snipping words to remove unnecessary digression, repetition or padding, but their authenticity remains intact. Nevertheless, to retain the authenticity of narratives, the quotes do not always map exactly onto the chapters' themes.

Purposes of and audiences for the book

This is a book that, in the first instance, is written for the BASSA cabin crew. In one sense, we are holding the metaphorical mirror up to reflect the participants' experiences, thoughts and feelings of their protracted struggle and, more specifically, of their involvement in strike action. Throughout the dispute, Robert Byford, a former BASSA cabin crew member and now a retired member and a skilled photographer, took many thousands of pictures. Consistent with the principal objective of 'giving back' to BASSA members, the selective photographic documentation should be an additional stimulus for cabin crew to recall events.

In this respect, this book is influenced by, and seeks in a modest way to contribute to, a tradition of British photojournalism that has given us unforgettable images of dramatic events surrounding workers in struggle, notably from the miners' strike of 1984–5.[52] Perhaps there is no single image from the BA–BASSA dispute that is as instantly striking as the miner in the comic policeman's helmet going head to head with a row of police, or the policeman on horseback assaulting the diminutive, cowering figure of Lesley Boulton at Orgreave. However, Rob's photographs convey to great effect the mass participation at rallies and meetings, and capture the mood on picket lines and the carnival atmosphere at Bedfont. Every picture does indeed tell a story.

This book contains multiple stories and visual images that should not be 'hidden from history',[53] to borrow Sheila Rowbotham's memorable phrase, reflecting our concern that the participation of women in struggle is not lost. These contributions seek to explain and describe the coming together of individuals with multiple life histories, experiences and identities to forge collective identity and action.

This is also a partisan work, in that the authors are trade union and labour movement activists. The issue of critically committed research and scholarship is a subject of interest and debate notably in Burawoy's call for a partisan organic public sociology that is part of 'a social movement beyond the academy'[54] and the late Bourdieu's appeal for committed scholarship in the service of the social movement against neo-liberalism.[55] This book chimes also with calls for engaged pro-worker, pro-union scholarship that should be an integral part of worker struggles.[56] These overall objectives, then, underlay the authors' role as empathic interpreters and 'active listeners' rather than dispassionate and distant interlocutors.

If the primary purpose was to give something back to the BASSA members, they are the book's primary audience, although not the only one. The second audience is a broad layer of trade unionists and activists interested in learning from the dispute. The affirmation of collective action that is the underlying leitmotif of the book has this audience in mind and reinforces the need for it to be written in an accessible style.

The book should additionally be welcomed by the academic community. Although not a strictly conventional work of industrial/employment relations, it does conform to rigorous academic standards. It makes a distinctive contribution to the industrial relations literature on strikes and specifically to an understanding of the BA–BASSA dispute as undoubtedly one of the most important conflicts this century. Further, as the first part of this chapter elucidates, the book contributes to the industrial relations and industrial sociology literature on the strike process, and to a body of work that has located strike dynamics in the experiences and meanings of strikers themselves. Thus, this book should be of value to industrial relations academics, but also to students taking employment relations courses. It is both a research source and a teaching resource.

The book is hugely affirmative of the actions that the crew took and, further, conveys the enduring and universal truths of the importance of collectivism, collective action, solidarity and the resilience of trade union organisation in defiance of the indignities heaped upon employees by management restructuring in an era of neo-liberal employment relations. Additionally, the book gives trade unionists and activist's meaningful knowledge of a recent strike that can help inform their understanding and practice. Books on particular strikes and episodes of industrial action are read and reread by those in the movement seeking to make sense of their own actions and to develop a better understanding of the effectiveness of mobilisation, strategy, organisation and action. The authors hope this book is more than a work of history.

Structure of the book

Chapter 2 situates the dispute and provides the context for Chapters 3–6, which are composed largely of the testimonies of the cabin crew. First, the chapter sets the BA–BASSA conflict against the broader strike trends in the UK, but challenges the received wisdom that would regard strikes as outdated, some kind of historical throwback. Second, the chapter evaluates the structural and economic changes that have characterised the global civil aviation industry of recent decades, necessary for understanding the strategic direction taken by British Airways. Third, the chapter turns to the level of the firm, providing an account of the company's history, its changed structure and revised priorities, as a preface to a critical review of its industrial relations and the role of BASSA. This discussion sets the scene for the subsequent chronology of the dispute.

Chapter 3 explores the erosion of cabin crew's organisational loyalty in the context of the transformed political economy of civil aviation and changes in the quality of the service they could provide. The chapter considers the factors, influences and perceptions that underpinned cabin crew collectivism including the organisation of work, the constraints on managerial control, informal working relationships, and the role of BASSA. Cabin crew testify to the deterioration of industrial relations in British Airways, culminating in the exposure of Project Columbus and the imposed reduction in crew members on both long and short-haul flights – by-passing negotiation with BASSA and the trigger for the dispute.

Chapter 4 focuses on BASSA's decision to ballot for strike action and British Airways' legal challenges to the right of cabin crew to strike. It considers the company's 'counter-mobilisation' against BASSA and cabin crew in the face of strike action, the measures it took to try to break the strike, to polarise the workforce, to 'decapitate' BASSA, to victimise activists and the use of sinister surveillance tactics.

Chapter 5 provides an account of how the union organised during the strike, cabin crew experiences of the picket lines and mass meetings held at Bedfont Football Club's ground. Here, the narratives suggest the importance of Bedfont as a 'home' for the strikers who lacked a fixed workplace and as a visible manifestation of solidarity. Accordingly, the chapter reports on what might be regarded as the 'conventional' withdrawal of labour, but also reveals mechanisms of organisation and communication and manifestations and expressions of solidarity that might be regarded as novel. These include the role of the two online forums used by BASSA members and the ways in which they allowed members to share anger and fears, to discuss tactics and developments, to provide emotional and political support, to challenge management's claims and to organise action, overcoming difficulties inherent in the organisationally dispersed workforce. Finally, the chapter looks at the strike 'counter-culture', how strikers communicated solidarity when at work in a hostile atmosphere.

Chapter 6 considers the settlement of the dispute and its implications. Crew reflected on the consequences of the dispute for their lives and relationships, and thus the chapter considers the neglected issue of the emotional cost for participants. This chapter also explores what is frequently termed 'consciousness': the extent and the ways in which attitudes, values, ideas and attitudes were transformed through experience of conflict and struggle.

Chapter 7 offers a conclusion. It briefly considers aspects of the longer-term significance of the dispute and its aftermath. It looks at the proliferation of industrial action in civil aviation, but in particular, it comments on the unionisation of the new 'mixed fleet' and provides a brief account of their remarkable action against poverty wages and harsh conditions, which saw them take 85 days of strike action in 2017.

2

Cabin crew collectivism

Introduction

This chapter provides essential contextualisation for the first-hand accounts of cabin crew and BASSA activists that form the core of Chapters 3–6. These chapters reveal the momentous impact of the dispute on its participants. From a sociological perspective, the dispute goes far beyond the fact of the 22 strike days and the reported £150 million in lost revenues.[1] Further, from an industrial relations perspective, the dispute and the strike action that was integral to it are of wider importance.

The cabin crew strikes took place against the background of a very low level of industrial action in the UK. For many commentators, trade unions had come to be seen as ineffective and incapable of mobilising their members in collective action. According to this narrative the late-twentieth-century workforce had undergone a 'dramatic transformation, from the traditional, class-conscious collectivism of the industrial manual worker to the self-interested individualism of the skilled, mobile and career-centred white-collar worker'.[2] The action taken by cabin crew thus challenged the depiction of Britain as 'strike free'[3] and lent support to the counter-argument that the end of collectivism perspective is 'seriously flawed and deeply misleading'.[4] The nature and composition of the cabin crew workforce, that it is organisationally dispersed and has no fixed 'workplace', added to the received wisdom that workers with such characteristics are very difficult, if not impossible, to organise. As the succeeding chapters powerfully demonstrate, British Airways cabin crew had a high trade union density and expressed a powerful unity of purpose and action that confounded the pessimists.

The dispute is additionally important because it is a compelling example of a struggle by workers to protect their pay and working conditions and to defend their union in the face of the intense inter-firm competition, the relentless cost-cutting and the perpetual restructuring that are characteristic of the era of neo-liberalism and global deregulation.[5] This dispute occurred as the global airlines industry[6] was buffeted by powerful forces in the wake of the financial crash of 2008 and in the midst of the subsequent great depression.[7]

The strike also saw the mobilisation of a workforce diverse in terms of gender, sexuality, race and nationality. Gender, particularly, should be commented upon in terms of the resilience of the cabin crew, who had been stereotyped as middle-class, Middle England, union-lite 'trolley dollies'. For one columnist, habitually hostile to trade unionism, cabin crew were 'the unthreatening faces of Middle Britain – sensible, orderly, down to earth people, as far removed from stroppy left-wing militancy as you could imagine'.[8]

Finally, the strikers encountered the sustained hostility of their employer, the opposition of the Labour government in the months preceding the 2010 general election and the antagonism of much mainstream media. In an extraordinary action elaborated on later in this chapter and reflected on by cabin crew in Chapter 4, British Airways initiated legal proceedings against BASSA that led to a High Court judgement in December 2009 that effectively threatened the legality of the universal right to strike in the UK.[9] Thus, resistance took place within the most challenging of contexts and against a formidable alignment of opposition forces.

This chapter sets out the wider context of the BASSA strike: the UK industrial relations landscape, the political economy of the global civil aviation industry, the specific history and strategy of British Airways and the background of industrial relations between BASSA and British Airways. It then provides a chronological overview of the dispute.

The BA–BASSA strike in context

At the outset, it is necessary to situate the BA–BASSA conflict within broader UK strike trends, about which Lyddon provides a helpful analysis and overview.[10] Over the last half century, four interrelated trends have dominated the character and trajectory of strikes: they have become far fewer, they now occur mostly in the public sector rather than coalmining and manufacturing, they have largely ceased to be unofficial, and, since the 1980s, the effect of legislation and the interference of the courts have been significant in dampening activity. Three phases of UK strike activity can be identified: the high period of 1964–79, the transitory decade of the 1980s (which resulted in historically low levels, according to all three statistical indicators, namely numbers of strikes, strikers and days lost), and the years since 1992. Since that signal year the number of strikes has fallen to only 100–200 per annum.

Action commenced at British Airways in 2010, the year that had until then witnessed the lowest level of strike activity since records began, with only 45 strikes occurring in the private sector,[11] a category that includes civil aviation. Although the BA–BASSA dispute continued until 2011, strike days were confined to the previous year.[12] Since the early 1980s the UK has passed through the most extended period ever of declining strike activity,[13] so that in only four years between 1991 and 2015 were there over 1 million working days lost to strikes.[14] Another indicator of the degree to which BASSA's strike action stands out is in terms of sectoral profile. In the UK over 80 per cent of annual days lost to strikes since 1995 have been in the public sector[15] and lasting largely for one or two days only.[16] Strike action in the private sector has been restricted to the company rather than sectoral level and therefore has involved smaller numbers. In contrast to the 1960s and 1970s, when strikes tended to be 'contagious', with successful action by workers in one industry, sector, region or enterprise encouraging workers elsewhere, the subsequent decades have seen an accumulation of a 'negative demonstration' effect where the difficulties involved in taking action and the uncertainties of outcomes have inhibited emulation. Given the context of an unprecedentedly low level of strike activity in the UK, the BASSA strikes of 2010 are all the more remarkable.

A core argument of this book is that the BA–BASSA conflict warrants examination on its own terms and that the strike action that was such a key part of it was a remarkable episode with distinctive dynamics. One notable aspect was the union's use of social media, considered below and in Chapter 5. The dispute was by no means a historical throwback to a lost era of industrial militancy.[17] Although the strike's roots inevitably lie in the decades-long legacy of industrial relations at British Airways, including, not least, the resilience of BASSA itself, members' grievances were fuelled by wholly contemporary concerns.

Furthermore, strikes as a general phenomenon merit study, even though academic attention has diminished as strike activity has declined.[18] In the influential volumes edited by members of the Warwick University Industrial Relations Research Unit,[19] discussion of strikes became condensed into a section in the chapter on trade unions and, in the most recent edition strike activity is subsumed within a section on collective bargaining.[20] Within the field of industrial relations 'the topic of strikes seems to have been largely forgotten',[21] so that in the Sage Handbook on Industrial Relations[22] not one of 34 chapters is devoted to strikes. Yet, despite supposed 'labour quiescence',[23] strikes remain a crucial subject for study because they and other forms of disruptive collective action 'reflect the fundamental antagonism at the heart of the employment relationship'.[24] To relegate strikes to a footnote is to mistakenly recast industrial relations as conflict-free, and fails to build on the knowledge of this important social phenomena that has developed over many decades.[25]

The inescapable fact is that strikes and other forms of industrial action still occur and, contrary to the unitarist perspective of industrial relations which asserts that employers and employees have the same interests, they are neither the result of mischief making nor the work of outside agitators, although of course the role played by leadership is central.[26] Strikes are purposeful and calculative,[27] and should not be counterposed to a 'normal' state of stable, ordered industrial relations. As the history of industrial relations at British Airways demonstrates, underlying antagonism regularly manifested itself in conflict. The withdrawal of labour by cabin crew exemplified the general truth that taking strike action is a rational form of behaviour designed to improve or defend the terms of the wage-effort bargain.[28] Of course, unions may embark on strikes or other forms of collective industrial action because of the failure to reach agreement with employers through negotiation, but strikes are not merely an extension of collective bargaining. In this BA–BASSA case, as so often, they were the action of the last resort and were animated by a clear purpose and specific objectives.

Related to this understanding of strikes as purposeful and calculative is acknowledgement of the centrality of trade unions. Industrial relations analysis emphasises the importance of a strong union with a sufficient strong membership as necessary to mobilise workers, organise activity and counter employers' attempts to undermine or break the union's action.[29] In the BA–BASSA dispute one precondition for strike action was the high union density that the BASSA leadership had fought to achieve over many years (see below) and, inextricably, the effectiveness of pre-existing union organisation among cabin crew.

It is necessary, nonetheless, to acknowledge the altered terrain on which industrial action took place in 2010. A general shift had occurred in the balance of power between employers and senior management on the one hand, and trade unions and employees on the other.[30] Part of the explanation lies in declining trade union membership. In 1979, UK union membership peaked at 13.3 million, a density of 55 per cent.[31] At the time of the dispute in 2010, 6.5 million workers were trade union members, a density of 27 per cent.[32] Women were on their way to comprising a majority of trade union members, largely a reflection of the enduring strength of public sector trade unionism, in which women are disproportionately represented. However, in the private sector, male union density in 2010 remained higher at 17 per cent, with 12 per cent for females.[33]

Union membership and recognition are inseparably bound up with collective bargaining which has undergone significant change over the preceding three decades.[34] A 'significant diminution in the scope of negotiations' has occurred[35] accompanied by the decentralisation and fragmentation of bargaining and a general shift from sector to firm and even to site/workplace level. Most marked is the reduction in collective bargaining coverage, from 71 per cent of the UK workforce in 1979 to 40 per cent by 2004[36] and 29 per cent by 2012.[37] Within this general trajectory, shrinkage of coverage in the private sector (including British Airways) is even more pronounced, so that by 2011 only 16 per cent of employees had their pay set through collective negotiations between employer and union.[38]

It follows that the reasons for the dwindling extent and substance of collective bargaining are bound up with the causes of the decline in trade union membership. Principal among these are deindustrialisation and the decline of sectors with historically high concentrations of trade union membership, in tandem with the rise of the service sector (broadly defined), in which trade union traditions have not widely been established or are weakly embedded. While economic restructuring, recession and the changing composition of employment are salient, trade union decline is attributable to a complex interaction of factors,[39] including the political and legal. Conservative governments (1979–97) introduced a battery of anti-union legislation, which curbed the ability of unions to pursue strike action. As BASSA found out to its cost, the Trade Union and Labour Relations (Consolidation) Act 1992 (TULRCA) introduced complex and time-consuming procedural rules for calling industrial action, designed to discourage unions.[40] Cumulatively, the effect of the legislation has been to create a climate which strengthened managerial prerogative and undermined union confidence.[41]

However, it does not automatically follow from union membership decline that workers' attitudes become anti-union even if these are not necessarily manifest in pro-union behaviours of membership, commitment or activism. A study based on a random sample of UK workers found two-thirds believing that unions were necessary to protect the interests of workers.[42] Such findings suggest an attitudinal disposition to the sort of collectivism evident in the actions of cabin crew who, in BASSA, had a union capable of and prepared to translate collective instincts and workplace solidarities into action.

One distinctive characteristic of the British Airways strike was the mobilisation of a diverse workforce with a relatively high proportion of women and LGBT workers. There are no statistics on the specific degree of involvement of women in private sector strikes in the UK. Historically, notable strikes by women workers include the sewing machinists at Ford in Dagenham over equal pay in 1968, by mainly Asian women at Imperial Typewriters and Kenilworth Components in Leicester in 1974 over differential treatment on the grounds of race, the 21-week long strike by members of the AEUW for equal pay at Trico in Brentford,[43] and again by Asian women workers in 1976–8 at Grunwick over union recognition and working conditions.[44] More recent disputes include women cleaners at Hillingdon Hospital who took action in 1995 over reductions to their pay following outsourcing to private contractor Pall Mall.[45] National one- or two-day strikes on pay and pensions taken by public sector unions in the early 2000s saw the largest mobilisations of women in UK strike history.[46]

As mentioned in Chapter 1, in civil aviation, Asian women were central to the 2005 dispute at Gate Gourmet, British Airways' main catering supplier. Here, workers at Heathrow Airport (who, prior to outsourcing, had been directly employed by British Airways) were sacked when they protested about the introduction of agency workers on inferior terms and conditions.[47] In this dispute, British Airways baggage handlers, members of the Transport and General Workers' Union (TGWU), now part of Unite the Union, staged a two-day walkout in solidarity, a move which may have constituted illegal secondary industrial action, which grounded British Airways flights. The effectiveness of this action pressurised the company into reinstating the Gate Gourmet women, although 200 labelled 'trouble makers' remained dismissed. Of these 200, 56 refused to take redundancy and continued to protest and picket over the next four years.[48] Gate Gourmet was hugely significant in that the legal implications cast a shadow over employer and union attitudes and behaviour in the BA–BASSA conflict. To summarise, in the general context of weakened trade unionism and unfavourable prospects for strike action, BASSA reaffirmed the historic significance of the strike.

Global civil aviation industry

To grasp the dynamics of the BA–BASSA dispute requires an understanding of the 'political economy' of the global civil aviation. Historically, the industry has been dominated by complex regulations based on bilateral (between two countries) air service agreements. The 'bilateral' specifies whether one (or more) airlines is designated by each country for agreed routes, but they must be 'substantially owned and effectively controlled' by nationals of the designating state. Agreements designed to ensure control over market entry and access and over-capacity and frequency have been related to tariff fixing through the International Air Transport Association (IATA) of airline companies.[49]

The principal factor underpinning the industry's decades-long transformation has been liberalisation. The Deregulation Act of 1978 in the US involved its domestic market and was followed by the opening up of transatlantic routes. In Europe, the first 'open skies' bilateral was signed in 1992 between the UK and the Netherlands and, by 2000, forty such 'bilaterals' had been agreed. In December 1997 the first 'package' of liberalisation measures was introduced by the European Community (EC). A further step change was the 'third package' enforced in 1993. In 2007, the deregulatory wave culminated in the EU–US Open Skies Agreement, which greatly influenced British Airways' thinking in the period preceding the BA–BASSA dispute.

European deregulation occurred in distinct phases.[50] A series of domestic reform initiatives, coupled with privatisation, occurred notably in Britain and the Netherlands. From the mid-1980s, the Civil Aviation Authority (CAA) sanctioned a degree of market entry to allow smaller airlines limited scope to compete. Privatisation and labour market deregulation offered flag carriers (e.g. British Airways and KLM) the potential to operate with lower costs and higher productivity. Over time, the arguments against 'exceptionalism' gained traction. It was increasingly accepted that civil aviation should operate like any international industry and its restrictive practices were both unethical and harmful. Structural changes, such as growing concentration, mergers and alliances, were part cause and part consequence of this trend. Still, despite moves to deregulate European and US skies, governments remained integrally involved in the decision-making of airlines.[51] Nowhere was this more evident than in the UK and in the government-driven privatisation of British Airways, as discussed in the next section.

Liberalisation led to fewer airlines competing on certain international routes, to less control over capacity and frequency and to greater pricing freedom.[52] Several major structural and market developments facilitated the creation of competitive inter-airline alliances during the late-1990s. These alliances mostly evolved into intricate webs that spanned diverse operational aspects and differing geographies. They were motivated by interrelated factors. Most obviously the marketing benefits of scale and scope, in which 'hub and spoke' operations centred on a major partner's home airport, providing transfer connections through code sharing.

Increased market power, enhanced synergies and sharing resources aimed to maximise revenues and minimise costs, while excluding (non-alliance) competitors. British Airways' Oneworld alliance, formed in 1998 with American Airlines, Canadian Airlines, Qantas and Cathay Pacific, was paralleled by the Star Alliance comprising, *inter alia*, United Airlines and Lufthansa.

The emergence of low-cost carriers (LCCs) placed enormous pressure on legacy full-service carriers (FSCs) to decrease costs. One estimate was that LCCs operated at 43 per cent of overall costs of FSCs. Among LCCs' advantages[53] are less congested airports, lower landing and handling charges, short turnaround times, online retailing, flexible pricing, high seat occupancy and using single aircraft types. All FSCs altered their business model, adopting elements of the LCC model. One study concluded that British Airways moved closer to the LCC model than Lufthansa.[54] Another showed how Qantas[55] had converged in business strategy and employment relations with its LCC subsidiary, Jetstar.[56] The scale of the impact of LCCs can be gleaned from Civil Aviation Authority statistics. In 2006 it reported that FSC international passenger numbers between the UK and the EU increased from 69.1 to 123.7 million between 1996 and 2005, while FCCs grew from 3.1 to 51.5 million.[57] LCCs accounted for 89 per cent of the overall increase in traffic compared to 9 per cent for FSCs.[58]

A significant outcome of intensified competition was the steady decline in the real value of airline yields. Consequently, cost reduction became the central priority for all airlines. While, historically, cost efficiencies had largely been short-term responses to cyclical downturns, in the changed structural and market conditions cost reduction become a never-ending and dominating imperative. Accordingly, strategies centred on reducing operating and labour costs. The focus on the latter is explicable by reference to the fact that labour costs constitute around 30 per cent of total operating costs.[59] Moreover, unlike most other costs (e.g. aircraft, fuel) labour costs are one of the few variable costs under the direct control of management.[60] Airlines concluded that labour costs could not be contained solely by raising labour productivity,[61] which led to the strategic objective of cutting unit labour costs. FSCs pursued this through salary freezes, cuts, and two-tier (or more) pay structures as terms and conditions of employment were continuously renegotiated. Perhaps 'the greatest challenge' faced by FSCs was how to reconcile 'the growing contradiction between controlling labour costs and enhancing service quality',[62] which preoccupied British Airways.[63] Heightened competition over customer quality between FSCs requires motivated staff, yet a high degree of engagement might be incompatible with the work intensification, downsizing, flexibilised schedules and inferior contracts that resulted from cost cutting.

The transformation of European aviation from bilateral agreements between governments and their national airlines into a single European market has impacted airline productivity and price. The 'product' has been redefined by unbundling services, such as business class, as passengers choose price over service. The use of secondary airports resulted in quicker turnaround times and more routes per day. Point-to-point services from local airports have meant local fares and reduced travels times, compared to those services operating through hub airports.

If these market and structural developments generated incremental change, the terrorist attacks of 11 September 2001 (hereafter '9/11') had a 'unique, unprecedented, devastating and immediate impact on all segments of the industry'.[64] It was a watershed for 'legacy' airlines. Following the precipitous decline in air travel, employers implemented dramatic cost savings, imposed redundancies, drove leaner staffing and revised employment contracts for many employees.[65] The logic for many firms was that, in order to cut costs, they had to pursue antagonistic employment relations and cost cutting, even if they jeopardised cabin crews' ability to deliver service quality.[66]

British Airways: history, market and strategy

British Airways' origins can be traced to the emergence of the civil aviation industry after the First World War when, in 1924, Britain's four nascent airlines[67] formed Imperial Airways. In 1935 several smaller operations constituted the privately owned British Airways. Then, in 1939, Imperial Airways and British Airways were nationalised under the aegis of British Overseas Airways Corporation (BOAC), while continental European and domestic routes were operated by the newly created airline, British European Airways (BEA). Following the Edwards Report[68] of 1969, BEA and BOAC merged in 1974 to form British Airways. Being the UK's flag-carrier airline bequeathed an important legacy for successive governments. As a key strategic asset, British Airways would have its fortunes intertwined with political-economic determinations of the national interest. The government could never be a disinterested observer of industrial relations when the negotiated order broke down, for conflict implied a threat, real or imagined, to the national interest. British Airways thus exemplified the general case of states developing airlines as national assets given the enormous costs of establishing them, their strategic importance and their early role as a quasi-military resource.[69]

If, during its years as a nationalised industry, British Airways typified the corporatist high tide of the mid-1970s, it was soon to be emblematic of what came to be known as neo-liberalism and the privatisation and deregulation it espoused.[70] Once Lord King, chairman of British Airways from 1982, accepted Prime Minister Thatcher's invitation in 1983 to privatise the airline, fundamental change was wrought in all aspects of organisational life, not least in attitudes to and relationships with trade unions. Dealing with unions was an integral part of the proposed transformation for King when he launched an assault on the established internal order. In 1976–7, British Airways had experienced 87 disputes and 52 stoppages of work and, in the following year, disputes accounted for the loss of 59,000 working days, equivalent to one day per employee. In a survey, 33 per cent of customers had put British Airways at the top of the list of airlines to be avoided at all costs.[71] Initial steps taken by King were brutal, with 16 international routes suspended, aircraft sold off, engineering bases axed, administration pruned and no fewer than 9,000 redundancies enforced. King's self-declared means of motivating his employees was to use 'fear'[72] as the cost-cutting exercise succeeded in slashing the workforce from 53,600 in 1981 to 39,700 in 1983, while ramping up profits to £77 million. King's strategy for British Airways 'umbilically connected to Thatcher's vision of "enterprise culture",[73] the strategic centrepiece being the company's privatisation.[74] However, privatisation should not be regarded as the unambiguous unleashing of 'free enterprise'. While King and Thatcher certainly employed such rhetoric, in reality, the project was concerned with eliminating domestic opposition so that British Airways could monopolise the British market. The government was central to developments. At an operational level it intervened, for example, giving British Airways £53 million to finance its redundancy programme. At the highest political level it interceded with the US government. British Airways' major transatlantic competitor, Laker Airways, had crashed as transatlantic fares soared. In retaliation, Freddie Laker had served an indictment in the United States against British Airways on the grounds of its predatory pricing, a move which threatened to stymie the cherished privatisation project. In February 1985, Thatcher travelled to Washington to lobby President Reagan on behalf of British Airways, so great was her commitment to ensuring the success of her flagship policy. Reagan duly cancelled the criminal investigation, a financial settlement was made with Laker and privatisation proceeded in 1987.

British Airways exemplified the general objective that informed all the major European flag-carrier airlines, the compulsion to dominate their home markets. It bought 40 per cent of Bymon Airways in 1987 (outright in 1993) and took over British Caledonian in 1987, the UK's second largest airline,[75] which became another sacrificial victim on the altar of the King–Thatcher privatisation. It was an acquisition that had significant implications for industrial relations (see below). Later, it purchased British City Flyer Express.[76] British Airways' route to domestic domination was path-breaking, a state-driven ideological project that was the prototype for much of Britain's nationalised industry. Although selected to be the first privatisation, other industries came to be privatised before it, but quite simply the British Airways project had to succeed given the enormous political capital invested in it.

The stakes for company and government remained high in the post-privatisation period. The departure of both Thatcher and Cecil Parkinson (as transport secretary), had weakened British Airways when it was faced with the next and more substantial competitive threat, from Richard Branson's Virgin Atlantic. British Airways' CEO, Sir Colin Marshall, admitted that its costs were 25 per cent higher than Virgin's and, in 1991, British Airways' profits nosedived to £130 million, down from £345 million in 1990. This diminished competitive advantage on transatlantic routes drove British Airways to launch a campaign to discredit Virgin, claiming it to be 'a dangerously overstretched airline, headed by an irrational eccentric who indulged in a range of physically and morally dangerous pursuits'.[77] As detailed by Gregory in a compelling account,[78] King as chairman, David Burnside[79] head of public relations and PA consultant Brian Basham were responsible for some astonishing actions against Virgin. Publicly, King instructed his legal adviser, Robert Ayling,[80] to lobby the CAA to prevent Branson from getting additional flight slots and from flying from Heathrow. More controversially, British Airways engaged in a slew of aggressive, questionable and illegal practices. A 'switch and sell campaign', which leveraged the company's powerful customer database, ultimately involved hacking into Virgin computers. Secret operations ('Operation Covent Garden' and 'Operation Barbara') were contracted to external 'security consultants'[81] and involved a 'small army'[82] of private detectives in 'dirty tricks'.

Provoked by an article Burnside had written for *British Airways News*, Branson sued for libel. The eventual outcome after British Airways' lengthy campaign of denial and its countersuit was victory for Branson and an out-of-court settlement in January 1993 that gave Virgin the largest libel sum ever awarded in British history. The company attempted to massage the verdict. The 'disreputable business activities' admitted in court were sanitised into an official position of 'regrettable conduct' that had been 'confined to a relatively small number of unconnected incidents involving a small number of employees'.[83] Basham was made the fall guy and Burnside, the most senior manager to face sanctions, was sacked. Although senior management underwent a reshuffle, the new order looked much like the old. Ayling, despite responsibility for the commercial 'dirty tricks', was promoted to group managing director, Marshall to chairman and King became president. David Hyde, the key link between the British Airways board and the 'small army of private detectives', who had even resorted to stealing rubbish from bin bags on behalf of British Airways in the hunt for compromising material and had launched illegal probes into members of staff, remained as head of security until 2002.[84]

Some questions arising from the Virgin affair for the longer-term conduct of employment relations and the 2009–11 dispute may be suggested. Engagement in dubious practice arguably might be applied as readily to industrial relations as to commercial matters. As discussed below, striking crew members in 1997 were subject to harassment and, in 2009–11, the *Daily Mail* published personal details of leading BASSA members in a clear attempt to vilify them, based on information that allegedly could only have come from company records.[85] Indeed, the question of whether the unacceptable intrusion into the profiles of individual staff had become a normative management practice is a legitimate one to ask.

The more general context of the Virgin events were the broader changes occurring in global aviation. The removal of state protection sharpened competition and increased market volatility leading to a perpetual process of restructuring and cost reduction.[86] British Airways, precisely because it was the first privatised flag carrier, had to confront the need for change much earlier than its competitors.[87] British Airways outsourced ground transport services to Ryder and in-flight catering to Gate Gourmet (owned by Swiss Air). In the 1990s it would have gone much further in its outsourcing strategy had it not been for union opposition.[88] The surge of low-cost new entrants, notably EasyJet and Ryanair, prompted British Airways to emulate the low-cost model, setting up in 1998 its own no-frills airline, Go, which was based at Stansted Airport.[89] European acquisitions (or part-acquisitions) included the German Delta Airline, the Finnish airline TAT and Air Liberté. The creation of the Oneworld alliance in 1998 was a crucial initiative. Over time, the responses of 'legacy' airlines to more challenging markets have included merger and acquisition which, in the case of British Airways in 2010, led to the formation of International Airlines Group (IAG), along with Iberia and Vueling airlines.

It was thus the freedom accorded British Airways following privatisation and the UK's 'liberal' labour relations environment that facilitated its concentration at European and global levels and which permitted it to pioneer management strategies in franchising, regionalisation, the creation of business units and outsourcing. As Europe's 'first mover' in respect of privatisation it was adapting to developments in deregulation and industry structure taking place in the US but 'arguably going further'.[90]

The privatisation of British Airways was Thatcher–King's 'jewel in the crown'. Forced monopolisation meant the drive to eradicate UK market opponents (Laker successfully and Virgin unsuccessfully) and the attendant dirty tricks activities. Concomitantly, the company adopted what became a hugely celebrated cultural change programme – 'Putting People First' – in its quest to become 'the world's favourite airline'. The programmes involved more than a formal commitment to customer service, more a thorough-going engagement of employee hearts and minds in what was explicitly termed the marshalling of 'emotional labour'.[91] The central idea was to refocus British Airways as a service rather than a transportation company, from being operationally driven to being market led.[92] The rationale was not to improve customer service for its own sake, but rather that excellent service was to be the connecting rod between greater passenger numbers, increased customer revenue and expanded profitability. Sir Colin Marshall, as chairman who headed the programme, articulated its basic terms as follows: 'to treat every single customer as though the entire airline is at his or her (the customer's) service, as indeed it must be ... this simple fact is that what we have to sell is a service to our customer'.[93] It became axiomatic for Marshall that the success of the airline was: 'entirely dependent upon the performance of our people from the quality of service we give'.[94] The cultural change initiative was feted as being responsible for transforming the airline from 'Bloody Awful' to 'Bloody Awesome'. The received wisdom has been that British Airways' programme was a resounding success, with its emphasis on employees' attitudinal and behavioural change, intensive training and the benefits of collaborative working on all aspects of British Airways' operations.[95] However, celebratory accounts in the manner of the 'Phoenix from the Ashes' school of company journalism were unduly influential. Radical cost surgery, where unions were compelled to accept workforce reductions, wage freezes and the implementation of new management strategies, were equally as important as cultural change factors in explaining the company's transition to profitability.[96] Even at the very height of 'Putting People First', workers in at least one bargaining unit annually were in conflict with the company. Industrial disputes remained widespread and involved British baggage handlers (1982), cabin crew (1982, 1984, 1989 – see below), engineers (1984, 1986, 1988, 1990) and pilots (1985, 1987).[97] British Airways' own surveys revealed that, while employees might be committed to the company and particularly the customer, many felt that the 'world's favourite airline' did not care about them as much as it should. Discontent remained widespread among all grades.[98]

So, when pursuing this high-quality change programme it was not simply the case that corporate management was freely able to select this strategy from a menu of options. Strategic choice was always constrained by structural and market requirements, particularly the imperative of cost reduction.[99] The early 1990s saw a sharp reduction in demand following the first Gulf War. To deliver the employee engagement strategy unions, including BASSA, had no choice but to accept cost-cutting initiatives that aimed to 'close the gap' between revenues and costs, even if this meant longer-term job loss as well as temporary lay-offs. However, not for the first time, and certainly not the last,[100] British Airways exploited this sense of external crisis with a unitary appeal to survival in order to justify the implementation, even though the 'Closing the Gap' campaign constituted one of the most painful episodes of corporate restructuring in the airline industry to date. To assert that employees positively assented to this downsizing programme,[101] though, is a misconception that conflates consent with compliance.

The shift to the 'market-led' realism of the Business Efficiency Programme (BEP) pursued by CEO Robert Ayling from 1996 brought industrial conflict (see below). However, BEP failed to deliver the profitability that had been expected, which in turn led British Airways to reprioritise customer service excellence ('Putting People First – Again'). The first mover advantage that had delivered success with the original strategy could not now be repeated. The new customer engagement strategy, including the ambitious 'Theatre and Flair' initiative, which encouraged cabin crew to fully express their personalities, failed to significantly improve profit margins. Subsequently, Rod Eddington, who replaced Ayling as CEO in May 2000, drove a new strategy in 2002 called 'Future Size and Shape', which sought to remove 'complexity from our business, competing more effectively with the no frills carriers and reducing costs, particularly through manpower reductions'.[102] The period of switching back and forth between an emphasis on customer excellence and investment in people on the one hand and an emphasis on cost reduction on the other hand was now at an end.

Strict cost reduction became central to industrial relations over the period. Indeed, the run-up to the 2009–11 dispute was dramatically shaped by the external shocks of 9/11 and the Iraq War, which led to 18,000 jobs being lost between 2001 and 2006.[103] When Willie Walsh took over as CEO in 2005, following apparent shareholder frustration with the pace of 'modernisation', a confrontation with the unions was widely seen as inevitable. As CEO of Aer Lingus, Walsh had severely cut costs, restoring the airline to profit in preparation for stock market flotation for which he earned the title 'slasher' from the Irish airline unions.[104] A historical analysis of industrial relations at British Airways with a particular focus on BASSA now foregrounds the overview of the 2009–11 conflict.

Industrial relations and BASSA

The dispute of 2009–11 was only the most recent episode in a history of antagonistic industrial relations. Overt conflict between cabin crew and company had occurred during the 1970s and in 1982, 1984, 1989 and 1987, and should be seen as part of a broader pattern of industrial action involving various sections of the workforce. If British Airways' early privatisation signified its importance as innovator in the global airline industry providing market leadership in business strategies and in cost reduction, it also implied first mover status in bringing industrial relations change.[105] This shift implied confrontation with the collective organisation of cabin crew in the form of the British Airlines Stewards and Stewardesses Association (BASSA).

BASSA had come into existence during in the 1950s during the state ownership of civil aviation. The Cadman Commission of 1938 had encouraged trade unionism and the extension of the Whitley Councils to the nascent industry and, at this time of industry consolidation, the standard framework of civil service collective bargaining and joint consultation was extended to incorporate the aviation industry.[106] In the post-war period when significant sections of UK industry were nationalised the dominant corporatist framework was accompanied by industrial relations systems, in which the actors (employer, union, government) recognised each other's legitimacy through mutually accepted processes of collective bargaining.[107] Trade unions had to balance protection of members' interests while sharing economic and job regulation with management, and recognising the overall interests of the industry, in this case a national flag carrier of strategic significance. To the extent that conflict occurred, or was permitted, it was to be 'institutionalised',[108] contained within defined parameters in a negotiated order. British Airways' subsequent development has to be understood against this backdrop and the breakdown of what has been termed 'quasi-regulated voluntarism'[109] following privatisation.

The formation of British Airways in 1974 led to the establishment of two independent branches of BASSA (both part of the TGWU) – Worldwide (long haul) and Eurofleet (short haul) – which mirrored the operational division of the constituent companies, BOAC and BEA. During the 1970s the incidence of industrial action declined among pilots and increased among 'less skilled' grades, particularly baggage handlers and cabin crew, whose combative strikes later in the decade and into the 1980s mirrored, to an extent, union responses to post-deregulatory activity in the United States. At British Airways, these responses also reflected the influence of the TGWU.[110]

When British Airways took over British Caledonian in 1988, the cabin crew were given the option of joining either branch,[111] but despite being essentially a long-haul workforce, the leaders organised a breakaway from the TGWU and, with support from the British Airline Pilots' Association (BALPA) and management, formed a new 'union', Cabin Crew '89 (CC89). This key development reflected King's contempt for trade unionism. He was most hostile to those managers, who he believed were indulging the unions, regarding them as obstacles in the path of his grand strategy. Prominent during the CC89 breakaway was Robert Ayling, later CEO, one of a cluster of managers whose antagonism to BASSA was captured in their anti-union soubriquet, 'the Miners Group'. Revelling in the defeat of organised labour, they sought to emulate the recent example of the Union of Democratic Mineworkers (UDM) in dividing the miners and undermining the NUM strike.[112] Acknowledging management's stratagem, BASSA reps referred to CC89 as a 'Trojan Horse', designed to introduce by stealth new agreements that would weaken BASSA's ability to maintain negotiations and produce stronger agreements.

While most short-haul crew remained loyal to BASSA, most long-haul crew defected to CC89 and only a minority stuck with BASSA and their branch (TGWU 1/1261). Shortly thereafter, they merged with their short-haul sisters and brothers to form BASSA 1/2000. The branch leadership then started work 'in earnest'[113] to win back members lost to CC89 and to recruit new starts. They emphasised CC89's essential weakness, which stemmed from the 'no strike' clause in its recognition agreement, which contrasted with BASSA's robust representation of members and its preparedness to take action on their behalf. A telling illustration of the differing approaches was the fact that CC89 reps were appointed while

BASSA reps were elected. The outcome of the recruitment campaign was a notable increase in net BASSA membership, from 4,079 in 1990 to 9,076 in 1997.[114] One year that stands out is 1996 (see Table 1), when cabin crew faced threats to terms and conditions from the BEP programme pursued by Robert Ayling.

A brief review of the context is necessary. While senior management had encouraged workforce division through CC89 and had sought to delegitimise BASSA, it was also sufficiently pragmatic in that it strove to enlist employee support for the cultural change programme Putting People First. While the King–Marshall quality strategy shaped British Airways' industrial relations policies, it did not solely determine them. The profound influence of deregulation and industry restructuring shifted the emphasis from quality to cost and a hard-nosed commercial approach, which went beyond the traditional peak and trough cycle. Through the Business Efficiency Programme (BEP) British Airways sought to implement a five-year cost reduction programme aimed at delivering £42 million of savings through restructuring cabin crew pay and conditions. Specific measures included the consolidation of overtime, reduced allowances, the implementation of merit-based promotion, the removal of long-standing conditions and the introduction of significantly lower pay for new starts.[115]

Table 1   BASSA membership: number of people recruited and leaving (1994–2011)

Year	Recruited	Leaving	Net
1994	955	406	+549
1995	804	315	+489
1996	1765	39	+1726
1997	1156	1445	−289
1998	1940	822	+1118
1999	817	357	+460
2000	719	401	+318
2001	711	525	+186
2002	195	257	−62
2003	408	636	−228
2004	1071	906	+165
2005	919	433	+486
2006	817	788	+29
2007	697	658	+39
2008	844	342	+502
2009	454	1057	−603
2010	117	1474	−1257
2011	231	346	−115

Epitomising the 'Trojan Horse' metaphor, British Airways struck a deal in 1997 with CC89, whose members voted in a postal ballot to accept these conditions.[116] Left to fight alone, BASSA secured an 80 per cent ballot vote to strike on a 73 per cent turnout, with action called for three days (9–11 July). Management adopted harsh 'counter-mobilisation' measures, including drafting in replacement staff and accommodating them in army barracks,[117] while withdrawing union facilities and refusing to de-roster union reps from flying duties in breach of the collective agreement. Senior management then threatened to sack strikers and to discipline 'stayaways'. Although only 300 did withdraw their labour, more than 2,000 reported sick in what became celebrated as the 'mass sickie'.[118] Despite limited industrial action, this dispute is estimated to have cost the airline £125 million. Reputational damage worsened when TV news showed managers filming crew on the picket lines after the company had denied using such an intimidating practice. Following a 'pause for peace', insisted on by TGWU general secretary, Bill Morris, but which broke the strike's momentum, BASSA agreed to the demand for savings, after the company had made some limited concessions.

If 1989 marked a turning point in industrial relations and the history of BASSA, then 1997 was no less definitive. It represented a qualitatively different initiative aimed at taking apart the employment relations architecture of the regulated era.[119] In multiple respects, the 1997 dispute foreshadowed 2009–11, most notably in the highly adversarial attitudes and actions of senior management, in the threat to derecognise BASSA and in British Airways' willingness to marshal substantial resources to undermine the crew's action, break the strike and intimidate crew members. It also prefigured the depth, if not breadth, of resistance, the repertoire of imaginative and satirical publicity, images and slogans ('Brutish Airways'), and the extreme hostility directed at the person of the CEO (in 1997 Robert Ayling, in 2007 Willie Walsh).

Not only did the outcome of the 1997 dispute fail to resolve its underlying causes, it actually deepened the resentment felt by cabin crew. BASSA's sense of grievance was stoked further by the dismissal of the branch secretary, Mike Coleman, and while British Airways proclaimed its desire to establish a good working relationship with BASSA, it still accorded CC89 preferential treatment. Yet CC89's membership was now in serious decline, due to the hard work of reps in persuading CC89 members to return to BASSA and in recruiting non-members. BASSA's charge that CC89's close association with British Airways rendered it impotent to defend members' conditions had been vindicated by its complicity in the 1997 dispute.

While BASSA did lose members in 1997, its determination to grow in order to increase its bargaining power produced positive results. The three years after 1997 saw a net increase of almost 2,000 members and the branch leadership easily exceeded the '10,000 for 2000' target of its recruitment campaign. CAA data confirms that membership density increased, from 43 per cent in 1991 to 73 per cent by 2001.[120] According to Duncan Holley, the branch secretary[121] elected in May 1998, once the immediate negative effects of 1997 had subsided (partly facilitated by the departure of Robert Ayling), a period of comparative industrial peace ensued under Sir Rod Eddington as CEO, which enabled BASSA to focus fully on building membership.

Yet, as indicated above, in the new millennium the business landscape changed dramatically following 9/11. British Airways was no exception to plummeting passenger volumes, particularly on transatlantic routes, an unprecedented crisis for an industry already entering a cyclical downturn. BASSA was compelled to make concessions over terms and conditions, agreeing to the 'temporary' removal of one crew member per flight and reluctantly complying with redundancies in order 'to save the airline'. The effect is evident in membership losses for 2002 and 2003 (see Table 1), although revival was recorded in the subsequent two years as some workforce expansion resumed. Nevertheless, 18,000 jobs were lost between 2001 and 2006[122] due to the effects of 9/11, although BASSA and many crew members suspected the company was using 9/11 opportunistically to impose rationalisation[123] and, in 2007, to justify proposals to reduce pay, pensions and sick leave entitlement.

From BASSA's perspective, the arrival of Willie Walsh saw industrial relations go into 'an almost instantaneous nosedive'.[124] Overnight senior managers became intransigent in their dealings with BASSA and in their interactions with cabin crew. As noted, over the preceding decades the company had periodically resorted to confrontation, notably in 1989 and 1997 and in the unashamed attempt to divide the workforce through the company's support for CC89. Nevertheless, there was an enduring legacy of the corporatist industrial relations structure established under nationalisation in which BASSA had been accepted, however tenuously at times, as a legitimate industrial relations 'actor'. Under Walsh's bullish leadership, British Airways allowed the collective bargaining machinery of the National Sectional Panel (NSP) to break down. At Aer Lingus, Walsh had established a reputation as 'slasher' and 'union basher'. His arrival exposed fault lines in the 'tripartite' industrial relationships[125] of British Airways, BASSA and BASSA's parent union, at that time, the TGWU.

The particular character of BASSA's relationship with the TGWU requires emphasis. While the TGWU was BASSA's parent union, historically BASSA was semi-autonomous, with its relative independence underpinned by financial arrangements which meant that while 70 per cent of subscriptions went to the TGWU, 30 per cent were retained for BASSA's own purposes.[126] A notable feature of BASSA is that its leadership and negotiating roles are held by elected reps, who remain employed as working crew,[127] thus obviating the necessity of having a corpus of full-time paid national officers wholly responsible for negotiations. Of course, at crucial stages of negotiations between BASSA and British Airways and/or when they had stalled, national TGWU officers, even the General Secretary, might become involved to broker deals. Such interventions occurring in 1997 and again in 2007 were not regarded positively by BASSA.[128]

Another notable feature of BASSA has been its role in the joint regulation of working conditions. Comprehensive and authoritative collective agreements covered Worldwide and Eurofleet operations and conditions in the finest of detail, including 'rosters and scheduling, pay, hotels, allowances and all working agreements and conditions'.[129] Such immersion in the day-to-day work lives of cabin crew and the familiarity that the reps and the union had with its members' concerns was key to the framing of the dispute and an essential resource that BASSA could draw upon (see Chapter 3).

Reflecting the origins and development of British Airways, BASSA's strength among both long-haul (Worldwide) and short-haul fleets was at Heathrow. Its membership base became even more concentrated there when the satellite bases were closed in Belfast (2001), Manchester (2007) and Glasgow (2009). By the time of the dispute, the workforce had a diverse composition, in part the outcome of Ayling's drive for international identity, which had seen the recruitment of crew from European countries and beyond. Evidence from the union's membership database suggests that European crew were just as likely to be union members as UK crew. Indicative of BASSA immersion in crews' daily lives is the fact that the proportion of members who were women (over two-thirds) did genuinely reflect the gender composition of the workforce.

As indicated above, Gate Gourmet was a significant conflict which, it should be recalled, took place only four years before the BA–BASSA dispute. While British Airways did not own and operate Gate Gourmet services it was obviously keenly interested in this dispute at a major supplier and came to be directly involved. Controversially, the outsourced caterer had sacked 670 workers, which prompted unofficial solidarity walkouts by baggage handlers employed by British Airways. In turn, the company sacked leading

TGWU members. Thus, the dispute contributed, to the increasingly hostile stance the company was adopting towards trade unionism.

Although the cabin crew dispute of 2006–7 did not lead to industrial action, it was far from an exercise in sabre rattling. The accumulation over many years of multiple grievances generated by cost-cutting, notably work intensification and eroded working conditions and terms of employment, clashed with the new CEO's determination to radically reconfigure work arrangements and contracts. After hostile and fruitless negotiations, BASSA registered 12 areas of a failure to agree, including pensions and the post-1997 salary rates. In the subsequent ballot for strike action, 97 per cent voted in favour on an 80 per cent turnout, reflecting the reps' and crew members' depth of anger. Three days of action were planned (29–31 January). In a reprise of 1997, British Airways responded by closing the BASSA offices at Heathrow and preventing the de-rostering of the union's reps.

Despite the fact that 'the membership was "up" for this dispute',[130] the BASSA Branch Committee voted by 6 to 3 in favour of suspending the proposed action, a decision attributed by some to the disinclination of the TGWU leadership to support the strike. It has been suggested that the circumstances of the Gate Gourmet strikes left the union vulnerable to British Airways, a threat of injunction still hanging over the TGWU for having, allegedly, breached the legislation proscribing secondary industrial action.[131] However, overt conflict was merely postponed. British Airways management then moved to clarify, indeed to toughen its proposals, set out in the Project Columbus strategy, which was leaked to BASSA in 2008. Meanwhile the union reunited its divided committee, increased recruitment and prepared its members for impending conflict.

In February 2009, the company formally announced its demand for £89 million of savings, and preliminary talks with BASSA commenced a month later.[132] Senior management created a conflictual context for these discussions by instigating disciplinary action against Lizanne Malone and Nigel Stott, in response to a complaint by the outgoing chair of CC89 (Andy Webb). However, British Airways' ability to foment division through using its 'Trojan Horse' had significantly diminished. Emboldened by the overthrow and retirement of some of CC89's old guard, who had been key players in collusion with management, a new breed of CC89 rep emerged willing now to collaborate with BASSA.[133] Although CC89 had shrunk, the coming together of its 1,500 members with the 11,500 of BASSA was more than symbolic, for it meant that 13,000 of the estimated 14,000 total crew workforce were now union members, shared a common purpose and were soon to be in the same union. Thus, combined union density at the commencement of the dispute stood at 92 per cent.

Of course, BASSA could not foresee the future course of the dispute and the costs and benefits of strike action for, to emphasise the general point, unions inevitably embark on such action without being able to predict developments and outcomes. Yet, with its strengthened membership and in tune with the mood of the cabin crew, the BASSA leadership was aware of the realistic level of support for strike action and its potential effectiveness.

Overview of the dispute

Two decades of cost-cutting had already eroded cabin crew conditions and introduced inferior contracts for those crew commencing their employment after 1997. Yet, management now resolved to radically reconfigure work arrangements and terms and conditions. Avoidance of conflict in 2007 had merely postponed the reckoning. BASSA first became aware of British Airways' internal document on Project Columbus (sometimes referred to as Operation Columbus) in early summer 2008. British Airways had engaged a US-based outsourcing and corporate restructuring firm to formulate a strategy aimed at dispensing with experienced cabin crew and eradicating their current terms and conditions, pay scales and existing collective agreements. At this stage, British Airways was considering 'setting up a subsidiary operation to "employ" all cabin crew at Heathrow and Gatwick'. Routes would be incrementally moved into the new organisation and crew would be bought out, forced to leave, or left behind.[134] An important aspect of the company's offensive was the need to tackle the specific problem of Heathrow, where management's ability to effect change had been more problematic. It was at Heathrow that the 'regulatory overhang' and with it employee expectations of labour contract, reward and conditions were the strongest and, of course, BASSA was most influential.

Then, in September 2008, BASSA's fears were confirmed with the receipt of a leaked factsheet spelling out new contractual arrangements for a so-called 'new fleet' to be introduced at Heathrow. New recruits were to work long-haul and short-haul routes and were to be employed on 'closer to market pay and allowance rates'. Crucially, Project Columbus stated these 'brand new agreements and reward structures' would provide 'a golden opportunity to break down some of the barriers to change that are a feature of the old agreements and the relationships that accompany them'.[135] These 'complex and restrictive cabin crew agreements' were regarded as obstacles to efficiency and a barrier to change and reinforced by the existing relationship with the trade unionism.

Over time, inferior contracts would supersede existing contracts and conditions, but the short-term would see the removal of 1,700 cabin crew jobs.[136] Existing crew would 'wither on the vine' as, through staff turnover and retirement, they were replaced by a new fleet working mixed short and long-haul (referred to as 'mixed fleet') on lower rates of pay and conditions of service.[137] The introduction of new tiers on different terms and conditions had become a feature of many UK workforces over the previous two decades following reorganisation and/or privatisation as a result of government policies and intensified market competition. In response, many unions had defended existing members' terms and conditions but often at the expense of new recruits, a concessionary course that BASSA was not prepared to accept.

As regulator of these 'agreements', BASSA was compelled to resist. Yet the strikes should not be seen as a simple and straightforward outcome of an unavoidable cost-cutting strategy meeting the immovable opposition of an intransigent union. British Airways had made record profits in 2007–8 and a 10 per cent operating margin.[138] Further, during negotiations BASSA made concessions which came very close[139] to meeting British Airways' target of £53 million savings. Walsh's rejection of BASSA's offer and the abrupt upward revision to a £108 million cut implied that savings were not his and the company's main objective. Rather, the principal aim was to break BASSA and its historical influence over regulation of contracts and working conditions. While Walsh insisted that British Airway's perilous situation necessitated the 'mixed fleet', BASSA countered by demonstrating that these were exaggerated fears, a position confirmed when the company's 2010's half-yearly accounts showed £158 million profit.

BASSA's determination to protect pay and conditions was hardly surprising considering the significantly inferior pay rates offered by LCCs and the pressure on wages resulting from intensified competition. Figures for 2008 from the Civil Aviation Authority (CAA) put the average total pay for British Airways' cabin crew at £29,900 per annum, compared with £20,200 for EasyJet cabin crew, which was by no means the lowest of the salaries offered by the LCCs.[140] Cabin crew were well aware of the harsh realities of basement pay and conditions among LCCs which could be a potential outcome of British Airways' 'race to the bottom'. Stories were emerging of conditions that were anathema to British Airways' cabin crew; of staff required to pay for uniforms and mandatory safety courses; of being paid only 'chocs off and chocs on' time; that is, the hours spent 'in the air' and not for preflight briefings, turnaround time, sales meetings and time on the ground caused by delays and flight cancellations; of being paid for only four days' work in a week and required to be on call ready to attend work at an hour's notice if required.

The trigger for British Airways' recourse to strike action was the imposition in late 2009 without negotiation, and in disregard of agreed collective bargaining procedures, of reduced crew complements across both Worldwide and Eurofleet. One purser was removed from Heathrow Worldwide flights, with cabin service directors (CSDs) required to perform customer service duties, while arrangements for additional crew on some long-haul flights were withdrawn.[141] For cabin crew, the company's unilateral action was seen not just as jeopardising the legacy of negotiated working conditions but also, inextricably, as dramatically increasing managerial control and threatening the existence of their union. Management was seeking the decisive elimination of the 'regulatory overhang'. To reiterate, it was not so much the substantive issue of the removal of one crew member that mattered, but the principle of the removal without negotiation and agreement that motivated the crew and union to resist.

Initially, BASSA had moved to secure an immediate High Court injunction against British Airways, on the basis that the company's actions were in breach of contract, but the court refused to grant it.[142] With this course of action blocked, BASSA balloted cabin crew on strike action in November 2009, leading to a huge majority (92 per cent on a 92 per cent turnout) in favour. The result was announced at a mass meeting of more than 2000 crew at the Sandown Race Course on 14 December and was accompanied by the decision of the BASSA Committee to take twelve days of strike action over the Christmas and New Year holidays. The committee was aware of the possible consequences of this decision in terms of public opinion, but calculated that the 'pros of taking such draconian action outweighed the cons [albeit] not by much',[143] because the extended nature of the proposed action would force the issue with British Airways and demonstrate the seriousness of BASSA's resolve. However, despite anticipating potential difficulties, the BASSA leadership later acknowledged that it did underestimate the sheer scale of the backlash against cabin crew, particularly from the media, and the extent of British Airways' counter-mobilisation.

The dispute became framed by highly politicised judicial proceedings resulting from British Airways' determination to delegitimise union action (see Chapter 4).[144] The circumstances were that, in the autumn of 2009, British Airways had offered voluntary redundancy and the union had included in its first ballot a number of crew who may have accepted this option before industrial action was due to commence.[145] Although no member had signed documentation either accepting or rejecting the offer, BASSA was presented with the dilemma of whether to include potential leavers in the ballot, for to exclude them would be to deny them a voice, while to include them might be deemed to transgress the legislation on balloting procedures. In addition, the union had no means by which to identify this cohort, who, it transpired, numbered only 1,003 out of a voting population of 10,286, of whom, 92 per cent voted in favour of industrial action.[146] So overwhelming was the majority that even if all those affected had voted against it would have made no difference to the overall result. Yet, British Airways won a High Court injunction under TULRCA, which prevented BASSA's proposed action on the grounds that it would be unlawful because it had balloted members who would not then be employed at the time of action.[147] BASSA thus joined a cluster of cases (e.g. Royal Mail in 2007, Metrobus in 2008, Milford Haven port strike) but unions were injuncted on minor technical grounds where no material difference would have been made to outcomes.[148]

In a High Court judgement on 17 December 2009, Mrs Justice Cox rejected the union case that the size of the ballot majority made no material difference to the outcome and ruled that the strike should not go ahead because of breaches of 'technical requirements'.[149] She introduced criteria that had nothing to do with legal process:

A strike of this kind taking place now, over twelve days of the Christmas period, is in my view fundamentally more damaging to British Airways, and indeed to the wider public, than a strike taking place at almost any other time of the year. For the reasons I have given the balance of convenience, in my judgement, lies firmly in favour of granting relief.[150]

This judgement raised fundamental questions regarding the right to strike in the UK.[151] The union was now compelled to reballot. The branch secretary, consistent with the terms of the collective agreement, which made provisions for him to undertake urgent union business, de-rostered himself in order to carry out the painstaking task of ensuring that the membership database was accurate. In the second ballot, announced on 22 February 2010, 81 per cent voted in favour of action on a 79 per cent turnout, with BASSA declaring seven days of strikes, commencing with three days from 20 March.

However, retrospectively, British Airways again legally challenged BASSA over the February ballot, this time on the grounds that it had not individually notified its members of the result, having posted the figures on the website. In addition, the company objected to the fact that BASSA had not informed members about 11 spoilt papers in a ballot in which 7,482 had voted in favour of action and only 1,789 against. Once again, British Airways was granted an injunction, to restrain four five-day blocks of industrial action but, on this occasion, the injunction was overturned by the Court of Appeal following an action by the union's legal team led by John Hendy QC.[152] The judge determined that to require the union to prove that each member should have been sent a report of the full ballot result was unrealistic. Had British Airways' action been successful the March strikes would have been deemed illegal and British Airways could have invoked the right to dismiss those who had taken strike action. Despite the ultimately successful outcome of this case, one of the blocks of action (18–22 May) had to be cancelled.

Table 2   BASSA's four ballots for industrial action.[153]

Date of ballot	Majority in favour of industrial action (%)	Turnout (%)
November 2009	92	92
January 2010	80	80
January 2011	79	75
March 2011	83	72

Consistent with union-busting strategies, notably those employed in the US, the legal forays aimed to throw the union into confusion, breaking the momentum of mobilisation and buying time so that the company could prepare its strike-breaking operations. Exploiting the detailed clauses of strike and balloting legislation was part of a broader counter-mobilisation,[154] which can be categorised as follows.

First, British Airways implemented a 'strategy of decapitation' against BASSA,[155] abandoning the long-standing collective agreement on de-rostering and time off for union duties. Confirmation came with the publication in the *Guardian* of a secret report by the company entitled *A Review of where British Airways are in the Relationship to BASSA*. The report's author, reportedly an industrial relations academic, was said to have 'encouraged British Airways to prepare for a showdown … with BASSA about three years ago'.[156] While the company distanced itself from the report and the *Guardian* printed a subsequent apology,[157] its correction was concerned only with the identity of the author/adviser and not the substance of the report, particularly this prophetic passage:

> The management team should agree and express a determination to force the issue with BASSA. Some consideration should be given to hitting the leadership of BASSA where it hurts. Ground rules for paid time off for trade union duties is an area which needs to be very closely examined.[158]

Management soon demonstrated the essence of its decapitation strategy. Several key activists and officers were dismissed or given final written warnings, including the branch secretary, the branch auditor and two other reps. In January 2010, the branch secretary, Duncan Holley, was charged with gross misconduct for having de-rostered himself. The level of personal intimidation was extraordinary. For example, on 11 February he received a 47-page legal report from British Airways that threatened him with court action if he did not disclose the names of 32 individual crew members who had made particular posts on the BASSA Forum. Four months later he was dismissed, having failed at an employment tribunal to gain interim relief to keep his contract of employment, pending the outcome of an unfair dismissal claim. Nicky Marcus, a BASSA representative, was suspended for gross misconduct and then sacked following a disciplinary hearing. Her case was another flagrant breach of worker rights.[159] She was charged with interfering in the employment relationship between British Airways and its employees, despite the fact that she was carrying out legitimate trade union representation duties on behalf of members.

The targeting of these key players was a matter of ruthless calculation. Holley, as Branch Secretary, was the figurehead of the union, while Marcus was central to rallying the crew, energising the picket lines and organising responses to the dispute-related disciplinary hearings. Mark Everard, another victimised committee member, had overall responsibility for BASSA's communications, which were so vital to organisation and mobilisation during the dispute.

Second, British Airways engaged in acts of retribution against the workforce as a whole and against specific individual crew members. Travel concessions were withdrawn in the immediate aftermath of the strikes, the company claiming that these concessions were gratuitous and not contractual. It was a spiteful move that reprised the company's action in 1997. Further, as many as 93 crew, it was calculated, were either sacked or disciplined for conduct relating to the dispute, often on the flimsiest of pretexts, such as private conversations being 'overheard' and 'misconstrued'.[160] The cases included long-standing cabin crew with exemplary employment records. A BASSA-commissioned report described 'an embedded culture of bullying and authoritarianism deliberately engineered from the top echelons of the company'.[161]

Senior management orchestrated divisions between strikers and non-striking cabin crew and other staff. The most infamous example was the graffiti board, known as the 'wailing wall', on which hostile and frequently personal comments against the strikers and BASSA were posted. Walsh endorsed the wall by being pictured next to it, with the sentence, 'the union should not be able to run ...' clearly visible. Compounding this practice was the fact that a number of crew members who raised concerns with managers were then suspended or even sacked. The climate of fear and division was deepened by the antagonistic behaviour of pilots, encouraged by management and made possible because of the lack of support for BASSA from their union, BALPA. Although only a minority of pilots did sign up as Volunteer Cabin Crew (VCC) the majority who did not passively watched these developments without protest. This TUC-affiliated union 'hardly lifted a finger to stop their members colluding with British Airways to break what was a legal dispute between one set of employees against their employer'.[162] During the dispute relationships between cabin and flight deck often dissolved into bitter acrimony.

Third, the company engaged in systematic, covert activity designed to undermine the strike ballots and weaken the union. This involved the Asset Protection department, British Airways' internal corporate security operation previously used to regulate and investigate theft of company or customer goods within the airline and which employed former Scotland Yard and security services' personnel.[163] BASSA reported that 'Asset Protection' had placed internet forums under surveillance for 'negative comments about the airline', and had dedicated 'teams of up to six people monitoring union activity and individual reps for any information'[164] that could be used against them. Perhaps 18 disciplinary cases were connected to Facebook postings, text messages, emails and postings on the BASSA or the BALPA fora, with three concerned with private Facebook postings to 'friends'.[165] A particular target for the Asset Protection department were crew members who posted on the BASSA Forum, the Crew Forum and the BALPA Forum. A notorious incident was over a post by 'Gespetto' on the BALPA Forum, which was objected to by a British Airways captain on the spurious grounds that it was bullying,[166] and led to 'Gespetto' being suspended and sacked. Sinister actions were alleged, particularly with regard to surveillance of cabin crew, who stated that the clandestine Asset Protection department had been responsible for following them to their homes. BASSA reported that it had 'unequivocal proof' of these human rights' infringements.[167] This charge is supported by *The Independent's* report that in 2015 British Airways paid £1 million to stop Unite the Union from suing it over the operations of its in-house security force, including the accessing of crew's private communications.[168]

Management actions bear the hallmark of the union avoidance and busting industry that has developed in the United States,[169] but is increasingly manifest in the UK.[170] Prominent in this pervasive and sophisticated industry is consulting firm The Burke Group (TBG). The exact nature of the relationship of the TBG with British Airways during the 2009–11 is not clear, not least because of TBG's preference for clandestine, 'beneath the radar' operations when engaged. However, it is known that TBG established an international division in 2005, it has advised airlines (e.g. Virgin Atlantic) and, in 2006, was hired by Flybe to defeat the TGWU's cabin crew organising campaign following the company's takeover of British Airways Connect.[171]

Fourth, British Airways abandoned existing disciplinary procedure that had been an integral part of the collective agreement with BASSA. New processes were introduced, known as 'Leiden' after the room in British Airways HQ at Waterside where cases were processed. They were reported to comprise 'secret criteria and frameworks unknown to the crew involved or to the cabin crew community at large or to their unions'.[172] Crew now subject to disciplinary action were unaware of the codes they might have transgressed, making it almost impossible for them and their union representatives to construct a defence. Leiden was a fast track to suspension and dismissal.[173] Like anti-union employers generally, British Airways was willing to take the risk of being taken to employment tribunals and to bear the potential cost of losing because, by the time those cases were held, the union would already have been damaged by the removal of key activists.

Fifth, the company invested substantial resources in measures designed to undermine the effectiveness of BASSA's action. As indicated, the perishable nature of the civil aviation 'product' – particularly passenger traffic – can be a source of significant 'bargaining power'[174] for unions. In this case, British Airways made strenuous efforts to reduce union power by finding alternative sources of labour, recruiting 'volunteer' crews apparently numbering thousands from among its pilots and ground staff.[175] So-called working crew and pilots were trained alongside each other in Cranebank. Indicative of the lengths to which British Airways was prepared to go to in order to break the strike, it chartered at huge cost more than twenty planes from other carriers, including its short-haul rival, Ryanair. Further, it drew on its Oneworld partners to carry passengers.

1. BASSA members in 1997 preparing to march past the Compass Centre where they would normally report for duty.

2. On 25 January 2007, a meeting of BASSA members cheer the 96 per cent vote on an 80 per cent turnout for strike action. The three-day strike scheduled for 29 January was called off.

3.   At the 1 October 2007 quarterly branch meeting following the aborted 2007 strike, BASSA members expressed their view that the January settlement had not resolved the issues that had led to the strike ballot.

4.   Steve Turner, Unite national officer for civil air transport, introducing himself at a BASSA branch meeting at Bedfont Football Club.

5. Carol Ng, general secretary of the BA Hong Kong International Cabin Crew Association, updating BASSA members at Kempton Park of its ultimately successful legal challenge against race and age discrimination involved in BA's enforced retirement at the age of 45.

6. At the quarterly branch meeting in January 2009 members engaged in intense debate about the basis that negotiations should take with BA management.

7. A branch meeting in July 2009 at Kempton Park saw a huge attendance crammed into two big conference rooms connected by a video link. Right to left: Duncan Holley, Nigel Stott, Chris Harrison, Adrian Smith.

8. BASSA members listen intently to the discussion on how to combat the threat of Columbus and a raft of other issues, including sickness policy, the loss of overtime and the general lack of respect shown to crew by management.

9.   On 2 November 2009, Unite and BASSA officers address more than 2,000 members at a branch meeting at Sandown racecourse, following BA's imposition without negotiation of reduced crew complements on Eurofleet and Worldwide. Left to right: Steve Turner, Nigel Stott, Len McCluskey, Lizanne Malone and Duncan Holley.

10.   At the branch meeting of 2 November 2009 members of BASSA and Cabin Crew '89 voted to ballot for industrial action.

11.   At Sandown racecourse on 14 December, Len McCluskey announces the ballot result with 92 per cent on a 92 per cent turnout voting for strike action.

12.   BASSA members listen to the announcement.

13–14.   Cabin crew express their jubilation at the ballot result.

15.   At a branch meeting at Kempton Park racecourse,
Lizanne Malone addresses BASSA members following
BA's successful injunction to stop the 12 days of strike
action scheduled to commence on 22 December 2009.

16.   Members listen intently to their officers' analysis of Justice Cox's judgement, which
blocked BASSA's proposed strike action and threatened the right to strike action more
generally.

17–21.   Discussion of BASSA's decision to ask members approval to reballot its membership. Clockwise from top left: Duncan Holley, Chris Harrison, Steve Cottingham legal adviser from H. R. Parsons, Oliver Richardson and Marcel Devereux.

Sixth, and reprising a response familiar over the previous two decades, attempts were made to divide the cabin crew workforce by setting up an employee organisation hostile to BASSA. Clearly CC89 could no longer play the divisive role it had done at its foundation and thereafter, particularly during the 1997 dispute. The Professional Cabin Crew Council (PCCC) claimed that it was set up by crew disillusioned with BASSA and, in terms and tones that reprised CC89, sought to foster a 'more positive, collaborative relationship with the company'.[176] It claimed not to be a trade union, despite its stated aim of seeking to negotiate pay and conditions. The PCCC strenuously insisted that British Airways had played no part in its establishment, had not given them any money and were not involved. These assertions of independence are questionable given the timing of its foundation, British Airways' long-term encouragement of CC89 and the absence of membership fees but the promise of free legal advice. Its creation is certainly consistent with the company's history of 'dirty tricks' and the character of union busting 'spoiler' activity. In terms of outcome, given the overwhelming allegiance of crew members to BASSA, PCCC made no headway.

Other forces were aligned against BASSA and the cabin crew. With a general election imminent, although yet to be declared, the government was firmly opposed to BASSA's action. Labour was obsessed by the memory of the so-called 'Winter of Discontent' of 1978–9 and the perception that ongoing or recent strike activity would damage its electoral fortunes. Prime Minister Gordon Brown declared that the crews' action was 'unjustified and deplorable'. The transport secretary, Lord Adonis, condemned BASSA for holding 'passengers to ransom', hyperbolically declaring that strikes would 'threaten the very existence of British Airways'.[177] New Labour's ingrained animosity to strikes had been signalled by previous Prime Minister Tony Blair's infamous 'reformers versus wreckers' speech.[178] The hostility of Brown, when chancellor of the exchequer, to the firefighters and their union (FBU) had been a signal feature of its 2002–4 pay dispute,[179] with Blair even considering the sacking of firefighters and their replacement with 'new personnel'.[180]

The cabin crew were on the receiving end of venomous press coverage and BASSA's leaders were subjected to harassment. On the day of the first High Court verdict, Holley was doorstepped by two journalists from the *Daily Mail*, which published personal information about leading BASSA members. A photograph of branch official Lizanne Malone and of her home appeared,[181] alongside profiles and pictures of Mark Everard and Nigel Stott.[182] Fundamental concerns regarding data protection and the right to privacy and human rights more generally were further raised with the publication of information on individuals' sickness records, annual earnings and holiday entitlements.[183] The predictable outcome was a wave of abuse directed at, and even attacks upon, cabin crew. If the *Daily Mail*, and to a lesser extent the *Daily Telegraph*, were guilty of 'crimes of commission', other media were guilty of 'crimes of omission'. Only the slightest coverage of the most significant industrial conflict since the national firefighters' dispute of 2002–3 was provided, and reports almost wholly failed to represent accurately the union's case.[184]

Seeking to break the silence, employment relations' academics had a letter published in *The Guardian*, which warned against 'underestimating the deep seated and justifiable anger of a loyal and dedicated workforce'. They pointed out that cabin crew understood that a victory for Willie Walsh's 'macho management strategy would precipitate a race to the bottom in terms of working conditions and job quality' and 'damage high standards of customer service for which British Airways' cabin crew are renowned'. Further, they reiterated the argument that Walsh's actions could be explained only by a desire to break the union. The letter argued that cabin crew deserved public support on the basis that 'the wider significance of a triumph of unilateral management prerogative would be a widening of the representation gap in UK employment relations, and a further erosion of worker rights and of that most precious of commodities – democracy'.[185] The authors timed the letter to coincide with the first days of industrial action.

This first strike was prepared for by a mass meeting at Sandown Park racecourse, attended by several thousand. Chapter 5 provides vivid accounts of the carnival atmosphere of strike days and mass rallies at Bedfont Football Club, the ways that strikes were organised and the dynamics of cabin crew mobilisation. Chapter 5 also focuses on the role played by union communications and social media, widely acknowledged by crew and BASSA reps alike, to have been extremely important, particularly in helping to overcome the problems of dispersion and distance.

A union website, email and texting were used to communicate to members, permitting the simultaneous dissemination of key messages. Of particular importance were two interactive internet union forums – the BASSA Forum and Crew Forum, which operated alongside each other for most of the dispute. The BASSA Forum, restricted to union members, had emerged as an important communication tool during the 2007 conflict. Initially, members had posted under pseudonyms, but the dominance of a small number of 'intransigent and aggressive' posters led to objections, prompting the BASSA leadership to close it down temporarily. It was restarted with members posting under their own names, a loss of anonymity which caused justifiable anxiety regarding members' vulnerability to management surveillance. The forum became the subject of what could aptly be described as a digital stakeout, leading to suspensions, disciplinary actions and sackings. In response, a BASSA member established the Crew Forum, where members posted anonymously and which was moderated, meaning that it was seen to be more secure. Moderators worked closely with BASSA reps and posts from the union were coordinated across the forums. It peaked at 5,000 active registered members.

In 2010, British Airways' solicitors attempted to force the moderators of both forums to release the names of members on the grounds of alleged defamation following the disclosure on Facebook, and subsequently on the forums, of the names of pilots trained to take cabin crew roles.[186] Both refused, but BASSA decided to close its forum to avoid litigation. As the testimonies in Chapter 5 reveal, BASSA members believed the forums were hugely important for advancing their interests, as a source of information countering British Airways propaganda, as a platform for debate and as a means of organising strikes. Continuous interaction between members reduced isolation, built confidence, fostered activism and offered emotional support in the face of hostility, so that, in the memorable words of one crew member who participated in our research, 'the forum broke the fear'.

The BA–BASSA dispute marked one of the first comprehensive uses of social media in an industrial dispute, prefiguring later widespread union adoption. The potential for digitally based communications and social media to strengthen trade union organisation, particularly in strike action, is an important subject for unions, activists and members. Early studies stressed the liberatory possibilities of communicative technologies. They were seen to engender 'distributed discourse',[187] by which communication flows could be facilitated, member participation increased, union internal democracy enhanced and the balance of power between employer and employees reconfigured in favour of the latter. Emphasis was placed on how technologies create 'e-spaces', or 'safe spaces', which enable employee participation without fear of retribution. A more critical, indeed pessimistic, evaluation, however, challenges the naivety of this idea of 'distributed discourse' and the notion of 'safe spaces'.[188] The truth may lie somewhere in between, for the use and consequences of digital communications are unavoidably a part of the contested terrain of employment relations. As BASSA understood very well, internet-based interactive media could be a powerful mobilising mechanism but, equally, as it found to its cost, management could invade supposed 'safe spaces' and exploit crew members' participation as part of its counter-offensive. Perhaps the main conclusion to be drawn, as evidenced by the rich testimony in Chapter 5, is that as the strike days came thick and fast in March, April and May of 2010, social media was a battleground bitterly fought over by BASSA and British Airways. BASSA and its members never considered the 'virtual' to be a substitute for the 'real', but internet-based interactive communication contributed to mobilisation in innumerable ways, not least to the organisation on the frontline of pickets and rallies on strike days.

After 22 days of strike action and no movement from the employer, BASSA informed British Airways of its intention to initiate a new strike ballot, a legal requirement as the union was introducing issues that had not been included in the previous ballot. The additional 'live' issues were bullying, the loss of travel allowances and the company's proposed 'mixed fleet' contracts. Yet the implementation of this ballot was postponed because British Airways made a new offer in late June, which was subsequently rejected by 85 per cent of those who voted. There followed, in October, another offer, which was so derisory that BASSA refused to put it to members. The only course of action open to BASSA was to conduct a third statutory ballot to sanction a further round of industrial action.[189] The ballot began on 21 December 2010, but the company immediately attempted to subvert the process. Consistent with its strike-breaking behaviour and its divide-and-conquer responses, British Airways offered non-union cabin crew two years of pay rises, and protection of terms and conditions of employment 'now and in the future'.[190] To qualify, a crew member was obliged to confirm that they were not a BASSA member, and to sign and return a form attesting to this by 31 January 2011. Individual crew were promised that union members could only become eligible for the offer, if they voted 'no to strike action in the Unite ballot and [encouraged] colleagues to do the same'. Even by the squalid standards of anti-union strike breaking, this desperate (and futile) attempt to divide the workforce was quite astonishing.

The outcome was a 79 per cent vote in favour of industrial action on a 75 per cent turnout. Despite this emphatic majority, British Airways declined to acknowledge the strength of feeling among cabin crew and refused to negotiate. Instead, it launched a legal attack on the Electoral Reform Society (ERS). Ewing[191] notes the unprecedented nature of this action against the ERS in its role as an independent scrutineer appointed by the union, as required by balloting legislation (TULRCA). Intimidated by British Airways' claim that the ballot was unlawful, the ERS qualified its verification of the result in order to protect its own legal position.[192] In turn, Unite and BASSA did not then pursue industrial action on the grounds that 'such a move would expose our members to sanctions by a bullying employer'.[193]

Once again, BASSA had no alternative other than to ballot its members, for a fourth time, the outcome being an 83 per cent vote in favour of action on a 72 per cent turnout. Although it is not possible to conclude definitively that this vote prompted senior management to sanction negotiations, such a tangible demonstration of the crew's resolve after almost two and a half years must have influenced its thinking. Simply put, the cabin crew were not going to be browbeaten into submission.

In April British Airways and Unite issued a joint statement spelling out their commitment to seeking 'an honourable and fair settlement'. One month later, on 11 May, the union and employer announced an agreement, *Working Together – A Joint Settlement*, with the issue of staff travel allowances to be resolved separately. On the positive side, BASSA had survived, maintained its organisation and ensured continuity in collective bargaining arrangements in the face of a concerted attempt by the company, backed up by the law and the legal establishment, to destroy the union and to ram through wholesale changes to contracts and working conditions. The agreement secured a two-year pay deal worth up to 7.5 per cent, plus independent and binding ACAS[194] hearings for sacked members and ACAS reviews for those disciplined short of dismissal. Further, guarantees were given that Worldwide and Eurofleet cabin crew would not be penalised in favour of mixed fleet in the allocation of routes and that existing contracts and terms would be maintained. On the negative side, however, despite certain limitations in the detail, BASSA did concede to British Airways the introduction of a mixed fleet on significantly inferior terms, and accepted the loss of a crew member and changed responsibilities for a CSD. BASSA accordingly acknowledged that the settlement was not perfect.[195] The creation of a mixed fleet would be the subject of intense debate within the union in the aftermath of the settlement, but, as Chapter 7 indicates, action by the mixed fleet constituted a remarkable future wave of resistance to British Airways. Chapter 6 explores crew members' evaluations of the settlement.

The agreement was overwhelmingly endorsed by a mass meeting of BASSA members and in June 2011, 92 per cent of cabin crew voted overwhelmingly in favour on a 72 per cent turnout.[196] In the face of a huge onslaught, cabin crew had defended their terms and conditions, albeit for existing crew. More importantly, their union had not only survived, but had demonstrated that it is possible to organise a dispersed workforce to stand up to the neoliberal forces that shape global markets.

3

Project Columbus

This chapter presents cabin crew members' testimony on the background to the dispute and specifically on Project Columbus. In explaining the remarkable resilience displayed by BASSA members during the protracted struggle the chapter delivers insight into the roots of cabin crew's solidaristic behaviour. BASSA was able to tap a deep reservoir of collectivism rooted, in part, on informal solidarities between crew that were continuously replenished in the performance of their work routines. Significantly, crew members reveal the embeddedness of BASSA and their representatives in the work lives of its members. BASSA's legitimacy, won over decades of defending members' interests and monitoring the detail of collective agreements, is crucial to explaining the dynamics of the dispute.[1] The chapter continues with participants' reflections on the broader economic context of the civil aviation industry which shaped, but did not determine, the business strategy implemented by British Airways and which, ultimately, led to the dispute of 2009–11. Crew recognised that powerful market forces and changed structural conditions influenced company policy across the civil aviation sector. However, crew also believed that there was nothing inevitable about British Airways' employment relations policies and the company's hostility to BASSA. The CEO, as the personification of senior management, was seen to enjoy considerable discretion and could exercise a real element of choice over policy.[2] Crew had been aware for decades of how company priorities shaped their work experiences, notably in the ways their work had been restructured and intensified. Such changes affected the performance of both physical and 'emotional' labour – the modification of emotions to meet organisational demands[3] evident, for example, in the 'Theatre and Flair' initiative which attempted to redefine the provision of customer service as performance. However, the appointment of Willie Walsh as CEO represented a step change in the demands made upon cabin crew in the context of driving the company further towards adopting elements of the LCC model.

Crew members conveyed often highly personal accounts of how the company's longer-term cost-cutting measures undermined a legacy of deep-seated commitment to British Airways. While crew's resistance to Project Columbus was provoked by the immediate threat it posed to their work lives, there had been a longer-term erosion of crew loyalty to, and identification with, British Airways. Interviewees spoke of their distrust of the company in its conduct of industrial relations. This legacy fed into crew fears arising from the company's determination to reconfigure work organisation and to recast employment contracts that were to be enshrined in Project Columbus. Of decisive importance was the introduction of the new 'mixed fleet' on different and less favourable terms and conditions that, in dramatic fashion, threatened to cut labour costs, to reduce cabin crew staffing levels, to dilute terms and conditions and to impose staffing flexibilities across both Worldwide and Eurofleet. British Airways' unilateral action would end the decades-long joint regulation of working conditions and simultaneously break the power and influence of BASSA. The trigger for industrial action was British Airways' *imposition* of reduced crew complements, as crew made abundantly clear. To a person, they viewed this unilateral action as a step-change in managerial control and, inextricably, an unacceptable attack on their union. In this chapter, they recall their reactions to this management offensive.

The cabin crew community

If formal collectivism was promoted by BASSA and BASSA reps, and their embeddedness in the joint regulation of working conditions, the informal collectivism that emanated from the routines of work performance was no less important. The cabin crew can be said to have enjoyed a degree of relative autonomy. Once the cabin doors were closed the crew, and in particular the CSDs who were effectively the on-board 'managers', could exercise a certain amount of discretion in relation to passengers, albeit within the general parameters of control and the protocols as prescribed by the airline. Crew reported that in general and in matters of task performance they had little contact with ground-based managers. These CSDs had risen through the ranks and were often union members, but even when not, were generally protective of collective agreements and the on-board 'frontier of control', so that they acted as buffers against the incursions of ground-based management. CSDs conducted preflight briefings influencing crew culture on board and setting the tone for the trip. The process of crew formation and the distinctive shared experiences of being a cabin crew member promoted cohesion:

We have to bond very quickly. We meet an hour and a half before a flight, and in that briefing room friendships, relationships, everything are formed. It's that simple, and again, I can fly with one person this week, next week I may fly with that same person but because everybody else is different, the group dynamics will be different.

(Rabea)

The fact that crew on most occasions do not meet those with whom they will be flying until the preflight briefing given by the CSD is fundamental to their work:

You could get on a flight and don't even know that person that you're working with down the back, four people, boys/girls, whatever. Crew have a certain personality and the majority, say 80 per cent, you get on the trip, you don't know any of them. Within an hour and a half, you all know each other's life stories. And you have this bond, this intrinsic bond of being there for each other. And it's a sort of synergy I suppose and you might not see somebody for four years and then you bump into them and they go 'Did you ever have that baby?' or 'How is your father?' And there's an amazing camaraderie, it's like a oneness that we all gel. This caring, it's quite spectacular actually. I can remember quite clearly this guy just saying to me one time, 'Get in that toilet, fuck the service, just go in there and cry and you'll be OK.' So I sat in there with a can of Coke and I remember crying for about twenty minutes and they covered for me. And I've done it myself a thousand times for other crew. Not necessarily crying, somebody else needed to go and just sit down and write a text or something and somehow we all tune into each other. And I think that's very special and I don't think it's something you obviously get in many workplaces, but I think it's because we all know what it's like to be away from home, whether it's one night or 26. We all know what it's like to be away at Christmas. We all know what it's like to miss your auntie's funeral. We all know what it's like not to be there for your little boy's birthday, to miss your son's first poo in his potty, to miss your daughter's first step. And I think people don't understand that and they are huge things, they're milestones but they might be tiny. You may not even really like that person but somehow we all connect on a level. And that's a hugely important thing and so I think that is a kindred spirit that we all share and that's what made our union so strong.

(Sally)

Sally highlights the fact that crew having no fixed workplace and do not work together regularly could be a challenge for union organisation, but in fact was a source of strength which made the role of BASSA all the more important. Will endorsed that perception and experience:

> Well you may not fly together for two years but you finish the conversation you started two years ago. It will literally be that feeling, fresh in that instant. And passengers have come up in between the service and said 'Oh, how long have you all known each other. Do you always work with the same group of people?' And of course I say, 'No, I haven't seen these people in my life before now.' And they can't believe it. They say if only we could have people with this bonding working for us. And I've said, you can start and finish a conversation two years apart and it still has a vibrancy, it's not old news. I've known people for 35 years, but I don't know where they live, I don't know about their children, or their backgrounds really. You don't meet up for a pint, it's not like a mining village. We do come from every different social strata, but what we have in common, I've always said, is a sense of what's right and what's wrong and they also have complete trust in BASSA.
>
> (Will)

Cohesion was also fostered by the social activities between long-haul flights – the infamous 'room parties' – which had helped to forge the occupational community. The informal bonds of collectivism, as generated by the shared experiences and, indeed, the intimacy of a distinctive labour process, facilitated union communication through what was widely referred to as Galley FM, promoting informal solidarity despite crews' residential dispersion:

> Attending BASSA meetings weren't always achievable because you commute. I would rely on the emails that BASSA would send to keep us informed and what was also really important was Galley FM, as we call it, the chat on board.
>
> (Louise)

Over and over, crew referred to themselves and their colleagues as a community, the use of this word being a reference point for multiple meanings of commonality and togetherness. BASSA was considered integral to this community and crew frequently testify to the union's role as a glue, making more tangible and explicit these inter-crew bonds.

I think BASSA were the guardians of the community. For example, if there was a dispute among the crew, we would say to those involved, 'Don't go to the management, come to the union office and we'll sort it out.' I remember sorting out lots of little stupid niggles like that. We knew what our job was in terms of defending the members and upholding the agreements, but sorting those things out was also our job. Because we were a strong community, we were a strong union, we were the gel.

(Duncan)

Cabin crew and BASSA

While informal collectivity was rooted in work solidarities, formal collective organisation was based on BASSA's joint regulation of the labour process, work environment and employment terms and conditions. Union-negotiated agreements encompassed every aspect of working life. The historically more collaborative environment permitted arrangements that intimated management support for unions and enabled BASSA to have access to potential members:

I joined during my training course and in those days, because it was a closed shop, the union was embraced and its input was welcomed. And as a consequence senior management allowed them to come into the training school and say we [BASSA] are the union, this is what the union does. I had never thought about the trade union. The unions for me had just been always blokes standing around a brazier shouting at buses on cold wintry mornings in the West Midlands. And this fella came in to speak and it was like this protective blanket had been put round you – somebody had your best interests at heart. This fraternal warmth just enveloped you and I can remember it and thought 'Bloody hell, that's fantastic, I'm joining. I'm joining, I've got to join.'

(Adam)

Crew provided a mass of evidence attesting to the embeddedness of BASSA in, and the significance of BASSA to, the work life of their members. BASSA was highly accessible and responsive to the concerns of its membership base:

It is just a case of taking a couple of minutes' walk down the road, because we had an office in Terminal 5 near our report centre where if you have an issue you can talk about it in person. Obviously you could also phone headquarters – BASSA are very contactable. I think that's a lesson maybe other unions can learn. We've basically got 24-hour emergency numbers if you need to. For example, if you're down route and there's been an issue on board, you want to clarify it or you want to discuss it with a rep, you can actually phone a number from anywhere in the world really and the phone is manned 24 hours.

(Jack)

The practice of industrial relations had certainly meant the involvement of union and management in consulting over and negotiating terms and conditions at higher levels of the company, but the spirit and more importantly the actuality of joint regulation extended into the domain of everyday issues for members:

You're rostered a number of hours, and you can only do a certain amount of hours in a certain amount of flights, otherwise you go out of hours, which means there is a delay. Say you are going to Singapore and there is a delay of four hours, you would be removed from that flight because it would be physically impossible for you to work 20 hours. But depending on circumstances, if you're diverted or you've got a delay you would check with the union as to what the hours are, because it depends on how many nights you would be away for and what the time difference is. So you would always double check with the union to say right, this is what's happening, is this within our agreement to do that? It's a visible union and it's an approachable union because all cabin crew can discuss anything about your job and your terms and conditions and they actually put it into layman's terms.

(Kate)

Recognition that management generally accepted joint regulation does not gainsay the episodes of acute conflict that occurred in 1989 or in 1997, nor the longer-term tendency towards cost cutting and its effects for employment relations and the performance of on-board work routines. However, it does highlight the legacy of collaboration at both formal and informal levels, part of the 'regulatory overhang', as discussed in Chapter 2. The fact that BASSA reps checked out every hotel where crew stayed between flights was not only appreciated by members, but symbolised the union's engagement in their everyday working lives:

Prior to the dispute I was the BASSA hotel rep, which meant that I dealt with hotels and I would visit them on behalf of the crew before British

Airways signed a contract and then we would discuss it at a joint meeting once a month. If the hotel wasn't suitable we would state our case and it worked very well. Sometimes, we pointed out things that the company had missed and then we would look at alternative hotels. I'd have crew members who would absolutely blast me in the office for accepting a hotel that they felt was substandard in whatever way. We had people who were product reps who would discuss the on-board product. And they would discuss with the management the crew manning levels that were necessitated by the product and level of service. And of course that was a big part of our dispute. For example, management might say that they wanted to put something on, and then BASSA with its experience, because we're actual crew ourselves, would say this would not work in that frame and they were very productive meetings. That form of collaboration has gone since the [2009–11] dispute. We used to be part of a joint meeting called Special Circs. There was a meeting every month on special circumstances – on when and whether to grant leave and a special one for Christmas. And we had two BASSA reps on that committee. The managers would present the case for the crew member who was asking for special relief, because leave is a big thing for crew because they might have someone to look after. We would have two people sitting on that [but] we're no longer on that committee.

(Andrew)

Crew members repeatedly attested to their familiarity with BASSA and its reps and to their effectiveness as they defended their members and carried out their representative duties:

And the people you work with, that probably is one of the biggest things. Every single rep I work with is just great fun, just really good support and the stuff that they listen to and hear every day and then the stuff they went through during the strikes, I just think I'm proud to be with those guys and work with them. Because in fairness, if it happened tomorrow, we'd all go again. And [Ben] makes it very easy for us. If at any stage it becomes too much, and you don't feel you can fulfil what the membership ask of you, then you can quite gracefully say I'd like to step down. And he'll accept it because there's no point trying to push people through situations that they don't understand. So every one of the reps who I work with has to be self-driven and they've got to want to be a part of it because if not, they're living a lie. And they're elected to protect the agreement and to look after the membership. That's why I suppose I have so much respect for each one of them.

(Max)

For Nicky, it was the embeddedness of the relationship between the union and members that underlined the importance of the collective agreement to members and, then, underpinned their resilience against aggressive management tactics during the strike:

What BASSA meant to me, and what BASSA does incredibly success-fully, is that it demonstrates its power every day. I remember the first weekend I was a rep. I had to stop an aircraft taking off because the company had tried to put a long-haul crew on a short-haul 767 with a short-haul configuration and a short-haul product. That meant putting passengers in hotels at Heathrow until they could get the right aircraft the following morning and it probably meant hundreds and thousands of pounds to British Airways. But it would have breached the terms of the agreement, and the crew phoned their union to ask whether they were allowed to do the flight and the answer was no. The fact that they phone BASSA as the first thing they do to check BASSA's permission is indicative of BASSA's power. Say there's a huge car crash or incident on the M25 and loads of crew are late and the company then runs out of crew on standby and they want to operate an aircraft with one less crew member, they have to ask BASSA for an elevation. Now, if we think it's a good enough reason, we'll give them the elevation, we will say, 'Yes you can do it on this one occasion, but if we grant the elevation every crew gets about four hundred pounds per sector extra.' That is to dissuade British Airways from doing it willy-nilly. Now of course crew love to work one down because naturally they have an eye on that extra money but they are not thinking long-term; that if they are constantly operating with one less crew member, they are teaching the company that they can operate with a crew member short and the company will simply remove that member permanently. So if a crew are tempted by a manager to work one down [for the money] without seeking the alleviation for doing so from BASSA, BASSA would stop them being paid the extra money. That might seem perverse but it's about protecting the agreement for all crew for the future. Because, BASSA demonstrates their power in making sure the company upholds the agreement on a daily basis, crew are in the habit of coming to us to check the detail of anything and everything. They trust us. That's why the first strike ballot was 92 per cent vote to strike and the last strike ballot was 87 per cent. There was barely a shift despite everything the company did to break us. I always think that this was the most extraordinary thing. After 18 months of outrageous she-nanigans; after consulting the Burke Group on how to break BASSA, after they very successfully created the climate of fear, the bullying and harassment, the sacking, taking out the key people, tying the union up in costly legal cases, injunctions, after removing the facilities time and trying to render the union completely ineffectual, after everything they did over 18 months, the last strike ballot was an 87 per cent vote to strike. Extraordinary! We just taught them time and time again that they will not break us. You just can't do it. And when you consider who BASSA is, that we don't have an industrial base, or that shared culture or shop floor or even know each other, that the crew are not fucking miners or dockers, they live in Ascot. They're mums. To me it's just extraordinary.

(Nicky)

Even crew members hitherto indifferent or even antagonistic to unions came to be convinced of BASSA's importance in defending their conditions. This realisation came quickly to some and more slowly to others, but could lead ultimately to a deep commitment to the union and its values, especially in cases where the principles of the union meshed with the strongly held values of individuals:

And then slowly I started to realise that what I had was very much thanks to the union. The hotels I stayed in, the terms and conditions I had were actually not through the kindness of British Airways, it was thanks to the union. But it took me a long time, it took probably a year or two to realise that. And then slowly I started getting really interested in it. I started to realise it by talking to other people and became aware of how many rules there were and the rules were in my favour. And when you talk to other people who work for other airlines you think actually, this is not bad. I became a rep two years ago exactly. So it took me a long time, the idea was always there but it took me a long time to actually go ahead and do it. For me being a trade unionist is nothing about the Labour Party, and workers' rights, it's about fairness ... I believe in fairness at work, respect and dignity at work. BASSA represented that. I wanted to become a rep because I don't like unfairness, I can't stand it. It wasn't because I wanted recognition, it wasn't to save the world or to have people be grateful for what I do or to feel good myself. I did it and do it because I believe in fairness.

(Sana)

BASSA's embeddedness in the totality of crew's working lives provided the organisational and ideological frameworks through which members critically understood and interpreted British Airways' actions.

Cabin crew and British Airways

All those interviewed saw the arrival of Willie Walsh, as CEO, as signifying an unwelcome change in direction at British Airways. Crew of differing lengths of service recalled their fears. They had been made aware from friends and former colleagues in the broader cabin crew community of Walsh's actions as CEO of Aer Lingus, where the perception was that he had transformed a national flag carrier into a low-cost airline, decimating employees' terms and conditions and defeating the unions. Given crews' own direct experience of British Airways' unremitting cost-cutting, the appointment of Walsh magnified the perceived threat to their conditions and represented a decisive intensification of the combative management style which had been encouraged by developments in the structure and competitiveness of the global civil aviation markets. Ian, a CSD and BASSA rep on Eurofleet, who had worked for the company since the 1970s, reflected:

> Obviously, I'm pro the company, it's been a good company for me to work for, I've always been prepared to work for them. Like everything, when they are good, they are fantastically good and a great employer. Over the years, I've seen this being eroded and a change in the management style which was almost drip-fed. It was a slow process. I understand why, because of cheap travel coming in and, like everything, you're looking to the future. But at the same time there's ways of doing it, of slowly changing the terms and conditions and the way the job works. Suddenly I realised that I wasn't someone that the company wanted anymore.
>
> (Ian)

All interviewees described, with varying detail, how their schedules and their work routines intensified. Like Ian, many attributed these incremental changes to the ways that British Airways responded to pressures from the operating practices of the low-cost, new entrant airlines. One recurring theme was the increase in work pressure:

> The schedules became much harder. British Airways seemed intent on minimising the gaps between flights on short haul. You could have done an 11-hour or a 10-hour day and they seemed to take delight in the fact

that if you landed at 10 at night they could get you back at 10.30 in the morning. If they've got a gap, some days, you would then have what is called 'available', so you came in at 10 o'clock at night and picked up what is 'available' the next day. They seemed to take delight in getting the maximum amount out of you. Passenger expectations with British Airways have always been sold as the highest, but within Europe we've practically become Ryanair and EasyJet, yet we're still charging these prices. Three crew on an aircraft is an impossibility when you've got the two class service. Ryanair and EasyJet have probably got the same number of crew members. If you've got a single-class service, or only economy you can do it with three. Once you are on the jumbo where it's got four classes, you need dedicated crew for each section, and it's impossible to give proper service with three crew.

(Andrew)

Lara, similarly, reflected on the reduction of crew members on short-haul flights:

You knew that you were operating within a very limited time frame and passengers often had and still have no concept of this issue. Because it does make a difference if two cabin crew are serving 100 passengers within 30 minutes, and those 100 passengers all want two drinks, that's 200 drinks to serve. Even in a bar you wouldn't be expected to serve 200 drinks within 30 minutes. On an Airbus 319 with 100 passengers on, say for example a Paris flight in economy, only three crew – one purser and two cabin crew – were then required. So that made it quite difficult. Well, I think it used to be a relatively agreeable working environment, which became increasingly, especially pre- and post-dispute, pressurised. Less crew. So obviously your workload increased. Less crew and also an ever-changing management. I've had about eight managers in seven years.

(Lara)

Cost-cutting and reduced staffing levels not only intensified work but, in downgrading service quality, had the additional effect of generating excessive demands on crew because of high expectations of service standards:

I think they gave the passengers an expectation that we could not necessarily meet. So people have a very high expectation, because it's not

Ryanair, it's British Airways. But what British Airways was doing was cost cutting, taking stuff out. Actually, a friend of mine has a good way of explaining what happens: 'You can only take so much wood off a match before it breaks and then it's no good for purpose.' They were taking out from first and club all the bits that the regular passengers knew should have been there. And they were still charging the same money or more, and the pressure on crew was horrendous to achieve something when they didn't have the goods to give. The intensity of the work, the constant intensity of what you had to do became magnified. You were spun faster and faster round the system, quite honestly.

(Ben)

James also reflected on the move towards a low-cost model in terms of the proposed introduction of the new mixed fleet crew on inferior terms and conditions and the implications for existing crew:

They've taken on that Walmart business model, in which you have one guy you pay reasonably well, like the store manager, but everyone else knows nothing, and the manager doesn't care. I suppose the closest equivalent here would be something like B&Q, where nobody ever knows anything and it's like eighteen-year-olds going 'oh I don't know, whatever'. And you're having to wait forever to speak to the one bloke who actually knows anything – it's that kind of thing. It's a promise of service without delivering it, so it's like that American thing. They all have these vests on that say 'How can I help?', and when you ever ask them they never can. It's not their fault, they never train them or they never give them an investment. What they did in proposing the mixed fleet was to say, in effect to the entire workforce of 15,000, 'You're not on the scrapheap, but it's just a matter of time.' It's probably one of the worst tactical business moves that the company could ever do. And, of course, the crew become more and more and more disenchanted and disillusioned, because there were to be no prospects, no hope and nothing new. It was a dying fleet, yet still carrying the flag for the airline.

(James)

The change at the top was reinforced by the reported removal, through redundancy, of managers who were deemed to be too close to the crew and who may have been crew themselves and their replacement by a layer of new managers from outside the company who willingly embraced the new management style. A number of long-standing crew attested to the positive interaction they had previously enjoyed with their immediate managers. Such collaborative relationships were a manifestation of the institutionalised order of employment relations, part of the 'old prevailing collective agreements and relationships', as Project Columbus described it. For Adam, a long standing crew member, the change in management under Walsh's regime was marked and signalled a departure from the joint regulation of terms and conditions between the company and union that had characterised previous decades:

> When I started it was a fantastic company to work for. I've had a brilliant career, I wouldn't have wanted to have worked for another company. And the management have been brilliant, up until the last six or seven years [i.e. since around 2005–6]. They changed because they brought in younger managers who have not had experience and have only had union busting corporate aggression training. They're completely different to the managers we had before because then in cabin services we promoted from within. So everyone that managed you had flown, which is by far the best way to go. Half of these people now have never been on a plane, they don't know what's going on and they're trying to tell *you* what to do and they're 25 years younger than you are. They don't know what's going on in an aircraft. They're training them inasmuch as they do the SEP [safety emergency procedures], but they don't know how to fly, they're not in charge of aircraft. Previously, everyone who had been a manager was a CSD and could have gone on to be a fleet director. And then they decided no, we don't like that, because they're being too soft on their crew. So they got rid of them and then the new style of management is what we have had for the last eight years, which regressed to what we have now, which is an absolute disaster. They are of the Willie Walsh ilk and they hate us, they make no bones about it. Don't get me wrong, not everyone is ghastly, maybe 20 per cent are decent and the rest would like to eradicate us.

> (Adam)

If union influence over joint regulation of employment relations was the central target for senior management, then replacing the over-familiar relationships between managers and crew were a related object of British Airways' change programme; the outcome was a dramatic cultural transformation:

[There were] a lot of good managers. We were well managed. You could go in and sit down and chat with them. They have brought in a different group of people. If you were in any way crew friendly as a manager, you were exterminated, eliminated, or shoved out. Three managers told me off the record why they were leaving. Lo and behold Walsh brought in what I can only describe as a lynch mob. A manager who was at a golf outing with me last week said he's never seen such a ferocious, cancerous, management style in 24 years of management at British Airways. You can see that as a community when you ring up for leave or you are sick – it's now real hard. They've changed, and people began to sense it. At work you came to look over your shoulder. They have created a horrendous atmosphere.

(Finn)

The change in management was reflected in the deterioration in the relationship between British Airways and BASSA, which had been based upon joint regulation embodied in the detailed collective agreements, that the company was determined to remove through the imposed implementation of Project Columbus:

Tony McCarthy, who was the IR chap who came from the Post Office, brought all his team in. He was running it. His sidekick, a fella called James Farren, looked at our agreement, the Worldwide agreement, which I think is 56 pages or something off the top of my head. And he said he wanted to get it down to four pages. Well, there's not wasteful stuff in the Worldwide agreement, there's nothing ridiculous in there, it's designed to cover every eventuality and everybody knows what to do. For example, if a flight diverts from Hong Kong into Amsterdam, what do we do? How many days off do they get? How many days off do they get after the trip? How many hours are they actually there? If you forget your passport, what happens to you? What happens to your roster because you've got a fixed life, you've got this roster – well shall we wipe all the rosters, so she doesn't know what she's doing for two months? Oh, but she's got childcare and she's got all her arrangements made. And it was all the agreements were there for the smooth running of the operation. It's not ladling it on, it's not all incidental stuff, it was important stuff. Well, when we started negotiating in June [2007], the Christmas before we'd had a tip-off that they were going for wholesale change. Also, the managers were canvassed regarding their willingness to embrace this new change

63

… If they weren't willing, or they didn't have the belly for it, they were given quite a handsome severance package.

(Adam)

Previously, industrial relations was perceived by cabin crew to have been 'collaborative' 'open' and the subject of negotiation and agreement.

I think there was a much more collaborative approach to industrial relations at the time. Your input was somewhat valued but since I joined [2005], they've created a certain number of processes that have changed things. For instance you can't now be off sick. If you are sick twice in three rolling months, you automatically are called in for an interview and ailments that we cannot fly with are not discounted, even though initially they had agreed to discount them. So all this added together makes for quite an unpleasant working environment.

(Lara)

The erosion of organisational loyalty

Cabin crew stressed how strong their loyalties had been to both British Airways and – by no means always the same thing – to its passengers. What emerges powerfully from their accounts is crews' sense of professionalism and their enduring commitment to delivering excellent customer service. Equally significant, though, is the manner in which cost cutting, the devaluation of 'the product' and the dilution of customer service eroded their allegiance to the company.

The product has got worse because with less crew, of course, you have less time to spend with the passengers. Whereas, I was initially hired for my ability to mingle with all sorts of people, give advice to passengers as to what they might want to sightsee in Paris etc., my job became consumed with extremely menial, almost robotic tasks. Because now there simply is no time, certainly on short haul, but sometimes also on long haul, to provide for anything else. There is absolutely no emphasis given now to the interaction between the customer and the crew. When I started, we were the face of the airline – sort of on-board ambassadors. It's no longer the company I joined and I only joined in 2005. But I joined under a different CEO and things were very different.

(Lara)

The impact of downgraded customer excellence on commitment to the company makes for some compelling testimony, none more so than in the case of Jade (Box 1).

Box 1 Jade – the story of Miss British Airways

I suppose I'm a little bit different from the rest of the reps in the sense that when I joined British Airways I became a customer service trainer. In 1999, I became part of the British Airways promotions team, so I've been in pretty much everything to the point of having my picture in the boardroom, all the photos, videos, everything. So from working closely with the board, running errands at their monthly meetings, knowing them personally to the point where I would pin a name badge on them, I have taken the step over to the union. Some people didn't trust me coming into BASSA. They wondered why I had done this. I get that now, but at the time I didn't quite understand why possibly people were a little bit hostile. I think people see the benefit of it now because there's so much that I know about how they work – brands and corporate identity all of that – because I was involved.

Basically brands drive the look, who we are as a company. It is a department within British Airways. We used to do promotional events, we'd work with corporate sales, we'd host events for them. The promotion team, they weren't liked by everyone [because] we were seen as goody two shoes, I was Miss British Airways, but that was in the good times, when they had the money to send you to places and we would do a massive launch of all the brands, all the different types of seats. It was great because British Airways were investing in the company and everyone felt good.

Then that started to disappear with Willie Walsh and Martin Broughton [British Airways chairman from 2004], because they started stripping back the assets. So there was no more investment into the product and there wasn't for a long time. We haven't seen anything on Eurofleet for years, it's shoddy actually. It was just so false, it wasn't heartfelt the way they were with their employees any more. There was no investment. It was all about cost cutting and what they could make savings on and you'd feed things back and whereas before they would listen to you and you'd say 'Oh no, that's not a good idea because …'. They did listen, that was what was good about the promotions team, because you met with the people who were actually doing the designing and were actually at the heart of it. So you were quite respected in that sense, but then the mantra changed, it came from the top, it was so obvious. I remember the last event I did and things were so bad and I looked at it thinking, 'Can I do this, can I actually stand there and promote something I don't believe in any more?' And I couldn't.

Working with these diminished resources had additional effects on crews' attitudes and behaviours, not least in the ways that it magnified their sense of professionalism. Perceiving themselves to be the custodians of front line service, they felt it their duty to make up for the shortcomings of the organisation, a process which deepened their disenchantment with the company, although not the customer nor the job:

And I think because the cabin crew are professional, they over-compensate for what they haven't got on board. There's never a 'no', and the cabin crew always compensate, they won't say 'no' to anybody. The product has dwindled in quality and quantity. The product – well mainly the food, the service standards of the food because we don't have enough food – are embarrassing. I am constantly apologising every time I go to work. When I started you were proud to fly for British Airways, it was like your badge of honour because they were one of the best airlines, it was respectable. You went to great destinations and always had the backing of the management. They respected individuals for their merit, but that doesn't happen now to be honest. You are under the impression you can be replaced very quickly and very easily and more cheaply. I like the job that I do but the trust has gone.

(Kate)

Further, for many of the crew, in the past there had been no contradiction between allegiance to the company and membership of and commitment to the union. However, cost-cutting undermined this dual attachment:

In spite of everything, although I'm a staunch unionist, I love the company. The brand is shrinking, but I still love British Airways, I wouldn't have given my life to it otherwise. However, I hate what's become of the company. I am a BA-ite, as I think you will find union people are.

(Sally)

Many of those interviewed drew the connections between the longer-term deterioration in the quality of customer services and the crews' motivation to take industrial action:

The big change that we went on strike for was crew manning levels. It's about expectations – on Ryanair you're going to pay for your hand baggage; you get nothing so there are no expectations. People still come on British Airways with massive expectations and we sell it as that. You can't sell people a Rolls-Royce and turn up in a Mini.

(Andrew)

Project Columbus

Project Columbus was presaged by British Airways' attempt in 2007 to introduce major changes to terms and conditions, although these proposals were much less far-reaching than those which the company sought to impose two years later. The 'deal' that ended the threat of strike action contained elements the crew found to be unacceptable in practice, the most notable being the tightened sickness absence management policy.[4] The outcome also brought criticism by some crew of the actions of Unite the Union at national level.

> So in 2007 we were about to go out on dispute, but we didn't. We had our strike action cancelled by Tony Woodley. He had the right then to be able to cancel a strike ballot without us – the membership – cancelling it. The union came to a deal with British Airways which led to them pushing through the draconian EG300 policy which deals with sickness absence. The company-wide EG300 policy was perfectly acceptable when you were on the ground, but was not acceptable when you're in the air, when you cannot fly with bad ears or an upset stomach or whatever because you are a food handler. They dangled a carrot for entrants who joined post-1997, who used to finish their increments on the 8 increment, offering them four more increments to accept this policy. I voted no to that deal because I knew that the policy would be a way for an aggressive corporate to manage staff out of the business. I don't know if the number of people, particularly among the cabin crew, who have been managed out by the EG300 policy, has ever been monitored. Since then, they were chipping, chipping away until the start of our dispute when we had the imposition, when they took the crew member off the aircraft.
>
> (Amy)

The proposal for fundamental change was articulated in the company's Project Columbus document that was leaked to BASSA in June 2008.[5] British Airways' strategic intention was to recast the utilisation of labour and employment relations primarily through the introduction of a new mixed fleet on lower terms and conditions. Unite national officer Steve Turner summarised the position of the union and confirmed that it had been prepared to negotiate in order to preserve the fundamental elements of its agreement with the company. However, this willingness to make concessions was thwarted by the company's intransigence:

> We were happy enough to sit down with British Airways and see whether we could resolve the problem of the post 9/11 decline in passenger numbers. But they had ulterior motives. Their view was to focus on cabin crew. They did not necessarily want a dispute with cabin crew, but they

were quite happy to accept the consequences of a dispute. If securing their objectives meant effectively taking BASSA off the face of the earth then they were prepared to do that. It meant imposing a new industrial relations framework, new employment terms and conditions and a new fleet operation to rebuild their airline. Mixed Fleet, as a completely separate fleet operation, was very dangerous for us. In response, we came up with a proposal around flexi fleet. We were prepared to concede – our people were prepared to concede – new starts on varying terms and conditions, although we would effectively have had a two tier workforce. British Airways had tried it a couple of decades before but they had been forced to incorporate the new crew back into the main crew again. Over time the new entrants had worked their way up. This was one of their fears, that [new starts] would be indoctrinated by BASSA when on board, so they wanted completely separate aircrafts on separate conditions.

(Steve Turner)

British Airways imposed these changes knowing that BASSA members would have no alternative but to resist them. An experienced CSD confirmed that the willingness to make certain compromises was not an approach that BASSA negotiators were adopting over the heads of the members. On this occasion the preparedness to make concessions involved widespread agreement with and buy-in from members:

Over the introduction of mixed fleet we came up with a perfect proposal of how we could work together, so they could get their cost savings. We would integrate the new people joining the mixed fleet on a new agreement. We calculated an hourly rate, so they'd get the benefit, they would save money because they wouldn't have to duplicate scheduling, management. It was actually a perfect solution. So British Airways got their cost savings for then and for the future. They said no. So then you realised that you were on a hiding to nothing. They wanted you to react, they wanted you in a strike situation, so they could just grind you into dirt.

(Will)

For all cabin crew interviewed, without exception, this imposed reduction in crew members on both long and short-haul flights – bypassing negotiation with BASSA – triggered the dispute, although they were clear that this was a symbol of a wider attack:

With Operation Columbus we were on a crash course over every aspect of our agreement. And then on the 16th of November 2009, British Airways said they would be implementing the reduction of a crew member on every Worldwide aircraft. That individual would be the purser. I still can't get my head around how they were able to do that because my contract of employment states that you will abide by your scheduling agreement. To this day I still can't understand how a court of law could look at our scheduling agreement, which states a minimum of 13 crew on a 747 and 12 on a 777, and then allow this blue-chip company to rewrite the law to remove an individual from a legal contract of employment.

(Max)

Taking off a crew member was the crux of the matter. But this was the first amongst many other things. It was the way they did it. We've always been used to negotiating and I would say if they'd come round the table and said to us, 'We have a problem, there's a massive recession, we need to cut costs, how should we go about cutting costs?' there would have been a willingness. Rather than invite us to make a contribution, though, they just said, 'This is what we're doing, take it or leave it.' And we thought, 'Well hold on, we understand, things are going to happen as a result of this', it was their attitude and the unfairness, which pissed us all off. This was the thin end of the wedge. If they got away with this, then what would be next? So if we didn't stand up against this suddenly everything would fall apart around us.

(Nathan)

While the imposition of the reduction in crew members provoked industrial action, it was the introduction of the mixed fleet that signified a watershed in employment relations and working conditions:

And I was one of the few who actually did new entrant training so I knew. As I saw it, the basic line was that they were taking our jobs away. Not necessarily mine, because let's be honest, I'm at the end of my career. But for goodness sake, you would have to be crazy not to see it and not to want to fight it, because it's a dilution of everything that we stood for, completely and utterly. People have fought for me previously, so it's my turn to stand up. We had already got four different contract types within the flying community at Gatwick and Heathrow, but to bring another one in, make it a separate fleet and then to bang down our throats that these are the elite cabin crew. No thanks.

(Stephanie)

The thing was that we didn't go into it [the dispute] lightly. Everyone could see what the introduction of the mixed fleet would mean. You can't take action over something that might happen, something that might have been planned but hasn't actually had an impact yet, so for legal reasons the action had to be over the imposition of the removal of crew. But obviously what was galvanising people was the thought that their job could rapidly disappear with the introduction of a new fleet that was a lot more cost effective and flexible. But there were other issues [especially] the bullish way the company went on to threaten the removal of staff travel.

(Catherine)

The implications of the airline's strategy for BASSA and the workforce were well understood collectively but, of course, collectivities are composed of individuals, for whom change might have particularly unwelcome personal consequences. Felipe provides a good example:

The reason for the dispute was that the company had breached our agreement. A lot of people believe that it was about money but it wasn't. Basically, they took a crew member off the aircraft, not necessarily a big deal. We all recognised that we could work harder for what we do, that wasn't the issue. The issue was that our agreement was signed by the company, by the union, and it is in black and white, but the company said it wasn't contractual. I supported the union 101 per cent because I knew that the moment you lost your terms and conditions you were never going to get them back. And that was the core of the dispute. The introduction of this new fleet obviously spelled the end of my career with British Airways. I was never going to get promotion, because our agreement stipulated that promotions are based on seniority, and I've been the most junior and now not having anybody coming behind me. So, in theory I could have a promotion if I transferred to the new fleet, which would be suicidal for me as I would lose out on my terms and conditions and financially big time and the new fleet would be run by fear. You would be told to jump and you would have to jump and I didn't and don't want to be part of that.

(Felipe)

A common perception among crew of various levels of experience and, indeed, of differing levels of involvement in BASSA, was that British Airways' intention was to break the union:

My interpretation is that it was purely a union busting exercise. I don't think there's any credibility regarding cost saving. Cases had been put forward to try and get us out of the failure to agree. And I think there was just a three line whip for management that whatever happens we're going to use this situation to try to destroy or dismantle the power base of BASSA. We were perceived as being too powerful and they wanted to get rid of that. The fact that they spent £150 million, whereas the savings were only about £70 million, speaks volumes that it was more to do with control. Of course, the mantra from British Airways, even now, we have the right to manage, which any employer does, it's how you choose to use that right.

(Rhys)

Nathan was very clear about the personal risks he was taking when he became a BASSA rep:

I knew when I stood [to be a rep] that it was going to be a volatile time ahead, I knew there was going to be uncertainty and I could lose my job because of being a union rep. The times were going to change. I felt I was putting myself in the firing line. When the dispute started I knew we would have casualties. It was so blatantly obvious what was happening and it wasn't about taking one person off the aircraft, it was about breaking the union. Everybody knew that. Well, some members shoved their head in the sand and they've still got them there. But the people who had common sense could see this was British Airways' plan, because once they bust the union they could do whatever they wanted.

(Nathan)

Preventing Walsh from breaking the union was essential for ensuring the maintenance of decent working conditions. This was the legacy won by the union over decades and many crew emphasised that it was this legacy that they wished to bequeath to their successors:

Technically the issue was over on-board crewing levels, but we all knew that it was about our future as well. If we let them get away with one thing, then it was going to snowball. So personally, I saw it as two things, protecting my future and protecting the people coming in behind, so that they would enter at least a decently paid industry. So there was the issue that we were balloted on and which we took strike action over, but everybody knew the bigger picture. The fact that they did it and there was no negotiation. So you just knew that if we just did nothing they would just start imposing across the board. Everybody was aware that Walsh hated the union and his focus was about the bottom line of the company and not about the workforce. I think he wanted to create this phenomenally profitable airline that would be the envy of the airline world. All at the expense of the staff and I knew what I was signing up for. It wasn't just the fact that it was about the numbers on board, it was about the future of my job and the future of the union.

(Guy)

What fuelled the sense of grievance was knowledge among the cabin crew community that the company was not in the parlous situation that, it claimed, was the justification the measures it was taking. Many crew had a good understanding of the financial state of British Airways taking time to read company accounts and to familiarise themselves with the statements it made to the City. Postings on both the BASSA Forum and the Crew Forum by the union leadership raised awareness and provided a lens through which to critique the supposed rationale for the staff cuts and which deepened animosity towards Walsh and senior management:

British Airways achieved a ten per cent profit margin before the strike, with the same terms and conditions and the same number of crew on the aircraft. Then they took the person off each plane, when that wasn't the problem. The fat cats were getting their profit and it was just so unfair. It was wrong, unfair, because we were making cutbacks, but they weren't cutting back themselves. You would see another increase [in dividends] half a million pounds or something. Well hold on, it doesn't seem quite right.

(Nathan)

Will reflected on the crew members' level of trust in their BASSA reps:

The strength we had was the fact that we weren't just union reps, professional union reps from a distance, we were part of the community. So whatever would affect them would affect us as well. And also I think cabin crew respected the fact that BASSA had tried absolutely everything and kept giving the company more and more and more not to strike, not to actually confront the company. And they knew it wasn't a knee jerk reaction to call the strike. In all the big meetings we had, it was the reluctance – we don't want to be here, we really don't have any choice now. So there was a total belief in the reps and the fact that if there were two versions of the truth we knew who to believe.

(Will)

4

Balloting, the right to strike and British Airways counter-mobilisation

Project Columbus was intended to undermine the collective organisation of cabin crew and weaken the strength of BASSA as a trade union. The removal of a crew member on each flight and the redesignation of the roles and duties of Purser and CSD were universally regarded as provocative measures, not least because they were unilaterally imposed. This chapter presents cabin crew accounts of the period of intensifying conflict that preceded strike action. It includes their reflections on the highly politicised judicial proceedings that played such a significant role in framing the dispute. In the first ballot in November 2009 crew voted by 93 per cent on an 80 per cent turnout in favour of taking strike action.[1] British Airways responded by securing an injunction (*British Airways v. Unite*, 2009) under the Trade Unions and Labour Relations (Consolidation) Act of 1992, which prevented BASSA's proposed 'twelve days of Christmas' strike action and, in a broader challenge to unions and human rights, threatened the legal right to strike in the UK. In the dispute employer counter-mobilisation took a number of classic forms; the use of the law, the employment of external anti-union consultants, the use of managers in one-to-one conversations with crew, a weighty propaganda and media campaign, and above all the suspension and dismissal of activists and members. There is evidence that the company acted beyond the law in its surveillance of union activists. These tactics undoubtedly created a climate of fear and, with the recruitment of substitute cabin crew to break the strike, presented the union with a series of formidable challenges.

The legal challenge: ballots and the High Court injunction

The decision to take twelve-day strike action over Christmas had not been an easy one for BASSA members. Yet, there was also a widespread feeling that, had the courts not intervened, a negotiated settlement could have emerged:

Nobody in their right mind wants to go on strike. You want it to be settled and the strike is your last resort. That's where we were at in 2009. We had the brilliant turnout, we had the brilliant result. We threatened them with Christmas. The injunction was typical of British Airways' heavy handedness and the upper classes beating us down with the law. I remember saying to people who maybe had questioned what we were planning to do, 'Well, when is a good time to strike then? Because sure as hell they'll tell you you're going to affect thousands of people no matter when you took action.'

(Ben)

The High Court injunction obtained by British Airways prevented BASSA from striking as planned following the overwhelming mandate for action. The decision was based upon the inadvertent inclusion in the ballot of members who had applied for voluntary redundancy,[2] despite the fact that the union was not able to identify who these members were at this point. The inclusion of these 1000 members made no difference to the outcome of the ballot. For the union nationally, the decision was not completely without precedent given the recent Metrobus case,[3] and huge obstacles were now placed in its path as it was compelled to comply with a highly restrictive legal decision. Steve Turner summarised the sequence of events preceding and immediately following the first ballot, and reflected on the union's decision to take twelve days of strike action over the Christmas holiday:

The ballot went through and overwhelmingly. We put out a notice that 88 per cent[4] had voted for strike action and that we would take twelve days strike over the Christmas period. They were our dates. There was a lot of discussion inside the union about whether that had been the right tactic to use. The undeniable truth is that if they hadn't won the injunction, this strike would never have taken place. There would have been a negotiated settlement.[5] People knew that the twelve days of Christmas was symbolic. This was the breaker and would have won the dispute for us. We knew that if we were to win we needed to take hard action. You needed to shut the airline. It is unquestionable that the twelve days would have won it. British Airways got this injunction on really spurious grounds, that 900 people who were later offered voluntary redundancy were included in the ballot, even though at the time of the ballot they had not been offered redundancy terms. They argued in the High Court that we'd balloted 900 people who would not be in a position to take action, despite our specific and written requests to the company for them to identify all the cabin crew who had applied for voluntary redundancy. We were buggered if we did and we were buggered if we didn't. If we hadn't balloted those who had applied for voluntary redundancy then we couldn't then have called them out. Either we've balloted people who might no longer be employed, or we can't ballot them and then you can't call them out. So we were caught between a rock and a hard place. We couldn't see it other than a perverse and political decision. We lost the injunction on the basis of 900 people we had no knowledge of. I gave notice the next day that we were going to reballot, that was our only strategy. Then we went through our figures again, we had people in working over Christmas on it. We only got the list of 900 eventually through the High Court, because they had to produce it as part of their evidence. Then we had to take those people out, rerun the checks on membership, give notice of intention and only then did we reballot.

(Steve Turner)

It is difficult to exaggerate the significance of the High Court decision, not merely in its impact on the immediate course of events, but also for its profound effects on crew members' attitudes. Richard, a BASSA rep and committee member, explained the union's tactics, reflecting long-standing labour movement discussions on what constitutes effective industrial action:

I think all of the outcomes of all of our postal ballots were key positive moments in the dispute, insofar as the returns consistently stayed really high in favour of strike action. On the downside, the real key moment was when the judge, prior to the twelve days of Christmas, agreed with the company to injunct us. At that time the company did not have any volunteer cabin crew trained up, so I think Willie Walsh would have been forced to have come to the table and actually negotiate a settlement that both sides could have lived with. The feeling we had at the decision was one of disgust, pretty much with British Airways, but equally with the courts. When Lady Cox said that our proposed action would be detrimental to people's travel arrangements over that time, it seemed to be a personal reflection rather than a decision based in law. People were completely outraged by that, but not put off. It was a key moment, because if we had been able to go ahead with those twelve days I truly believe that we would have had an agreed settled document to deliver to the crew. I don't think British Airways would have allowed the strikes to have gone ahead, that they would have had emergency talks with us and an emergency resolution would have gone through. But because we lost that injunction, it allowed them to rapidly build up this volunteer workforce in preparation for the next proposed strike. So I think that was the pivotal point against us. But the consistency and the determination of the crew was overwhelming. A lot of people were shocked at the twelve days because I don't think we'd ever done twelve days before and at Christmas too, which is obviously an emotive time. But I think because of the degree of support that we had we were able to show what Columbus was about and how bad British Airways were. The majority of the crew saw our proposed action as a key tactic. You make it so bad that it forces British Airways not to have the strike, whereas if you have a one-day strike in mid-November, they'd say, 'Yes, we'll take that'. So we had to make it so bad we couldn't escalate it, we couldn't start one day then three days, then seven days and then ten. We had to go in hard right from the beginning because we had to try and nip it in the bud.

(Richard)

The legal sanctions against BASSA had the effect of hardening the resolve of the cabin crew community. The outcome of the first High Court judgement confirmed their deeply held grievance against the company, but also challenged the views of those who believed that the legal system would deliver impartiality, or 'fairness', to use the word that crew members often chose to express the rationale for their struggle. A BASSA rep, originally from Italy, recollected:

The saddest thing was the High Court judgement. I was there. The judge said quite clearly, 'I need to take into consideration the consequences of the industrial action', which was not the reason why we were in court. I hold that particular judge responsible for 18 months of misery for everybody, because this issue could have been resolved so quickly. Had she taken away the numbers of those who were included in the ballot, the overall majority would have gone from 92 to 91 per cent. It was minimal. She disregarded the higher percentage, not because there were mistakes during the ballot, but because of the consequences of the national ballot, which is not why Willie Walsh took us to court; he took us to court over the technicality. I just felt so let down. I had always held this country to be the most fair country. Whenever I had been abroad and I used to talk about how fair this country the UK was, and that day just broke my heart.

People were crying, because of the injustice of the judge saying, 'I have to take into consideration the consequences of your actions.' That was not what she should have been there for. She was supposed to be there to see whether the way the ballot was done was fair or not fair. And 91 per cent of us had voted for industrial action.

(Felipe)

Many crew saw the High Court decision as a more fundamental challenge to the UK's system of justice and strengthened their growing conviction that they were up against forces more powerful than just British Airways itself:

One of the key events was the first time we went to the High Court and our strike action was turned down by the judge. A lot of people then realised that this dispute was not only about fighting the company, but was also about fighting the establishment. You've got to be very naive if you think that government and big corporations were not applying pressure to certain judges and departments within the government to have certain decisions made.

(Asad)

Crew came to see the reaction of the legal system in broader terms as an attack on the labour movement, with Unite the Union's subsequent appeal crucial to the survival of trade union rights. Sarah reflected the views of many when she reasoned:

I took industrial action to protect my job and to protect the labour movement. Well, because we challenged the High Court injunction and then got permission to take legal industrial action, we protected all trade unionists in the future. If we hadn't done that and hadn't taken industrial action then nobody in this country would ever have been able to have gone on strike ever again. Well, as someone who has followed the dispute all the way, like 92 per cent of us followed the dispute all the way, BASSA kept us informed all the time. And if you're an avid reader like I was, and wanting to know every second of every day what progress was being made, then part of it would be information that they would be giving you, but part of it would be because you were intelligent enough to realise what the bigger picture was.

(Sarah)

The 'wailing wall'

The judicial offensive against the union was combined with an attack on the material conditions of union members, namely the termination of long-established crew benefits. The withdrawal of staff travel subsidies from those taking strike action was an acutely perceived injustice which affected crew both resident abroad and those in the UK living some distance from Heathrow. British Airways' closure of its Manchester and Glasgow bases in 2006 and 2009 respectively had increased the importance of travel benefits for many crew residing in the north of England or Scotland:

> As the first ballot was running, British Airways said they would remove staff travel privileges. Being French, that alone infuriated me. So OK now we have a company that's hell bent on intimidating their staff against exercising what I believe is a human right. And they know that many of their staff rely heavily on staff travel because they can't afford to live round here, it's too expensive. And they live in Spain or in Scotland and that was to me an indirect lockout anyway.
>
> (Lara)

A small group in BASSA, called Crew Defence, felt that there needed to be a legal response to the loss of staff travel:

> We lost the staff travel, but Unite was not quick enough to respond to that. So this group called Crew Defence was set up to fight legally with the staff travel situation and people donated money to this crew defence, – almost £90,000, for cabin crew.
>
> (Uwe)

Academic John Logan has described how union avoidance consultants, like the Burke Group, work behind the scenes training supervisors in how to 'interrogate, intimidate and terrify employees'.[6] For British Airways planning for strike action meant putting managers on a 'war footing', to use the phrase of a cabin crew activist, later sacked on the most trivial of grounds. Preparation involved a battle for the hearts and minds of the workforce but, given the high degree of union density and the strength of crew members' commitment to BASSA, simplistic appeals to the community were unlikely to succeed. Instead, the company sought to weld the diverse managerial grades, but especially those with direct responsibility for the crew, into a dependable force who would intervene forcibly on its behalf. However, realising this objective was not necessarily straightforward, as this BASSA Committee member recalled:

> British Airways decided to segregate the cabin crew community and get all the managers to phone every single crew member and tell them not to strike. But it also seriously upset these managers because a lot of them saw it as a thankless task, when they knew that overall BASSA would prevail on fairness. There was enough trust in the community with the work we've done over the years at BASSA that if we were asked to deliver the service with half the amount of crew then the crew would probably agree to do it if there was a long-term gain. Eventually I guess with that onslaught of anti-crew propaganda directed at managers, some were going to buy into parts of it or managers might come to believe that for some reason the cabin crew were malingerers. So it wasn't until a manager said to me, 'I'm best friends with a short-haul rep and I can't believe the way they're treating him. Is it the same for you?' that I said 'Yes, I've had people sitting outside my house for days on end with the car running, just doing surveillance on me.' So about that time when we knew that we would ballot again, in February 2010, British Airways put up the 'wailing wall' at Waterside where they could put down their thoughts and 'I'm backing British Airways' lanyards were brought out.
>
> (Max)

As Max indicated, at the same time that the strike-breaking crews were being formed and attempts were being made to secure the loyalty of more immediate managers, senior management instigated measures aimed at sowing further division:

> A white board was set up at Waterside, called 'the wall', where managers and hostile crew wrote 'Cabin Crew Scum' and things like that. All of that has been swept under the carpet. This was a big thing for me. I thought it's never going to come out, what this huge company have done to their workforce.
>
> (Gemma)

The interviews are replete with crew members' abhorrence of these provocative initiatives:

> Well the wall basically was set up by British Airways, again, I suppose, to create this in-group and out-group. The in-group was perceived as

'you're backing British Airways, you're wearing the lanyards'. All the screen savers on the PCs around Crew Report[7] changed to 'Backing British Airways'. Any email that was sent out had at the bottom 'Backing British Airways'. My manager, on her voicemail, had the message 'My name is ____ and I'm backing British Airways'. It was very subtle, but it was done to chip away at our confidence. And then of course this wall appeared on which people could write their comments about 'backing British Airways'. But it very soon deviated to become a hate wall. It was basically a big white board and they just wrote anonymous comments which could say quite mild things like, 'I support British Airways' or nasty messages like 'Cabin crew are scum, how can they do this to us? We will fight you, we will destroy you. You're mindless thugs'. Anything and everything was allowed.

(Rhys)

For Steve Turner, Willie Walsh and British Airways' corporate leadership were drawing on an anti-union narrative that had been used in the 1980s by the Thatcher government in its counter-mobilisation against the miners and their union, the National Union of Mineworkers:

Inside the company Walsh had waged this war against the cabin crew, so that they were 'the enemy within'. It was a very Thatcherite approach, this enemy within – this was about the future of the airline and this group were bringing down your airline. He had this 'wailing wall' that he put up and he encouraged big white boards that went up and down in Waterside. And it encouraged everyone who passed to write comments about what they felt about the cabin crew, like 'Fucking waste of space. Sack them all. Fucking disgrace'. It was horrible, dehumanising, they tried to dehumanise them.

(Steve Turner)

Decapitation, victimisation and the Facebook 15

Pressure on crew members intensified in the run-up to strike action, with concrete steps being taken to marginalise the union and to render its actions ineffective. The company revoked the decades long facilities agreement with BASSA and then suspended and/or sacked activists in what labour lawyer Keith Ewing termed a 'strategy of decapitation'. Senior management's thinking would appear to have been that the sacking or suspension of officers and activists would profoundly affect BASSA's capacity to organise, while raising the cost of activism for the wider membership. A chastised and leaderless membership would be unable to take determined action. British Airways disciplined union reps, activists and ordinary BASSA members using procedures that were subsequently (post-dispute) deemed by employment tribunals to be illegitimate. The most notable act of 'decapitation' was the dismissal of Duncan Holley, branch secretary of BASSA. When the first strike was called Duncan withdrew from his rostered duties as was his right according to the company-union collective agreement. He was promptly sacked. Another BASSA committee member remembered the sequence of events and how Duncan's principles could not be compromised:

> Now Duncan, he was the one person that did what he did knowing what the consequences would be and British Airways said 'you do it, we'll sack you'. Tony Woodley [joint general secretary of Unite the Union] said, 'Duncan, Don't do it, they're going to sack you. Don't do it, just come in to work' and Duncan said, 'I'm a union rep, I'm the branch secretary, how can I bottle it and then turn round to people and say go on strike? I can't do it. I'm going to stand by my principles.' And I take my hat off to him.
>
> (Tom)

Crew were particularly offended by management's instruction to train volunteer cabin crew, and by the fact that this training took place at Craneback, the company's training centre, in full view of cabin crew having annual checks:

> Then they created voluntary cabin crew [VCC]. They had the audacity to ask us, the whole crew community, to train the VCCs on board our flights. If I, or my fellow crew members, were perceived, subjectively perceived that is, to be hostile or uncooperative, that would be our jobs on the line, purely on the credence given to these VCCs – strike breaking cabin crew. The message being given out was that anyone who wished to could do my job. Only very minor checks were being made on the quality of their work. We were easily replaceable, that was the message.
>
> (Lara)

In preparing the VCC for strike action, British Airways' motivation, according to interviewees, was to antagonise BASSA. Unsurprisingly, crew responded angrily and some were provoked into actions that gave management the pretext for suspensions and in some cases dismissals – the 'Facebook 15', as they came to be known:

> So some ground staff and engineers and pilots thought that scabbing during the strike was a great way to see Hong Kong or New York, or that they would get a leg up in the company or whatever. They forgot about solidarity and not undermining their fellow workers. They forgot about their own disputes and how turning the workforce against each other would only play into the company's hands in the long run. Pilots we worked alongside every day, who BASSA had supported in their own dispute with the company a year before, volunteered to work as cabin crew. There was definitely an element of them; intelligent, knowing men, having a valid dispute but when it came to cabin crew, how dare a bunch of girls and queens have a word to say about the company. So all the 'volunteers' had to be put on courses in Cranebank to train as cabin crew and extraordinarily, the company chose to do that alongside existing cabin crew. The identity of the scabs wasn't a secret. They were right there training alongside crew on their annual checks who were just about to go on strike and it emerged that there was a list of pilots on the first training course. A class list existed and the list might have come from anywhere. Regardless, the list got passed around. Eventually there were two Facebook threads discussing the list, 'Have you heard there's this list?', 'I've got the list, do you want the list?', 'Send me a private message with the list', 'What do you think I should do with the list?'. 'Don't do anything with the list, give the list to BASSA', 'No, I think we should name and shame them.' What became known as 'the Facebook 15' were 15 crew members who were all suspended and some dismissed for daring to even discuss the existence of a list of pilots working as crew to undermine the dispute. That was the start of the climate of fear during which crew were met off the aircraft by managers who suspended them for things like using a BASSA pen on board the aircraft or discussing the dispute in a bar and being overheard, both of which in the new Stasi world constituted bullying and harassment. In the meantime pilots were writing, and I quote, 'Fuck off BASSA you lying, malevolent bunch of hypocritical self-serving cunts' on public forums with complete impunity.
>
> (Nicky)

This final quote is referred to in Kevin Cook's employment tribunal judgement as an example of a posting on the BALPA website,[8] for which the pilot was merely given an informal written warning. At the same time individual crew members were being suspended and dismissed for unwittingly being party to discussions on VCCs via social media, the victims of a vengeful management focused on providing salutary reminders of the consequences of defiant behaviour:

> There's one young lad I know who was suspended for Facebook postings and he was off for four months. He didn't have anybody to talk to. He couldn't tell his parents or his partner he was so ashamed. He was in such a state. I trained him, he's a lovely lad. I spoke to a couple of other people, because otherwise it's all word of mouth and you never really know whether he was surviving. He was found guilty. I think all he had done was to have accepted a text and responded with a phrase that expressed his shock, 'oh my God'. I spoke to him when I flew with him shortly afterwards. He told me that they had found him guilty, but they said that he had obviously seen the error of his ways so they gave him a three-year written warning. It was all to do with the Facebook thing. I wasn't part of that, thank god.
>
> (Gemma)

Actions taken against crew under British Airways' established bullying and harassment policies were universally regarded as vindictive and unnecessary. In addition to the sackings and suspensions, many crew were given warnings of varying degrees of severity. Some had their seniority and promotion revoked:

> I was a cabin service director but I was demoted and made a purser. At the very start of the dispute, I received a text message listing the VCCs. I forwarded it to two girlfriends and one forwarded it to somebody she knew who was a VCC and they took it to the company. Hence I got demoted. I appealed against this demotion that meant a £6,000 cut on my basic pay, but I was given a final written warning. And I was not even allowed to apply to be a CSD for standby. I appealed the decision again and they reduced my final written warning from three years to 18 months.
>
> (Rabea)

Not only do the interviews illustrate the impact of victimisation on individuals, they also demonstrate the effective defence of these members by BASSA. Reps were often overburdened by the excessive number of cases taken under British Airways' disciplinary procedure – known as EG901 or

'901s' – for which they were responsible, at the same time as dealing with the daily demands involved in handling the dispute:

> I probably did 50 per cent of the cases during the dispute. So at one stage I had sixteen '901s' going on. About three of those were final appeals, seven were in hearings, four or five were in preliminary investigations. So I was managing those sixteen people as well as day to day problems. Every single day I was doing a different disciplinary. A couple of other reps were doing bits but the other reps were just gone, sacked or suspended. Apart from all these time consuming demands, I was manning the 24-hour emergency telephone.
>
> (Max)

Senior management held arbitrary hearings against crew in the specially commandeered 'Leiden room' in Waterside, which according to crew testimony, commenced before the first strike days, but became fully operational thereafter:

> We'd never heard of Leiden until after the fact. We now know that any disciplinary case related in any way to industrial action was called by the company a Leiden case. Ordinarily, what happens in a disciplinary procedure is that there will be the precautionary suspension, then a preliminary investigation and the preliminary investigation manager conducts some investigation. They take some statements and then hand the file to a case-to-answer manager who then decides whether there is a case to answer or not. If yes, the case goes to a disciplinary. In 'ordinary times' in British Airways preliminary investigation team exists only to carry out preliminary investigations of alleged wrongdoing by cabin crew. With the Leiden cases, the Preliminary Investigation team were not involved. They did not investigate a single case. They carried on investigating cases of nicking stuff or drinking, but they were kept out of anything related to the industrial dispute. A special team was brought in, initially made up of engineering managers, who knew nothing about cabin crew and clearly nothing about preliminary investigations. They didn't conduct proper investigations. They would do things like opening a meeting by saying, 'Can I confirm you are a member of BASSA?'
>
> (Nicky)

Kevin was dismissed for producing *Scabbin Crew News*, a spoof of British Airways' *Cabin Crew News* (see Box 2). *Scabbin Crew News* satirised volunteer pilots and was apparently deemed by an anonymous pilot to be bullying and harassment. Kevin's subsequent employment tribunal judgement wondered 'whether or not there was ever a genuine complaint' and found his dismissal unfair because the company had circumvented its procedures. As the judgement proposed in the cases coordinated by the 'Leiden Unit', existing procedures 'did not suit the company's purpose'.[9] It also found disparities between the treatment of Kevin and the pilot who had posted the offensive comment on the pilot's website as quoted above. It concluded that the decision to dismiss Kevin but not to dismiss the pilot 'was so irrational that no employer could reasonably have made it'.[10]

Box 2   The case of Kevin – sacked but vindicated

While I was at Bedfont, I produced a magazine for a joke called *Scabbin Crew News*. After the first strike days, a couple of people emailed me and said, 'I've lost my copy, can I have another one', and other people would say, 'I never saw it, can I see one?' So, rather than produce more paper copies, because I wasn't going back to Bedfont – or rather we didn't know we were going back to Bedfont at that time – I created a website with the same stuff. Then somebody inside British Airways copied it onto a pilot forum. A pilot then made a complaint and I got suspended, and was later sacked. I was sacked for bullying and harassment just like everybody else. Every single person who got suspended or sacked was suspended for the same charge. It was a satirical magazine about pilots and managers volunteering to do our job, it was just taking the mickey out of them. I don't officially know the identity of the person who made the complaint. They used a pseudonym so they were anonymous. I don't know who that was, but I can make an educated guess. The person described themselves as a British Airways manager who somehow had access to the union, the BASSA forum, illegally, and copied the link to my website from the BASSA forum onto the pilots' forum.

I got back from a trip to Phoenix and two managers were waiting to meet the aircraft and they didn't tell me what they were there for. I actually thought it was because my mother was seriously ill and I just assumed it was something had happened to her. So I was taken through the airport and into a room where they read out a letter of suspension. They took away my ID, and sent me home. When they actually suspended me, my first reaction was relief that it wasn't that my mother had died. My second reaction was disbelief, but when they read out that I was being suspended for bullying and harassment because I'd published this joke magazine I actually said 'This is a joke, right?' I couldn't believe that anyone would ever think that that was harassment or bullying. They just stared at me blankly and I realised this wasn't a joke at all. So my reactions were relief and then disbelief and I left the room totally confused and angry, really angry. I was angry at the company for what was going on, but I didn't feel angry for me personally. To be honest, I just thought of it in terms of the dispute and I was just another one. It seemed like every day somebody was being suspended.   ▶

They were monitoring the BASSA Forum and shortly afterwards we knew they were monitoring the Crew Forum. People actually saw them doing it. But they'd probably been watching me for some time I think because I had been very vocal in support of the strike, on the union forum. Everything I ever wrote on the BASSA Forum was produced at some point in my disciplinary hearing. When I posted later about having been suspended, they tried to use it against me. When I posted after I'd been dismissed they used that against me as a reason for not reinstating me because I'd posted on the BASSA Forum. At times, they went to extreme lengths to identify people through the forum – looking back over two years' worth of rosters to see where people were. When crew mentioned in posts that they were in Hong Kong that narrowed them down until they were able to identify individuals.

In the disciplinary hearing the manager started to read out this eleven-page letter of dismissal including some of the jokes that were in the original *Scabbin Crew News* and, bizarrely, if a dismissal can ever be funny, it was, it really was. He was reading things out that the BASSA rep hadn't heard before and he was sitting there with this fixed expression on his face. And I was desperately trying not to laugh. Eventually the BASSA rep said, 'Look I'm going to have to stop you. Kevin already knows that he's being dismissed. Can we just have the letter and go? It's too difficult to sit here trying to keep a straight face listening to you.' And the manager said, 'But I have to read out the whole letter!' The BASSA rep said 'He already knows he's been dismissed, it's probably on the BASSA Forum by now!' So he left and then I read the letter and, of course, I was dismissed, but it was funny, honestly. It was a very bizarre thing. I'm being sacked and laughing about it, it was odd.

That's when we started to find out about Leiden, because I was allowed to ask 'What is Leiden?', because it appeared in my notes twice. The first time I saw the word Leiden it was in the written notes which were sent to me of the disciplinary interview. They were sent to me for correction or for comments so I corrected them and they didn't bother to even look at them until after this happened. So out of the blue I said 'Can I just ask you a question, can you tell me what Leiden is?' And she just sat there frozen for a few seconds and then went 'It's a room', and the Unite officer said 'To do with the industrial action?' and she replied 'Yes'. That was it. But just by the way she reacted I knew that we'd hit a very raw nerve so then we started digging. So I started asking about Leiden more and more, and not just about me. I passed the information to other sacked crew who also started asking about Leiden. We actually mentioned it at the preliminary investigation and at the disciplinary hearing, and they came out with a form of words that said 'We're not changing the procedures, we're just doing it in a different way.' We knew that things were different, but we weren't quite sure how or – well we knew how, but we weren't sure why. And then we found out they'd set up a special unit just to deal with the industrial relation cases.

I was resigned. I didn't feel sorry for myself, I have felt sorry for myself since a little bit sometimes, but at the time I just felt angry that I was being used to make a point to the union membership – 'This could be you next'. I was well known, not as well-known as I am now, but I was fairly well known by then because of the forum and the fact that *Scabbin Crew News* had got me the sack. I then produced more editions of it! And I had learned lessons, pilots were in the vanguard of attacking cabin crew and getting cabin crew sacked, so I made a very specific point of not mentioning pilots much at all, but going for Willie Walsh and management and the whole bizarre nature of the whole thing. They got better, much funnier and much more professional.

It politicised me more than I thought was possible. I wasn't a traditional union activist, I was a member of the union, I would go along to certain meetings and do stuff. And I was a believer, but it's made me more aware of how dirty politics is. How the union operates, and not everything that I found out about my own side is good, mind you I didn't find anything out about British Airways that was good, so I have to qualify that one.

My partner's been a real bedrock – absolutely 100 per cent solid behind me. It's been tough, it's been tougher on him than it has been on me, because I got the sack and had to stay at home. Since I was sacked, he's had to go back to work and we used to work together, we used to be on the same flights all the time. So a lot of people know us as a couple and every flight he went back on, people were saying, 'Where's Kevin?' and he was having to say 'Oh, have you not heard, he's been sacked', so it was much tougher having to explain and to defend that – even from – some of our friends. It's broken friendships that we had before.

I didn't even realise I was stressed until I went to the doctor and I can't remember what I went to the doctor for, I think I had a stomach upset – yes, I did. And I went to the doctor and said 'Look, I've got this stomach upset'. She asked me a question and I just burst into tears for the first time. And if you think about that now, it was a revelation to me that I'd been carrying around all this stress without even realising it. That was before I was dismissed and there have been a couple of occasions since where for absolutely no reason I just burst into tears – looked at the dog or some stupid thing.

British Airways strike breaking

The delay to BASSA's strike action caused by the High Court decision gave British Airways the opportunity to strengthen its position by recruiting 'volunteer' crew from the ranks of ground staff, management, the small minority of 'loyalist' crew and, most controversially, pilots. Even some call centre agents were included in the ranks of the would-be strike breakers. As the Facebook 15 episode demonstrated, members had strong views on the creation of the VCC:

> The VCCs that Walsh built up were a strike-breaking force of ground staff, of Waterside management, of former pilots and American-based employees as well. So that when we were due to go on strike, he reckoned he could fly a full worldwide schedule. He started planning that from about Christmas after Lord Justice Cox overruled our strike ballot.

(Max)

British Airways' counter-mobilisation inevitably intensified once BASSA took its first strikes in March 2010. Senior management initiated (dis)information campaigns directed at 'stakeholders', both external (customers, shareholders) and internal (middle managers, pilots, crew themselves), with the purpose of challenging BASSA's case and undermining proposed action. There were rumours that the first crew to go on strike would be sacked. In interviews, crew used the term 'ideological offensive' to describe managements' response and recalled the opposition they encountered from not only management, but the media, politicians and in some instances the public.

> My poor old mum, she likes the crossword in the back of *The Daily Mail*, I think that's the only reason she gets that newspaper. And she kept phoning up and saying 'Oh, I never knew you earned £54,000 a year.' I said 'I don't, Mother!' So they really did go overtime and the whole thing they did with Lizanne was incredible, chasing her to her home in LA. Things like that were dreadful.
>
> (Guy)

Here Guy refers to a number of stories appearing about key activists in the press which, as Lizanne recounts (Box 3), appeared to be based upon personal information that only the company could have held. Cabin crew reported on the impact on them of a hostile press which influenced public perceptions of the strikers.

Box 3   The case of Lizanne – harassed and victimised for being a BASSA leader

I was getting targeted left, right and centre. I had one disciplinary, I was accused of bullying and harassment and interviewed over that. And it took them a year and four months to come back to say that it was not found. So for a year and four months, which broke all procedural rules, I had the pressure of waiting for this decision. This wasn't a Leiden case. It was because the ex-branch chair of Cabin Crew '89 section said that I had bullied and harassed him. He had actually left the company, but the company proceeded with the grievance.

Then they did me for a data protection breach. I posted a mixed fleet roster on the Crew Forum with the names blacked out, but because of the pixilation, the names could be seen. But unbeknown to them, the crew member in question had given me permission to do it, but I wasn't about to tell them because it would have got the crew member into trouble. And I'm still waiting for that outcome, so that's about a year and four months now and they haven't come back to decide, to tell me whether I'm guilty or not. These were just grievances that the company took out,

---

that certain individuals took out during the dispute. So I was called in a few times to answer various allegations. But I was absolutely prepared to be sacked because I felt it was – I was fighting for my rights and Duncan had been sacked for doing his union activities. And I felt that I was prepared to be sacked for doing my union activities, and nothing would stop me from doing it.

We gave the reps the choice before we went into dispute. We said to them. 'This is what we're going to be coming up against, this is what we're expecting of you. If you don't feel you're up for it, or if you've got family concerns, your family is concerned about you, step away now.' And not one did. But once the dispute started, one did – he went on strike and everything, but he resigned as a rep.

I did come across Asset Protection. I went in as I had to post the results of the ballot for accepting the deal. And whereas we hadn't been allowed into T5, the Crew Report Centre, unless we were working as crew, I'd been given permission to go in. And I couldn't post it on the BASSA notice boards until exactly two o'clock. Asset Protection followed me from the minute I got into the building. And then I sat down with some crew at a table while I was waiting to post the results and they sat down at a table opposite to try and listen to the conversation. So I just went over to them and said 'Would you like a copy of the ballot results, gents?' and they said 'Oh yes, that's good, thanks.' They're all ex-coppers, they're allegedly ex-bent-policemen, employed for security purposes. They've been there forever. If a crew member's been stealing or anything like that, they get involved.

Also, at the shareholders meeting at the Queen Elizabeth Building, they were filming me outside while I was talking to a shareholder. Two members of Asset Protection had a video camera and were filming me. So I just waved to them. They seemed to get involved in every single disciplinary regardless and they were all involved in the Leiden disciplinary cases. They were doing investigations, were following crew. We knew that because they were using pictures of crews' houses and cars parked in their driveways and things like that and these things would come up in disciplinaries. I'm sure they were following us, I'm sure they were up here during the dispute, watching us coming and going. We were very careful about what we said, no doubt about that. I think our phones were tapped, I think they tried to get into our computers. I wouldn't put it past any of them, and even now I don't put my bags down anywhere.

We got a call from a crew member who used to be a BASSA rep years ago. He wasn't really involved and he didn't go on strike, in fact he broke the strike. But he phoned Duncan about a week before the *Daily Mail* published the notorious BASSA bashing story, although we'd been told about a year before that that they were going to target myself, Duncan and [James (a pseudonym), a senior rep]. Myself, because I was grounded at the time, [James] because he took long blocks of leave, and Duncan. And then this individual phoned Duncan two nights before it went to press and said 'They're doing a hatchet job on you, [James] and Lizanne.' He didn't mention Tom. He obviously didn't know that he was going to be included. He said he had been at a do with the top British Airways people and somebody had told him. That we were being targeted.

My husband phoned me and he said that he'd come out at 8 o'clock and was going to walk the dog, and had seen a car parked across the road. He'd thought it was a bit strange. About an hour later as he came back, the two reporters approached him and asked if that was the house that I lived in. He said 'Yes' and they said 'Well where is she?', and he said 'She's in London at work'. The issue is I've got a house here in Twickenham but British Airways don't have that address, they only have my American address. So of course, they sent them all the way out to America and they could have sent them to Twickenham, because I'm just round the corner from [James]. They could have done the two of us in the one day!

And then the journalist phoned me that night and said 'We're running an article about you in the paper tomorrow'. And I said, 'I know, you were talking to my husband. Who gave you my address in America?' And he said, 'No, no, I just want to talk to you about how much money you earn.' And I said, 'No, who gave you my address in America?' And he said, 'No, it's basically around the money aspect, I need to talk to you.' And I repeated, 'Who gave you my address in America?' I just kept saying that to him, and in the end he hung up. And then he put in the article that I had no comment. Without a doubt, without a doubt British Airways gave our address, because nobody else had my address in America.

Nobody else had my medical history. Well, they said to my husband, 'She's been grounded because she's had a serious foot operation.' And they put it in the paper that I had osteoporosis or something, but it's osteoarthritis I've got, but they were just boxing clever and they got all the information from the company. There is absolutely no doubt about it. Nobody else knew. I don't use my married name so how did they know my husband's name? He's down on my staff travel. All this stuff came from them, our personal details. That day I came up here on the train and it was front page, my picture was on the front page of the [Daily] Mail and it was rush hour. I sat on the train with [James] while everybody was looking at my picture. And then on the way back, it was front page of the Evening Standard, so I got a double whammy. Of course it did affect me, the invasion of privacy.

I was shocked by how vindictive and vile some of the public were towards us. One guy came past when we were on the picket line, he was on his bicycle, he spat at us. Got back on his bicycle and rode away as quickly as he could. There were cars coming past with kids in the back giving us two fingers. What had those parents told those children?

(Rose)

One crew member suggested that, as a European national with different traditions of industrial action, she was more resilient than some of her British colleagues. Nevertheless, in responding to this psychological pressure crew strengthened their bonds of solidarity. Lara recalled:

Strike breakers were never particularly intimidated even though the company was absolutely hell bent on describing the striking crew as mental bullies who were threatening everyone's well-being. It has to be noted also that the adversity we faced from the media, from the company and from the political world was absolutely ruthless. When you think of the vulnerable single mothers and gay men who are in this profession, the violence with which we were attacked was quite incredible. This was especially true for me, because I am not British and, coming from a European country, I had no idea that this would be the reaction. And consequently, in adversity, people bond together. My immediate involvement was due to the fact that my partner was a 'day one' striker and his shift was starting at six in the morning and, being British and Scottish, a strike probably had a far greater impact on him psychologically than it did on me because, being French, I don't see political confrontation as a problem. I think it is part and parcel of democracy. So we went to Bedfont at the time he was supposed to start his shift on the first day when the company was spreading rumours that the first 500 strikers would be sacked. Needless to say because of this union busting tactic he was quite concerned. Ruling by fear, basically. The media coverage, everything, was absolutely appalling. I felt that I was living in some sort of dictatorship. We unleashed such bile from every part of the establishment – on the picket line with people driving past giving us the finger, being rude to us on the radio and in the media. We were on the receiving end, but that was not going to deter me from continuing, because if anything it made me more determined.

(Lara)

Studies of strikes which focus on developments alone may miss the ground level changes in attitude and action that occur on the front line between the contending parties. British Airways marshalled considerable resources to undermine the strike, chartering planes from rival airlines including Ryanair, in addition to the creation of volunteer crew, as indicated above. Contrary to the company's intention and expectation, the consequence was a reciprocal 'escalation' as crew who had not initially gone on strike were drawn into the action. The testimony of a BASSA health and safety rep is compelling:

Tony and I are the Worldwide health and safety reps. We had received a lot of reports from crew during and after the first three days of strikes. Crew who had gone in to work were disgusted at the lack of knowledge of the VCC from an SEP [safety and emergency procedure] point of view and from the information and instructions they had been given at their briefings. They felt that it was completely unsafe to be on board the aircraft. Subsequently, they didn't go in for the second lot of strikes. They wrote to us and also to the Civil Aviation Authority to complain. We informed British Airways that we were going to do a workplace inspection of the briefing rooms because of these safety issues and gave them notice in writing of our intention to do so as safety reps. So the following week during the next round of strikes we turned up at Terminal 5. There were Group 4 security guards at the doors of the Crew Report Centre. We approached them, introduced ourselves quite politely and showed them our union and health and safety credential cards. We explained the reasons why we needed to be allowed into the building to do our health and safety work, but we were refused entrance. We asked to see a manager who we could talk to and they came back five minutes later with Bill Francis [the head of in-flight customer experience]. He is basically the head of the cabin crew. We knew Bill as he sat on the level III Health and Safety Committees and because we've been reps for a long time. We explained that we had given prior notice in writing, we were there as health and safety reps, not as industrial reps, and intended to do a health and safety workplace inspection of the briefing rooms as was our right and because of the numerous reports we'd received. He flatly refused to give us permission to enter the building. The conversation went on for approximately ten minutes, not heated, just pointed. We then realised that we weren't going to gain access. We informed him that we would write to the CAA on this matter and that we would now be leaving the terminal, which we did. Three days later Tony and myself received letters from our own managers saying that we had attempted to gain access to T5 during the dispute, contrary to the instructions given to all cabin crew that the only people allowed to go to T5 were people who were reporting for duty. We were told that if we made a further attempt, we would be subject to disciplinary proceedings. That left a hollow feeling in your stomach, knowing that you're going there legitimately as a health and safety rep and yet they are threatening you with gross misconduct. Obviously by that stage, Duncan had already been suspended and was going through his disciplinary so we knew they were serious. You knew that the stakes had been raised to such a level that they were looking for any reason to try and get rid of the leadership. They were trying to decapitate us from the top down. They'd taken Duncan out and they'd taken Tom out. Graham and I felt that we were probably next. It was before Nicky had had her event, but we were clearly aware that it was British Airways' solemn intention to remove anyone they saw as obstructing them. It did give you restless nights. My wife flies and she was 100 per cent supportive of everything we were doing.

(Richard)

Dirty tricks

If British Airways' 'strategy of decapitation' contravened due process within its established procedures, other measures reported by individual members were flagrantly illegal. Kevin's employment tribunal judgement conceded that British Airways at times monitored BASSA's website. Many interviewees commented on the sustained campaign against BASSA as an organisation and the targeting of its officers. By virtue of his national position in Unite the Union, Steve Turner was aware of the bigger picture of British Airways' 'dirty tricks', as he and others put it:

British Airways had leaked information to the *Daily Mail* about individuals, they personalised it. Information was published that could have only come internally from the company. We knew about it at the time and were really concerned. I wrote to the Information Commissioner about the information that had been leaked and we never received a response. We kept it all on file. We said it was a serious breach of the Data Protection Act because private and confidential information that could have only been in the hands of the company was being provided to the *Daily Mail*. [For example] the photograph they used of Tom was his British Airways photograph. It was him in uniform, the photo that was used on his security pass. They couldn't have got it from anywhere else other than British Airways. We also wrote to them about issues surrounding the use of volunteer crew and the way in which they were recruiting them. They tried to dehumanise them. They were tapping phones and all that. We know that they were tapping phones. And we know that Walsh was up to his eyeballs in it. They'd got into people's private phones. We know that they did that, and we know that Walsh authorised that.

(Steve Turner)

As Lizanne's testimony in Box 3 indicates certain information, including her home address, published by the newspapers could only have come from British Airways.

Many BASSA members reported on the activities undertaken by Asset Protection, British Airways' corporate security department, which took on the role of industrial police during the dispute:

> I knew of Asset Protection because being a rep, when crew members were caught thieving, nicking and so on they would be the group of people that we would have to communicate with. I did get on alright with Asset Protection. I would represent a crew member who had been taken off the aircraft with a carton of fags in his pocket. I would be thinking, 'I can understand why they do what they do, they are there for a purpose.' But since the dispute, seeing how far they've stepped over the mark, a lot of their efforts were done to monitor crew. And some of the crew that had been monitored and they found information about them, they must have spent months on the computers trying to sort out the information.
>
> (Tom)

Claims by crew that the company, through Asset Protection, had undertaken surveillance of individual crew members have been confirmed by recent newspaper coverage of Unite's subsequent legal action. In 2015 *The Independent* stated that British Airways had paid £1 million to stop Unite the Union from suing the company over the operations of the airline's in-house force, many of whom had been former Scotland Yard and security services' personnel.[11] It was reported that the private communications of ten crew, some of whom were union officials, had been accessed:

> There were dark forces at work and in order to take out people who were obviously active union members, active on the BASSA Forum at the time, very vocal at work, etc., they tried any tactics. They were getting rid of as many people as possible and making examples so as to put the fear of god into the workforce.
>
> (Amy)

Crew members vividly recalled the ever-present atmosphere of managerial intimidation and fear of reprisals:

> I was followed in Cranebank. I was sat in the restaurant. There was a man, quite big built, who was just on his phone like this, just sat behind us, trying to listen to our conversation. And we then moved to a separate part of the building, and stood in an isolated position. And he comes and stands right next to us on his phone like this. He was recording

us. It sounds paranoid, but what is that man doing? So we reported the incident to our instructors and they didn't know who he was. None of them knew who he was, he was an outsider and did not have an ID on. But it was in the midst of the dispute and people had been suspended for questioning 'What are you doing there?' So we were scared to actually question someone. Then we were listening to his conversation at lunchtime when he was talking about his exploits in Bosnia and stuff like that. An ex-union rep was with me and said to me 'He's classic, he looks like Asset Protection.' He might not have been but his behaviour was very suspicious. The trainers asked security who he was. It was like he was above the law within British Airways. Our perception of Asset Protection is that they were working above the law.

(Carrie)

Reps, in particular, reported surveillance, as Max remembers:

People were sitting outside my house, just staring in with the car running. The first time I saw them was on a Monday morning. I saw a car sat opposite and there's not even enough room to park a car opposite, because there's two driveways. And when I came back an hour or so later, after I had been to the gym, I think, the car was still there with the engine running and about 5.30 that evening it finally left, but the engine had been running all day. Then the next day it arrived about 9 o'clock in the morning, again engine running all day. So I went out and he was there again when I went to the football. At 8 o'clock in the evening and he was still there. So I said to him *'Do you want a cup of tea or anything, you seem to have been here a while? What are you up to?'* He said *'That's not really any of your business.'* I said, *'It is, you've been here a couple of days now.'* He said, *'Well I'm waiting for someone to come out of that house.'* I said, *'Oh that's strange, because that house has been empty for a year now. No one lives there and you know that.'* After I spoke to him he drove off about ten minutes later and I never saw him again. I didn't really mind, but for my wife with a one-year-old and the amount of work that we were doing anyway, that was pressure. She's far more outspoken towards people than I am at times, so it was a good job I went out there and she didn't. There was stuff like that. You think about the telephone tapping and perhaps you should actually go to the police and say my phone might be tapped. If Sky or anyone wants a story, well there's only going to be about five or six people that had their phones continually in contact.

(Max)

Action taken against individuals had tragic consequences, as in the following case reported by the BASSA rep who had most responsibility for representing members in disciplinary hearings:

> One of the girls I was representing killed herself two weeks ago because she couldn't go on with it any more. I got a suicide note that came through to me via the chair of the disciplinary panel. She phoned me up and said, 'The person you're representing has written to me to let me know that by the time you read this letter she will be dead. And she wants to thank you for your hard work and the amount of cases you've done for her. But she couldn't go on with the fight.' I think it just goes on and on and on. She was a crew member for 30 years, never had a mobile telephone, just used the internet to write a couple of things. In her particular case, which was brought to British Airways as a grievance, all she said was 'she wanted to see his [a particularly vindictive opponent of BASSA] blood boil'. That's all she said, that's the most derogatory line in it. There wasn't a case. The next thing she knew was that on other forums, he [the same antagonist] was asking for the true identities of people who had posted. She decided that she couldn't continue. The crew went through so much. So we [BASSA] are very lucky to have them support us but, at the same time, we appear to be the only people that listen to them. They can trust us because we do the same job as them.
>
> (Max)

5

Collective organisation
The XXXX campaign

In the face of employer hostility, the resilience of cabin crew, underpinned by BASSA's organisational strength and innovation, was remarkable. This chapter shows how BASSA organised industrial action and cabin crew discussed their experiences of taking strike action, of the picket lines and the mass meetings held at the ground of Bedfont Football Club.

The fact that cabin crew are geographically dispersed and have no fixed workplace offered a particular challenge to BASSA, so that collective organisation took a combination of 'traditional' and more 'modern' forms. Electronic and digital communication – mobile phones, email and internet forums – ensured attendance at mass meetings and contributed to high levels of participation at rallies and picketing on strike days. Crucially, these forms were not just organisational tools, but served to promote collectivism, reinforce beliefs and engender confidence. An organic link developed between the real and virtual. Electronic media used to mobilise for Bedfont was then used to report back the numbers at Bedfont to galvanise those who were unable to attend and might be scattered around the globe. This chapter describes the two online forums used by BASSA members, one established by the union and another independently. These complementary forums played a crucial role in the mobilisation of cabin crew, but also in allowing members to share anger and fears, while providing emotional and political support to this dispersed workforce.

Taking strike action

The testimonies of cabin crew are probably unique in revealing the emotions and fears of workers taking strike action. They show the role of union reps in reassuring them. Sana was a relatively new BASSA rep when the dispute began. She talked frankly about her own worries and how she had to deal with members' anxieties about going on strike. She also discussed how the media attacked female strikers in terms of their role as mothers, expressing moral outrage that they might take industrial action to defend themselves as workers:

I was really, really bad, I was really panicking because there were rumours about British Airways sacking the first 500 strikers to set an example. They knew it would be unlawful, but it was better to pay out six grand or whatever. And there were days that I believed that rumour and I remember thinking that I was going to lose my home, my children – they would have to change school. I'm thinking 'How do I pay for nursery fees?' And I remember I was on the picket line and the nursery rang up and they said 'Oh, by the way, we've changed the policy now so you have to pay the £2,000 and then you get the money back in July when you leave', and I said 'You know what, I'm on strike, I can't', and she said 'Well can you put your circumstances in writing?' I didn't sleep at all, I was really panicky, I was crying constantly. And then March came and it was stressful and everybody was like calling constantly. I remember I had an emergency phone ringing all night, people were worried, people were scared, people were asking questions, scared of being sacked. 'I don't know what to do, am I doing the right thing, will I lose my staff travel?' 'Yes you will, probably.' 'What happens if I do go in?' I was like, 'Well I can't answer that.' Or people were trying to make you understand, 'Well I've got a holiday booked and my mum lives in Paris ...' 'Well so does mine but ...' They were trying to justify themselves to you. They wanted me to say 'That's OK, I understand', but I couldn't say that. 'What happens if I go to work?' I will say 'Well, I understand your fears and I have exactly the same ones, but you have to do whatever you feel is right for you. For me personally, I can't tell you what to do, I would prefer if you went on strike and I think as a union member you should do it.' But I always said 'Come to Bedfont' to everybody. I would say 'Come because you will be part of a group, you will be part of a community.' And one guy, I remember, rang me up at one o'clock in the morning and said 'I went to work yesterday' and I said 'OK' and he said, 'It was the wrong thing to do' and I said 'OK', and he said 'Can I come?' and I said 'Of course you can.' He then said 'Well you're probably going to shout at me', and I said 'No, I won't. You've admitted to it, you've made a mistake and you want to rectify and nobody is going to know anyway.' I said 'Come, and then you will realise that you've done the right thing.' And most people actually came up and said 'You know what, coming to Bedfont really made me realise I'd done the right thing.' Because he was sitting at home and he was scared and I understand he was scared and he watched TV and there was all this propaganda. But as soon as they came to Bedfont they realised that it was a really good feeling and would say, 'I feel proud of what I've done, I really, really do.' I think it must have been awful having to go into work and look around and think, 'I hope I don't meet anybody today, I hope nobody recognises me, I hope nobody knows.' And people are ashamed of it because they lie, it's so obvious that people lie, they say 'I saw you at Bedfont' and I thought, 'No you didn't because I know you went to work.'

I was at Bedfont every day, but my partner was more with the children because the children came at weekends, but we could not justify paying for somebody to look after them when we weren't earning because obviously we had a massive hit because neither of was earning. So we brought them at weekends and sometimes during the week, Obviously, the oldest one was in school at the time. So they experienced it. They experienced so much and the *Daily Mail* put my youngest daughter on their website and I wasn't happy, it took a long time to get her picture removed. She was at Bedfont walking along with me and she looked as glum as anything, and they put a picture on there saying about mothers dragging their children too young to understand the picket line and said this little girl looks glum or doesn't look very happy. And the comment was 'Can we go home please Mummy?' or something along those lines. I was really angry and eventually they removed it, but they removed it as a gesture of goodwill not because they had to. I was so cross. In the newspapers, you can go on their forums and readers can put comments. I read some of them but I stopped because it was like questioning my ability to be a mother. Like 'Are these people really suitable to be parents if they think it's OK to bring a child to a picket line?' But it was the reality.

(Sana)

Camille was one of only 34 cabin crew who took strike action at Gatwick. Historically, cabin crew at Gatwick were on different terms and conditions from those at Heathrow, so the impact of Project Columbus was not necessarily regarded as seriously by crew based there. She is French and was a purser on short- and long-haul flights (which are mixed at Gatwick), but because she was not a rep, she felt particularly vulnerable both before and after the dispute:

Well I was scared, I was always scared you know – oh yeah, for more than a year. And during the strike and after the strike for more than a year

I was always scared. I was never talking about the strike with my crew because I'm in charge also so I don't want them to say I'm bullying them or something. I was never talking about the strike, never talking about anything. Talking about the weather, nananana, rubbish, because I was scared that they would find an excuse to get rid of me, I didn't want them to get rid of me like that, they are not going to get rid of me so easily. So I was really, really, really careful. And I was careful with the pilots with everybody really. And now it did become more laid back, but I had a rough time at some point to be honest. In my head I knew that the scare-mongering like *'Oh yeah, if you go on strike, they're going to fire you the next day or something'* – I knew that was rubbish. But I was just thinking OK, I've just got to be careful that I don't make any mistakes or anything like that that will just compromise myself.

(Camille)

How BASSA mobilised

Combatting members' fears and building confidence and solidarity were crucial. One way BASSA did this was in the staging of mass meetings in the run-up to strike action, drawing upon the artistic and creative backgrounds of a number of BASSA reps. As James described:

As the dispute became more and more likely, meetings grew from 500 to 1,000, and then we had to find a venue for 2,000. By the end we had to have a venue for thousands which is a hell of a lot. They were like rock and roll shows, they were incredible. They were so big I think at Sandown we had 6,000 on the top floor and then we had to have a whole other floor with video screens. Then we had to have video screens outside. I can remember walking in there and thought, 'My God, it is literally like U2.' We had the music and it was almost tribal. We had the sound system, which was about £10,000 a go, because it was a high-tech sound system, it was so rock and roll. But that was my doing really because of my theatre years. I know how important the staging of it is. Because if you make live theatre it captures people's imagination. If you just walked about with a bit of a cloth cap and go 'Well brothers and sisters what we're going to do is …' We made it an event, and it worked. We had T-shirts, it was like a rock and roll show, it literally was, and people really loved it.

(James)

Another way of encouraging resilience was by countering and subverting British Airways' actions. BASSA committee member Nicky described how the four capital exes (or kisses) – XXXX – became, for cabin crew, the symbol of the dispute, but was also another battleground:

British Airways could have just wiped our rosters but they didn't. What they did was, when you went on strike, they put four exes through every line of your roster. Overnight that became a symbol of the strike, they handed it to us. So the next day we had done – in the manner of the *X Factor* television programme – XXXX Factor T-shirts, XXXX Factor mugs and pens and banners. And so everyone was bringing their rosters in, and one of them had their roster framed, four exes through it because they were like 'ha ha!' So we used the symbol, we inverted the symbol. So it then became that, in those days following the first days of strike action, if you then used a XXXX pen – a pen that had four exes on it – you got suspended because that's 'bullying and harassment'. They hated us, absolutely hated us, so you'd get suspended for using the XXXX pen, they lost the plot, and they couldn't bear the symbol, so they were saying 'We can't have it. We will not have these XXXX luggage tags.' For them they had to go because they couldn't stand the strength of the symbol. So on Facebook no one will ever talk about the strike but they will put XXXX or they will sign everything with XXXX. Four exes were just everywhere, but just in a subtle way. And people still say 'Four-exer or no – you think not?' instead of saying scab or something.

(Nicky)

The XXXX campaign, which drew on the popularity of the reality television programme, *The X Factor*, was also a prime example of the responsiveness and inventiveness of BASSA in immediately producing witty and relevant publicity material and what became coveted merchandise. For Elizabeth, a purser on Worldwide:

When we didn't go to work and we went on strike the company would put on your roster four exes, so BASSA very cleverly produced these XXXX key rings that you could put on your luggage tag, or they had these T-shirts, or they had a yellow pen with XXXX and the company were desperate. They actually suspended people for producing the yellow pen. They were desperate to suppress any knowledge of what the support for the strike was – the pens, the T-shirts, loads of stuff, we had stickers – kisses on your roster. The company were pulling their hair out, they couldn't stop it as much as they tried. The company wanted to monitor it, they monitored everything, I've still got it now, I've got my yellow pen. We'd get to the briefing and I'll get my yellow pen out and I started to write and I could see people looking at me.

(Elizabeth)

Elizabeth illustrates how strikers communicated solidarity at work between strike days in a hostile atmosphere, where any discussion of the dispute was out of the question. It shows how the strikers produced a counter-culture. Tom was at least partly responsible for the BASSA publicity machine and reflected on how the stickers became another battleground:

We had key rings so we thought, let's do some more key rings but key rings are boring, so I had an idea, let's do stickers. And knowing what crew are like, we did loads of stickers with things like 'Walsh is a bully' and 'BASSA is THE union' and things like that, which people liked. We did print off thousands of them, but we restricted them going out. So people would get to the briefing and go, 'Have you got any stickers?' and then people would stick them everywhere – everywhere – that brought the union again to the forefront, people were talking about it. And I've always said that you've got to do something to get people talking about it – you've got to make it interesting and exciting and the stickers took off so well. The company hated it because it was costing them money to remove them. As fast as they were removing them, people were sticking them on. And it was the time when Terminal 5 was just opening, we were doing the trial runs and someone managed to sticker the longest escalator in the world. Someone managed to sticker the handrail. And the funniest thing was when you saw cleaners, or members of management, running down the escalators cleaning it and it disappears around the other side, so you would see them run back up to the top again. As they cleaned it you would see someone walking down and they'll look at you and they sticker it. So you'd see the management taking that sticker off and there'd be another sticker coming down again at them. So it made it fun and we had about three different sticker campaigns. We had bright orange, red and yellow, green and the company hated it. And of course if you're Willie Walsh, you get on board an aircraft and you see 'Walsh is a bully' stuck everywhere and you get a bit pissed off. I did all that, then [James] did the more subtle communications in the newsletter showing Willie Walsh as a second class salesman and stuff like that. And then we did pens and then lanyards, and the first lanyards we did the company were saying 'No you can't have that, it's the wrong colour.' So then I copied the exact colour of the British Airways corporate lanyard and just made it the same colour as the corporate lanyard; one side was plain and one side was BASSA. So people could wear them and then just turn them over to show BASSA and they went down a storm and we did about 20,000 of those.

(Tom)

While more traditional publicity material lent visibility on the ground and in the aircraft, BASSA's use of information technology was vital to the organisation of this transient workforce. While crew members' distrust of management meant that many had refused to give the company their email addresses, they readily volunteered them to BASSA, giving the union a notable advantage. The union would email members on a daily basis. Duncan, the branch secretary, began a daily blog, aware that his days of employment at British Airways were numbered:

I did my blog every day. When I came home from Bedfont, I was pretty knackered at the end of the day, but I posted it online that same evening. It took me about an hour, and I'm not just saying this, but I got so much feedback from it, crew said that it kept them going. People logged on to it, they religiously followed it wherever they were. I wrote this blog all through the days we were actually on strike, every night and the crews liked it because I was personalising it. I decided to put my name on the end of it, talked about my tomatoes and gave it a sort of a human perspective. And the crew told me they appreciated it, it really went down well. And I realised it was leadership of sorts, but I was really taking the mickey out of British Airways and particularly ridiculing Walsh at the time. They had said they genuinely thought I was out of control and so I deliberately acted like I was just to unnerve them, a bit like Marlon Brando's mad Colonel Kurtz, up the Mekong in the film *Apocalypse Now*, because I wanted to show I wasn't afraid of Willie Walsh in particular. And I enjoyed them thinking I was out of control and I knew that I was hung as far as my job was concerned, so for me it was a case of might as well be hung for a sheep as a lamb while at the same time, hopefully, it upped the morale of crew and gave them strength knowing that actually British Airways don't control everything and everybody.

(Duncan)

Asad expressed BASSA members' appreciation:

> How he was able to sit down at the computer and write it up after spending the whole day on the picket line, I do not know. He did it as an update – day 12, day 14 – and that was really appreciated.
>
> (Asad)

Access to members' mobile phone numbers also became a necessary part of union organising, although expensive and used sparingly. Duncan recalled:

> I could text every member, but it cost £1,000 each time so we texted them every night before strike days – 'DON'T GO IN', simple effective messages, and the belief cascaded down.
>
> (Duncan)

Jack, a crew member on Worldwide, talked about the importance of mass texting to a geographically dispersed workforce during the dispute:

> Down route, because in a lot of the hotels you couldn't maybe get access to a computer, but you would get to your room, switch your phone on and 'ting' a text from BASSA, telling you what is happening at Bedfont today or if they were in negotiations, this has happened, because we're divorced, we're not in a central place, and people don't live together, so that was vital. BASSA played a blinder there.
>
> (Jack)

Will, a Eurofleet CSD and BASSA rep, suggested a collective dimension to union texting:

> I was on the crew bus, so there are say ten people on there, we all got the text messages come through at the same so 'ding', 'ding', 'ding', 'ding', 'ding', 'ding'! There might be one person who didn't have a text message. Now that doesn't mean they went on strike or they didn't go on strike or not, but it meant they weren't in the texting system or they weren't a member or they hadn't gone on strike or whatever. And of course the flight deck would be there and it would be very intimidating in the nicest possible way, because it meant that also we just looked at each other realising we were in this together.
>
> (Will)

The forums

BASSA members believe that the forums were hugely important for advancing the interests of cabin crew in the dispute; as a source of information countering British Airways propaganda, as a platform for debate and as a means of organising the strikes. Crucially, the continual interaction between members reduced isolation, built confidence, fostered activism and offered emotional support in the face of hostility. Sally commented:

> Across the world we planned a dispute by BlackBerry. Unbelievable. The whole thing was done by phone and our laptops. Because we're all over the world, it was just amazing, absolutely amazing. But we are all techies, except for me of course, but our lives are planned that way and we're very adept at it. The average person probably couldn't plan a dispute of that nature between Sydney and London, but that's how we run our lives.
>
> (Sally)

In 2010, BASSA temporarily closed the BASSA Forum when British Airways' solicitors attempted (unsuccessfully) to force both Forums to release the names of the Facebook 15 for alleged defamation of character following the disclosure on Facebook (and subsequently the forums), of the names of pilots trained to take crew roles during the strike and following an apparent leak of posts to management. Both forums refused to release members' names, but BASSA decided to close its Forum to avoid litigation. Alex reflected on how the forums became yet another site of conflict in the dispute:

> The main thing for me, I find with the forum is that propaganda gets squashed straight away because there is that real time communication. So basically British Airways' propaganda gets dissected and discussed openly on Crew Forum, and this is the reason why the company actually wants to shut us down, and they have tried several times. BASSA decided to close the BASSA Forum in 2010 -- British Airways' solicitors asked for 32 names from the BASSA Forum, they wanted those members to be identified. And they also contacted me, asking for four names from the forum. They contacted me via email and telephonically as well. They sent me the document on the same day, I think it was probably about 3 or 4 o'clock in the afternoon, to ask me to release the names. And so immediately after that, I contacted Lizanne. Lizanne was in Los Angeles at the time. I said to her 'Oh, by the way Lizanne, I've actually got a letter

from the solicitor to ask for four names.' And she said 'Oh yes, I've just been on the phone to Duncan, they've actually asked for 32 names.' I said 'What are you going to do about it?' and I said to Lizanne 'Well I'm not going to be giving the names so that's how I'm going to operate.' I said to Lizanne 'So what are your plans?' and she said to me, 'We are going to close the BASSA Forum, there's too many people involved, 32 members is a lot of members to actually sacrifice, so we are closing BASSA Forum.' I said, 'Well actually Lizanne, just to let you know, I'm not closing the Crew Forum, over my dead body will I close Crew Forum.' Those were the words I used to Lizanne, I said 'Yes, I'm going to fight them, I will be fighting them.' Obviously I did not release the names and basically I stonewalled British Airways so they couldn't do anything. We got together because of that problem, because of the common denominator during the industrial action, so the whole industrial action thing. The intention of the forum was never to undermine the union, but to actually fight against the injustices that were happening.

(Alex)

Carrie was a Worldwide crew member who also became involved with Crew Forum and once again highlighted its role in countering British Airways propaganda, but also in building confidence and bonds between the cabin crew:

Everyone always mentions how they couldn't have even gone on strike without the support of the forums. On the first day of the strike there was talk that we were going to be sacked. There were people going 'Oh my goodness, am I going to be sacked'? Everyone was phoning each other up. But the one place was the forums. Everyone flocked to the forums saying how many people there were at Bedfont? How many people? Word got around that there were loads of people here, you're in good company! And then British Airways were saying 'No, no, we're getting all these flights off', well the reality was they weren't and they were empty flights. The forums completely negated what British Airways were saying to the press. We created a sub-forum called industrial relations and it's probably the most active sub-forum, even now. Because what it's done, it's made people interested and aware of what's going on. Not everyone, because a lot of people don't use the forums or just come and have a quick read. Not everyone contributes, but it discusses rumour that becomes fact. People use it like a blog and post their thoughts, they go and find information. We had a period where everyone was writing to their MPs during the dispute to serve an early day motion; whenever you wrote to your MP, you included your MP on it so you knew that that MP had been written to. And it was an organising tool. There's been numerous things like grievance letters; 'Right, what do we do here?' 'OK, this is the one I used.' So it's a way of organising and in terms of trade unionism, it's the ultimate in unifying a workforce. It's very pro-British Airways. It's not anti-British Airways, it's anti-management, it's anti-bad-management. And when the dispute was wrapping up there were massive arguments on the BASSA Forum and on Crew Forum about whether or not we should accept the deal. And there was a minority of people, but very vocal – well it all got quite aggressive – who said 'No we shouldn't, we should carry on, it's the only way to get what we want', but the majority of people were saying 'No, we've got to at some point give peace a chance.'

What the forums have done, in my opinion, is that they changed the whole nature of this dispute because it enabled people to be more informed. So the propaganda that British Airways were releasing was instantly dismissed; lots of people contributed and said 'No, no, this is the reality.' So it really informed people which totally cut down any propaganda from British Airways. And also it provided a real support network. We've had people threatening to commit suicide on the forums who have been supported straight away by the community that's developed. All know and we all accept that they probably know who we are and we've been profiled, but it's the risk that is worth taking, and everyone who contributes puts themselves at risk because we know we're being watched. But it's the camaraderie that's developed and it's a community that's been developed through Crew Forum. We're such good friends, there's a massive network of people now, all friends. Some of us have never met but we're like family literally, it has become like a family, like a real strong solid community. In a weird way, what British Airways has done to break us has actually made us stronger, but thanks to the forums.

(Carrie)

Sarah, a CSD on Worldwide, confirmed the importance of the Crew Forum in providing social and emotional support:

It's a very helpful website, not just from an industrial point of view. It's a place where crew can come and talk about absolutely anything. People with bereavements, with health problems, it's a place where people seek advice on anything. But at the height of the dispute, it was where everybody went to see what was going on. People would turn to the forums. The forums were our lifeline. Even if they weren't expressing themselves they knew that they could listen to somebody else that was. Not everybody would say what they really felt, because they didn't like to, but then somebody else might have said what they were thinking. So they were able to see well, that person is suffering the same as me, although I dread to think how the sacked and suspended were coping.

(Sarah)

For James the role of the forums was heightened during the dispute – when BASSA members could not discuss the dispute at work they could release their frustrations and emotions online:

People drew strength from the forum where they could talk openly and let off steam and rant and rave. It evolved from heated discussion into almost an underground movement during the dispute.

(James)

Jack underlines how the forums succeeded in sustaining collectivism wherever members may have been located across the globe:

BASSA had a vibrant forum, which we logged on to nightly or daily to catch up. You'd go away for two, three or five days, you're in Singapore or Los Angeles so you're obviously divorced from events in London. The first thing you do is log on and you're personally involved again; the forum was humming, just zinging some nights. So we could hit the ground running when we returned to Heathrow.

(Jack)

Melanie, a cabin crew member on Worldwide, talked about how she had become an activist through her persona on the BASSA Forum:

I just became a lot more animated on the forums, it was a bit of a laugh posting on there and I just became a little bit more confident with the written word, so it just naturally progressed to the spoken really. Almost like being bipolar, because I am quite quiet really. In briefings people might have said, 'You look like a scab.' Once they started talking to me then I would become more animated and they were like 'I didn't realise how militant you are.' We all sized each other up, you do that just by their faces, it's dreadful isn't it? My first post got slammed down actually, it was about the disruption agreement, I asked because at the time we were talking about going out on strike. I said 'Are we balloting for the disruption, is the disruption agreement part of the set up?' I got a reply back going 'Don't you read your emails?' – that was what the BASSA site was like. I remember thinking, 'Bloody hell I don't want to write anything more on here.' I left it a little while and just read it and that gave me a bit of confidence actually. I quite liked it, and interestingly my first post I did in my real name, and then I changed to a pseudonym and when I changed to a pseudonym I got better responses from what I posted. People were nicer to me, it was really bizarre. I remember one post I put down, oh my God, it was like 'I am chatty today', this pseudonym had brought me out of my shell or something. My pseudonym was 'Flopsy', so it was kind of a bubbly persona, it was very different. It was nice to have that and people responded to it. In fact if I tell people what my pseudonym is now people are like 'Oh', they're surprised. There were quite a few funny threads that I don't think were union related, I think it was something silly, somebody was taking the piss out of Walsh I think and we just all joined in, yes, and all with the same sense of humour. I would make a joke and you'd always have a wingman, you'd say something and they'd say something and it would be like 'Ha, ha, ha, that's great.' That other people were there, that you weren't alone, it wasn't just a bunch of lefties, it was real people. I would not consider myself a militant person, no. I wanted a decent agreement, I wanted to go back to work. I don't think they were a bunch of lefties, no, I think that they did their best with the negotiations and stuff. I think there was a lot of propaganda at the beginning, but no I didn't think they were going out on strike for the sake of going out on strike. I don't know, I am not like, maybe it's the persona, I don't know what I mean. I wouldn't down tools for the sake of it.

(Melanie)

The foundation of the picket lines

A feature of the dispute was the animated and also glamourous picket lines around Heathrow Airport run from operational headquarters at Bedfont. BASSA had no difficulty getting members to volunteer for picket duty, a willingness by cabin crew to participate in action which challenged the widespread contemporary presumption that union activism was a thing of the past. The picket lines contributed to the high visibility of the dispute, often in freezing weather. For Rhys, a CSD on Eurofleet and BASSA rep:

I would say we've got our ten per cent who are like our gold card holder BASSA members, who would burn the building down for not having running hot water. British Airways have their ten per cent who would probably sell a kidney if they asked them to. Then in the middle you've got the 80 per cent and they're the quiet moderates that just plod along. For me, to get that 80 per cent mobilised to the degree that we did, speaks volumes. Bearing in mind we are people people and live off our emotions so we're not the miners, ours are not hard core macho environments. Our demographic, our girls and gay guys mostly, are not probably the most militant of people. We used the miners' strike as an analogy, as probably the last dispute that probably would come anywhere near to this was the miners' strike, and you could draw comparisons as it was purely about breaking the union, and about personalities – between Thatcher and Arthur Scargill. So we did, but then we didn't want to go down that route of the image of the aggression and the image of the fighting element with the riots and the police and all that sort of thing. I remember one of the papers I think titled it as one of the most glamorous picket lines they'd ever seen. You got stewardesses in Chanel sunglasses and there was the joke on the phone-in. On one of the London phone-ins, this guy rang in and said, there's no foundation to this, there's no foundation to that picket line. And one of our girls rang up and said 'I do have to correct you on that. There is more foundation on that picket line than you would get in Debenhams and that's just the men.' The reporter just fell about laughing. I remember standing there once and this steward walked past in bright pink wellies, waving his flag, and you think, 'What picket line is like this?'

(Rhys)

A further challenge for BASSA was how to organise the European and inter-national crew, who were dependent upon staff travel concessions to travel to Heathrow, concessions which had swiftly been removed by the company. Yet, as Sally (a long-standing CSD on Eurofleet, but recent BASSA rep) described, European cabin crew did participate:

Some who had lost their staff travel were already in their homes and obviously stayed there. They couldn't keep going backwards and forwards because at one point I think some of the Greek crew were paying a grand, some were in South Africa and so on. Obviously when they had to work they were having to come over, but during the strike those that wanted to be involved were staying either in a bed and breakfast to start with, but then between us we were networking, 'Oh, I've got a sofa, I've got a spare room, come and stay with me.' I started it a bit on the picket lines, I said, because I was running the buses, I would say when I had got 14 people in the bus, 'If there's anyone here that doesn't have anywhere to stay and if there's anyone here that can lend a bed, can you all please talk.' You have to push people because it was a very uncertain time at the beginning of a strike and because people got very nervous, they were so worried. That first day is the worst day because people are so scared and that's why some people go in. The proudest moment of my life was, apart from my children, it was bitterly cold, it was torrential rain and they were queuing ten deep to get on a picket bus. And some of them didn't even have coats, it was just the most amazing thing I've ever seen in my life – and everyone was laughing, they were all singing. But the fact that we're in the hospitality business if you like, we had the chuck wagon, the toilets, there was nothing that we didn't think about. And then we had the open air bus, so the kids could go out, bring your children, the bouncy castle, activities days. We had everything and then we had all the other unions visit us, it was brilliant, brilliant. We had John McDonnell, he came down loads, he's a great guy, I really liked him. Obviously Lenny came down. We had, I think the RMT came a couple of times. I can't tell you the names of all the unions but we had huge support, they were all down with their banners.

(Sally)

Elizabeth also commented on the humour, ebullience and carnival atmosphere of strike days:

We got the masks of Willy and they put it in the gents' toilet – a picture of him on the urinals. So every time anybody peed it went straight onto him. We had him in the ladies toilets, if you did anything else it went straight on William. And the pants, we had his face put on a pair of pants, we got the ones where he was like Hitler. He hated it.

(Elizabeth)

Richard, a BASSA rep, alluded to the support of other trade unions and individuals in the context of a strike marked by the hostility of political parties and the media:

On strike days, I tended to run minibuses around the different picket points because we were only allowed a certain number of pickets as per police instructions. We had five or six picket lines dotted around the airport, but because we had so many people based at the Bedfont Football Club, as our headquarters, so many people were there coming to picket and were wanting to play their part in the whole dispute. We had hired a series of about five or six minibuses and then we would rotate people round normally on about an hourly basis to allow everyone the chance to say that they'd been out on the picket. So we needed five or six drivers so I was one of those. It's normally the other way, you're scratching to get people. Yes, and even in the freezing cold people just came in in all their North Face stuff. We didn't leave them out too long, they were going out to wave their flags for an hour, because they knew they were going to get picked up in an hour. And then there would be the next lot. And I think people gained so much strength from that because again, because we are a vagrant workforce, we don't often get together. Well we don't get together apart from when we're at work so having that Bedfont base and having hundreds of people there and on occasions it was well over a thousand people there. People could see that they weren't on their own. When you're lying in your bed at night, thinking the world is collapsing around you, it gives you strength. Lenny McCluskey came down on many occasions during the dispute. Even down to, there was a little Indian chap who worked in Gate Gourmet, called the samosa man – I don't know what his name was, but he was christened the 'samosa man' and he would come down to Bedfont and deliver hundreds of samosas as a sign of solidarity, I can only assume that he had been part of the Gate Gourmet dispute. Also all the letters from around the world, from other trade unions and the generous cheques that they gave towards the strike fund for us.

(Richard)

In this context the letter signed by academics and published in *The Guardian*, which highlighted Willie Walsh's attack on workers' rights, was very important to cabin crew. Julianne recalled, 'I tell you what I cried, I cried, I couldn't believe that people out there cared.' Similarly for Elizabeth:

There was the academics when that letter got written, there was a first class passenger that was a gold card holder that actually used to come to the meetings and he donated. Eventually we started hearing of other unions and bodies donating. But I must admit apart from ourselves we felt completely isolated.

(Elizabeth)

And for Stephen, a long-standing BASSA rep and committee member:

The Guardian were a major help, because we felt that the media was just bombarding us and we had no one, we had a gold card holder stand up and support us, and we had your [the authors and colleagues] letter that was published in *The Guardian*. What you did, it gave it credence, it gave us some sort of legitimacy. That we're not just a bunch of airheaded left wing idiots, we've actually got a legitimate reason for doing what we're doing. We're not doing this for fun, we're not killing ourselves for fun.

(Stephen)

The biggest room party: Bedfont

Cabin crew have repeatedly emphasised how Bedfont was integral to the organisation of the strike. In the absence of any fixed workplace, BASSA needed a base near Heathrow and found and rented the football ground on strike days. As Nicky put it:

Bedfont was hugely important. Bedfont was because we don't have a shop floor. And we couldn't be – because of the security – we couldn't be actually at the terminals, in the airport. So Bedfont was the shop floor if you like. It was a football club, it was a random place, but that was the place that we had. We organised all the vans to go out to the picket lines from Bedfont, so there were six picket lines. So we had hundreds and hundreds of crew at Bedfont and we had about half a dozen mini vans. And in the first strikes it was freezing, freezing cold and so we decided to only leave people out at picket line for about an hour and we'd have people driving vans, people at Bedfont, people on the picket lines and then the vans bringing them back, picking 12 more up, exchanging them, so taking 12 more. I was on the picket line all day every day for the whole 22 days, wearing a pair of old men's underpants with Willie Walsh's face on my arse. We also had the open-top bus driving around the airport. And we had a demo up Bath Road one day to the corporate headquarters, past the hotel where they were housing all the scabs. You'd have crew coming in, crew driving over from France, wherever they lived. We had the best buffet, we had a mountain of food that crew would bring in or they'd bake stuff or they'd bring over cheese from France. And there was a bar there as well and there was a burger van and god knows what. Everybody missed it desperately when it was over, no one wanted to go back to work. They loved it because you got a sense of community that we don't have as cabin crew. You have to remember that when we fly, we don't know each other whereas there it was like a family and because we don't have a shop floor it just meant all the more to us. Because you saw people that you hadn't seen for years and suddenly you were just all together. The solidarity was quite astonishing really.

(Nicky)

Laurent, a CSD on Eurofleet and BASSA rep, commented on how Bedfont, was in part a result of lessons learned in previous disputes, but he also conveyed the party atmosphere and the fact that it encompassed both those with or without families:

We were talking about Bedfont the other day and there's a couple of days we nearly lost crowd control, it was unbelievable. We had, I can't remember, it was either theme days or there was certain occasions when we said look we do need a big push, for whatever reason. Because I was organising the buses and minibuses going out, it was just mayhem. I've never seen so many people and the camaraderie and it was just, it was great. It was their frustration because at work it became that if you mentioned the word strike or BASSA and British Airways, you thought you would be suspended and it was an awful, awful atmosphere and it was just a total release of tensions out there. On the picket line people could shout whatever they wanted and they just felt no intimidation. It was a total release of pent-up anger. Barbecues, bouncy castle, one day family things for the kids. The main theme that Bedfont was about was for people, because I've never been in this situation, but again we were quite wary of the people who we represent. There are quite a few single people out there, because of the job, people don't have steady boyfriends, girlfriends and that kind of stuff. And we all believed, and we learnt this in 1997, that people are sitting in their houses, flats, on their own, petrified because nobody ever wants to go on strike if they can help it. So we thought, right this time we'll get somewhere. Again this was down to Tom, who organised Bedfont. And people could just come along and be with people who were in the same situation as themselves. That was the plan, but I think most people wanted to get out on the picket line, especially the good days, I can't tell you the amount of times we had to turn people away. The highlight of the picket lines, I don't know if you ever saw it, we had an open top double decker bus. I used to organise that and I'm not exaggerating, I used to have over 100 people queuing to get on that.

(Laurent)

Stephen highlighted Bedfont's importance in countering isolation and fear:

> People came down to Bedfont in tears, really nervous and they saw the atmosphere down there. And it's almost like you're frightened, you're sitting at home on your own frightened, worried, scared, thinking that you're the only one that thinks this way. Then there's hundreds of people there that are putting their lives on the line just like you. How reassuring is that? The company used not only the media, they were using the British Airways forum and also the database so they'd be emailing you these threats. So we all had a phone and they'd phone up and you'd talk them around. The amount of people I've said to in the middle of the night, 'Alright, just calm down, just listen.' 'I don't know whether to go on strike.' 'OK, well let me explain my situation, let me explain.' Bedfont was the bedrock of our dispute, it became the focus where people could gravitate to and people could feel a part of the dispute and also feel that they weren't isolated and alone.
>
> (Stephen)

Stephen's views were confirmed by Annie, a purser and BASSA member on Worldwide. She underlines the social nature of strike days and the sense of liberation:

> It was a place where you were surrounded by people who just took real joy in the fact there were so many of us who felt the same way. Not joy in not having to go to work today or being on strike, but just being able to speak so freely. And real pleasure in seeing people who you hadn't seen in years who you'd flown with and you had massive respect for. They did their job really well and finding out they were strikers was great, some really terribly pro-British Airways people who any passenger would look at them and think they were real role models for the rest of us and they were there, it was great. Standing on a picket line with people I really admired, it was great. I remember there was somebody who I hadn't got on well with a couple of years previously and I'd argued with her. She was a CSD and I felt I had a real bone of contention with her and we passed each other in the corridor and sort of you know, obviously the animosity was still there. I saw her at Bedfont and we were really pleased to see each other, it was lovely. It's so weird you know, booing when a British Airways aircraft went over. You know you're being a bit childish, but it was just fun as well. Yes, it was a real mood lifter because if you stayed at home you wouldn't have had that sense of comradeship. People

would come down from the rest of the country as well and their arrivals would be announced and everybody would be cheering the bus from Manchester and so on. Yes, it was great … it was great. I remember one day I did sleep badly, generally I was fine, but one night I'd really slept badly. I was worried about the possibility of losing my job and so on. My husband doesn't work at the moment, I'm not living on some sort of cloud, I know what it's like. And I had a sleepless night but it was a really sunny morning so I just got up really early and went to Bedfont and it made me feel a lot better.

(Annie)

Another Worldwide crew member, Uwe, underlined the particular importance of Bedfont for the successful first day of the strike and reflected on how Bedfont was reminiscent of the parties held in hotel rooms during the stopovers which were part of Worldwide flights:

I think it was being here, Bedfont, everyone. They were fighting for the same reasons, I think that's what kept the support. The first day that we went on strike I was there, there was not a lot of people there because the first day I think is the most important one. If people think that people are going to work, they want to go to work, too. But when the support starts to gather, and people say yes, we are serious about this, that's when the support starts to grow. We called it the biggest room party we've ever had.

(Uwe)

6

Outcomes

Worlds turned upside down

Following 22 days of intermittent strike action, an agreement was reached in May 2011 by negotiators representing British Airways and BASSA/Unite the Union. In the subsequent ballot of members, 92 per cent voted to accept the terms of this agreement on a 72 per cent turnout. This chapter presents responses to this settlement, which reveal both cabin crew members' sense of achievement at what was successfully defended and, at the same time, some disappointment at what had been lost. The chapter then discusses the participants' broader reflections on the dispute, how it had impacted on all aspects of their lives, including their physical and mental health, their political perspectives and their broader views on work and society.

As emphasised in the introduction, prior to the dispute cabin crew had been depicted as a rather conservative and 'unthreatening' face of middle-class Middle England. The conflict certainly challenged these perceptions, not least because of the mobilisation of large numbers of women and gay crew members. This chapter explores the extent to which the strikers talked of themselves in terms of class, gender, race and/or sexuality, and how far these identities, and their values and ideas, were challenged and transformed by their experiences.

As the testimony amply demonstrates, many who were actively engaged in the strike did not consider themselves as 'activists' and were reluctant to be described by others, as 'militant'. Crew rejected this negative media characterisation because they saw their actions as entirely legitimate given the unfairness of British Airways' actions. While to observers they might be seen to have engaged in militant action, crew suggest that the 'militant' stereotype trivialised their cause, undermined the legitimacy of their actions and potentially weakened public support for them. The chapter considers these nuances.

Finally, the chapter provides reflections by the crew on the legacies of the dispute. These include widespread disillusionment with the legal and political system, and with the Labour Party and Labour Government in particular. What emerges most powerfully, though, from this testimony is the conviction that taking strike action was the right thing to do and, allied to this conclusion, a wider belief in the power of collectivism.

The settlement

Working Together – A Joint Settlement was signed by BASSA and British Airways on 11 May 2011, with the restoration of staff travel allowances negotiated separately. The Agreement secured a two-year pay deal worth up to 7.5 per cent, plus independent and binding ACAS hearings for sacked members and ACAS reviews for those disciplined short of dismissal. With many cabin crew emotionally and physically exhausted by the action, the settlement was endorsed by a huge majority at a mass meeting at Bedfont, and the sixth ballot of the dispute, in June 2011, produced a majority of 92 per cent in favour of the settlement on a 72 per cent turnout. The settlement provided assurances on British Airways' commitment to collectively agreed arrangements for Worldwide, Eurofleet and London Gatwick crews, in addition to the provision of union facilities. It also guaranteed that Eurofleet and Worldwide cabin crew would not be unfairly disadvantaged by the allocation of routes to mixed fleet. For Laurent, one of the Eurofleet reps:

If there's a football analogy that can be used I think it became like a 1–1 draw. British Airways didn't win, we didn't win. We didn't have a choice and I think looking back now there were things that we put on the table and they turned round and said 'no'. And that's when we knew, and that's when we thought, this is all about survival in our view. Obviously the company would say something totally different. Looking back on the negotiations I think, putting our hand on our heart, we did the best we could. To me the positives were and still are the fact that the crew have a union. We're a different shape to where we were before the dispute, various personnel have lost their jobs, which was horrendous. We ended up in limbo – there were things that weren't followed up, and there were things that were followed up. So we ended up in a better place than where we were during the dispute. We were able to get in there and talk to managers, we were able, after the dispute, to put our point of view across, but it is a different place to where we were pre-dispute as well. We have to acknowledge that.

(Laurent)

Larissa, a main crew member on Worldwide, in common with the majority of those interviewed, was in favour of the settlement on the grounds that it meant that the union had survived:

> I felt that we should take it. I felt obviously it was probably the best we could achieve. I think it was a question of saving face in that BASSA was protected and because pilots hate BASSA, or dislike the fact that they are still here. Well guess what, BASSA are still here!
>
> (Larissa)

Gemma, a Eurofleet crew member, was quite representative of those crew members who were genuinely conflicted over how to vote, torn between acceptance rooted in loyalty to and trust in the union, and rejection, based on a critical reading of the detail of the proposed settlement. She had supported the settlement at the branch meeting, but then reconsidered and voted against in the ballot. She referred to the clear majority in favour of industrial action in the ballot that preceded the settlement; at the time the action was called off there was a strong mandate for further strike action:

> I went on strike and I would have gone on strike again and again, whatever they said to me. We seemed to be in a position of power so to speak, I don't know whether it was 78 per cent or something back from the ballot. We won that majority for further action and then they went back to negotiations and they came back and we had a meeting in a tent at Bedfont. Everything was called off that day. This agreement came and that's when I really started to question what was going on. In terms of the last ballot we had got a slightly higher majority and I thought this is great; people are still up for it. The way I saw it was we had to fight on, we had no choice. We had to have one almighty battle and that was it, we just had to. We asked, 'What's going to happen to the people from Gatwick?' We had to ask that question because there were only about 34 that went on strike from Gatwick, and I think at this stage they were going to be cut off, cut adrift from the union a wee bit. The 34 people that had gone on strike I thought there should have been some way, I suppose this is naive, that they should have been able to bring them up to Heathrow. Because it must have been unbearable for them, I don't know, what with those 1,200 or 1,400 crew down there, and to be in a minority group like that – I would say it would have been very easy to victimise them. We were told 'Don't worry, we'll talk about that at the end of the meeting.' They said we've got to vote on this agreement or we want to call the strike off

so that we can send this agreement out to everybody to vote on it. I didn't understand why we had to call the threat of the strike off, because you just weaken yourself if you do that. I didn't understand why they couldn't still talk while that threat was running in the background. We had to vote on more or less accepting this agreement, calling the strike off and we didn't know what was in the agreement. We voted on it [i.e. putting the agreement to the members for a ballot vote] and I voted yes, and I wish I hadn't. Some people abstained. I think maybe half a dozen people abstained and I don't think anybody voted no. Because we thought it was pitched in such a way that you have to give us the chance to put it to the membership, which they did. I voted no to the agreement [i.e. when the agreement was then put to the members]. That was a very hard decision to make for me because I felt like I was going against the union, and that was quite difficult for me because if the union said 'Do this, vote yes', I'd do it, but this was so important and something where I made my own decisions.

(Gemma)

Sarah, a CSD from Worldwide, gave an example of the powerful and conflicting emotions that were evoked during the settlement process. The emotional investment that crew had made over the best part of two years was inevitably going to arouse passions given the importance of the outcome for their future working lives:

I was very, very upset about the settlement because I felt we should have stayed out on strike, but I voted 'yes' to save BASSA because if we'd voted 'no' then BASSA would still be out in the cold and they wouldn't be in a position where they could be inside and fight from the inside. They would have always been on the outside. So we knew – so it was tactical.

(Sarah)

The size of the ballot majority for acceptance of the settlement should not deflect attention from the impassioned discussions that preceded the vote. Crew members reported vigorous, even rancorous, argument on the forums and at branch meetings:

And when the dispute was wrapping up there were massive arguments on the BASSA Forum and on Crew Forum about whether or not we should accept the deal. And there was a minority of people, but very vocal, well it all got quite aggressive who said 'No we shouldn't, we should carry on, it's the only way to get what we want', but the majority of people were saying 'No, we've got to at some point give peace a chance.'

(Carrie)

Louise, of the Worldwide crew, was surprised by the fact that such a large majority voted in favour but believed that the physical and mental exhaustion of crew members played no small part in this outcome:

People were run down and they were fed up. They'd been run into the ground and people wanted the dispute over. But I had spoken to quite a lot of people who said that they had voted 'no' and the result showed a very small percentage to reject. I did think it was going to be really close. I think the majority could have been about 87 per cent, something like that, and I really thought it was going to be more 60-40, so I was really surprised. At the same time a lot of people I spoke to were just sick and tired and just wanted it done. And, of course, there were people who were scared in case they get called to go on strike who hadn't been on strike so far because of the way their rosters worked.

(Louise)

Lizanne, chair of the BASSA Branch and involved in the negotiations, indicated the double edged nature of the agreement and the importance of protection for existing staff against the new mixed fleet:

I don't think it was the best we could have done, but I don't see what else we could have done. I think it was really important to get the contractual terms put in which were never in there before for the money, for if they take routes off of us and give them to mixed fleet. Our money is guaranteed for the length of our contracts until the day we leave, because it is a dwindling workforce now.

(Lizanne)

Travel concessions were restored in a separate settlement. Those crew members suspended or sacked during the dispute were, after Employment Tribunals found the procedures that British Airways had used against them illegitimate, reinstated or offered compensatory packages. For Oliver Richardson, the Unite the Union officer responsible for civil aviation:

I thought it was extremely timely, I think it would have been extremely difficult for both sides had that opportunity not been taken. No, I think essentially what we sought at the time, which was protection for existing crew from where the company wanted to go, protection for the existing community, was critical, absolutely critical. And I think that has been proven, protecting those people who had been damaged during the dispute, protecting the existing crew, protecting those who have been subject to unfair treatment by the company and dismissed – we did that. Most importantly, we ensured the survival of the union. I think that has been critical and within the wider movement I think it has been extremely valuable in terms of an employer with a clear agenda trying to break a union and not being able to do it.

(Oliver Richardson)

The aftermath: the 'mixed fleet'

The settlement meant the introduction of new contracts for a new mixed fleet, which have been described as 'remarkable, both for the pay differential, but even more so for the flexibility demanded by the company'.[1] As Duncan commented:

They wanted to turn us into Ryanair. I'll give you a perfect story to illustrate what I mean. A friend of mine has just come back from Vegas, day before yesterday. And Vegas is one of the routes operated by the new crew, I'm talking about the post-2010 crew, they call them 'mixed fleet crew'. During the dispute British Airways created this third fleet, this new mixed fleet, and it's full of 21-year-olds. And my friend has just flown on it and I said, 'What were they like?' And he said 'Well, they were all quite young, they all looked very smart, they'd all got hats and they all looked very presentable', which is what British Airways want. My friend started speaking to them and they said, first of all they're knackered. They go to Vegas, they have 24 hours in Vegas, they come back, they have a night off and go and do it again. They're knackered, but British Airways know that and they know that in two years' time these people are going to leave. Probably a lot of them are graduates or they're trainee doctors and they've come into the job for two years to have a bit of a look around, see Vegas on British Airways' expense, but then they get to 25 and think, 'The jet lag is killing me now, I'm going to leave and do something else.' Their terms and conditions are completely inferior to ours – I couldn't do it.

(Duncan)

After the ballot vote to accept the settlement a vigorous debate took place among members as to whether BASSA themselves should organise the mixed fleet or whether the crew on these new contracts should be recruited into a separate branch of Unite the Union. For some the *raison d'être* of the dispute had been opposition to the introduction of mixed fleet on lower terms and conditions. Lizanne referred to the fact that immediately after the dispute mixed fleet were not unionised:

> We couldn't actually get involved with the mixed fleet because that would have been a contradiction of what we were doing. They are on a horrendous contract that we should have nothing to do with. If we were to get involved in the future, because the company are not recognising any union for mixed fleet, it would be about improving their conditions because they're just horrendous.
>
> (Lizanne)

A number of BASSA members were so raw emotionally that they felt unable to welcome these new crew members on inferior conditions into BASSA so soon after the strike. However, they did recognise that the mixed fleet was now a reality and its crew had to be organised:

> It's very, very sad that all these new people are joining British Airways now and they're earning a pittance and they've got no future. Obviously it's not good for us because their numbers will eventually grow and we will be unemployed one day. I think the timing isn't right for them to be brought into BASSA at the moment. I think it's good that they're joining Unite and they're being parked to one side. But when the timing is right, I think it will be good that we would all be together.
>
> (Sarah)

Oliver Richardson, the Unite officer responsible for the aviation sector, considered the situation from the parent union's point of view and the issues involved:

> At the end of the dispute, or more specifically during the dispute, but at the end, there was a real sense that this was too difficult an issue to deal with at that time and was too raw for members. So therefore, if people asked, you would say *'Yeh, contact Unite, this is the person to contact, and off you go'*. We didn't want to expose BASSA members because, partic- ularly when the dispute was still happening, you didn't want somebody

sacked for trying to speak to a mixed fleet crew member. You wanted to avoid those things happening. And stranger things happened in the dispute. You would think, *'Oh well British Airways can't do that, but then they would'*. We didn't want to put anybody's neck in the noose. Nobody had sat down and asked, *'How are we going to deal with these people or otherwise?'* So, it started on that basis and then there was a debate in terms of if and when and how we organise them and what is going to be the relationship with existing BASSA structures. Once we were in the position to have that debate, then that's what we needed to say. It is not just about whether they were in the branch or not in the branch. It was and is about how you deal with those issues because they may be in the branch and then you have a large branch meeting and there are 5,000 people at the branch who are mixed fleet saying we want your terms and conditions. And there were 4,500 who are old fleet saying we don't want to give them up. So there needed to be quite a considered approach to it.

(Oliver Richardson)

In fact Unite the Union won union recognition for 2,000 mixed fleet in September 2013, after it had recruited over half of the workforce, the proportion needed to secure recognition under the statutory recognition procedure. The agreement covered terms and conditions including pay, holidays and hours of work for all new and future cabin crew at British Airways working on European and worldwide routes with destinations including Los Angeles, Rio de Janeiro, Las Vegas, Tokyo, Hamburg and Manchester and operating out of Heathrow. The recognition deal included an increase in holiday pay entitlement.

The impact of the dispute: personal costs and consequences

As intimated in the comments on the settlement, the company's actions against crew took its toll on individuals. Members reported the fall out which, in extreme cases, involved an appalling human cost. Lizanne recalled:

People were just completely stressed out, tired, worn out. Some of them were thinking 'I just can't be doing with it any more, any of it. I'm just going to come to work.' Some of them are still really angry. Loads of them are getting counselling. Loads of them have been off sick for long periods of time and that's not just the ones who have been suspended and have come back. A lot of the ones who were suspended were really good poster

British Airways crew who had been flying for a long, long, long time and were caught up in this mess and, for making a comment on the aircraft, they were treated like dirt. And that really has, well it's changed them for life, because whereas they'd been really loyal to the company, they can't believe the company treated them in that manner. Nothing was taken into account about loyalty, you were a striker, you were guilty, you were the enemy and all of that. It was outrageous the way people were all treated.

We had one girl who died. I did my Christmas trip with her, [Monica], she was a lovely girl, really good fun. But obviously she was a striker and stressed out, and she went on the British Airways website and was looking for part-time contracts. Accidentally she pressed that she wanted a 50 per cent contract. And when she pressed that button, there was no facility to undo it. So she got herself into a state, she emailed me, I got her in touch with a rep, we asked the company 'Please, it was a mistake, she realised straight away, can you change it? She can't afford a 50 per cent contract.' She's been on strike, she's single, she's got a mortgage, the whole lot. The company said, 'No, once it's pressed, it's pressed.' There was no flexibility whatsoever. She then went with a rep into the Crew Report Centre to meet with her manager, because she really was making herself ill over it. This was after the dispute, and the response was, 'We're not interested in you guys and what you want any more.' She just collapsed in the Crew Report Centre. She didn't die until she got to hospital but she never came out of hospital, she was 41. I blame them. I definitely blame them. They are totally inflexible; 'We're not interested in what any of you people want, we need to get the numbers down.' That's what this is all about, cutting costs, getting rid of the legacy crew. You pressed the 50 per cent contracts, so that helps'. So there has been lots of casualties, there's been marriage break-ups, there's been friendship break-ups. It's caused untold damage and even now, the crew won't socialise with the pilots.

(Lizanne)

One recurring theme in the interviews was the longer-term damage to crews' health. Several reported how in the months following the settlement they had experienced illness as a delayed reaction. Alex, a Worldwide crew member, described how he had been off sick for six months because 'the stress had actually got to me in the end'. Crew also talked at length of how the dispute had placed pressures on their partners and families. Kat, a main crew member on Eurofleet, recalled:

You went from euphoria to fear. The euphoria was always your Bedfont days, the fear was putting that uniform on and worrying, 'Have I been spotted in a paper, have I been spotted in uniform?' I made page three of the paper, I've always wanted to – unfortunately it was *The Financial Times*! You jumped, it was energising. It would be very interesting for you to interview the families of the people who went through this, who didn't have wives and husbands for nearly two years because they were entranced by a union website, petrified of leaving it. It became almost obsessional for everybody. There were an awful lot of divorces because these sort of things were happening where partners would be saying 'Can you get off it and make a cup of tea now, can you get off it and sort the kids out?' From the minute you woke up in the morning to going to bed at night, it was obsessional. My husband was very, very supportive, but it did put a strain on us. He was a financial adviser who lost his business because of the recession. But thank God, he's also a truck driver so he's been doing some work as well. But it's a busy household and Mum was needed, but Mum was involved in a bitter dispute with her employer that took over everything unfortunately. He wasn't really a trade unionist until this dispute, he was very middle of the road, but he is very unionised now.

(Kat)

Laurent also talked about the consequences of the dispute for his well-being, the pressures placed upon himself and his family and the importance of a supportive partner:

Physically it's aged me 20 years inside, maybe not outside. It's just worn me and I feel permanently tired, drained, worn out, paranoid, totally paranoid about what you can and you can't say at work. It's made me feel let down or saddened because of the way British Airways was, the way it had been a great, brilliant company and you felt proud to work for them. And god willing, we may get back to that stage in the future, but it's going to take years, and probably not in my lifetime, to get over it all. So home life just went out of the window because I've got two youngish kids, eight and eleven. You have to somehow switch off at some point to look after them. I've never known anything like this – 1997 we thought was tough, but this was just a killer. And we're still here. My partner she's brilliant, she used to be crew; she left ten years ago. But I'll be honest with you, without her I personally couldn't have got through this. I went home every day, dinner's there, not a problem. In the run up to it, we were up in London week after week, night after night. I never heard her complain once, ever, and she does like to complain so there you go! It cost me a fortune in the clothes I had to buy her! My dad was great, he was on the picket line. He loved it.

(Laurent)

Not all partners were as supportive as Laurent's. Savi, a purser on Worldwide, highlighted the damage the dispute inflicted on the relationship with her partner, and how work and home identities became intertwined:

> My husband was completely against it, just did not want me to be part of this at all. I said, 'No, you can't tell me what to do, this is me and my dispute', but he said 'We're going to be affected by it, we've got a mortgage, we've got children, but yes, fair enough, we'll see what happens.' It did affect my relationship and still does even now. He was dropping me off today for the interview and he didn't want me to talk. I said 'Why shouldn't I talk?' It's probably about fear more than anything else, and he didn't want me to get involved. I said 'How can I go to work and not get involved with something which is so central to my life? How can I just disengage myself from something like this?' I couldn't. I'm not one person here and one person there, it's the same person. Oh, it put a huge strain on my marriage, it really did. My children know what I'm like, they know I'm very passionate about things I get involved with. They actually respect the fact that I stood up for what I believed in. I said, 'Look, I'm doing it as much for you as well so you know that whatever you believe in you have to put your foot down and you have to stand up and be counted. You can't just say things and then not do anything, it's wrong. You've got to go all the way. There's no point going halfway and then not doing anything about it.' So I think my children have grown up with that background, they're older now, 26 and 19. But they've grown up with that now and I think it's stuck with them how ill I was with it, but how I continued and they have said, 'We really respect your views, although we don't agree, but we respect your views and we like the fact that you've taught us morals and principles.' I said 'Yeah, so you should!'

(Savi)

Melanie from Worldwide spoke for many when she described the emotional fall-out arising from the conflict between her commitment to the strike on the one hand and to her family on the other hand:

I'd like to turn the clock back and spend a bit more time with my dad. I spent a lot of time with the dispute and I was scared of asking for dependency days when we weren't in dispute, because at the time the company were being really nasty and so I couldn't spend as much time with him as I wanted to. I didn't want to lose my job. They were getting very tight. One time I phoned them up asking for a dependency day just before the strike and they just laughed at me. My husband then said, 'You can't take that dependency day if you're going to go out on strike the next day, you do one or you do the other, you can't muck the company around like that, you're with it or you're not.' That was hard. That was hard because I felt that it was my employment right to have the dependency days and fit my roster around it, but we were just so scared of doing anything wrong. It was very, very stressful. I did spend an awful lot of time going to meetings or AGM's and I did spend an awful lot of time on the forums, I still do. That had an impact. A few times I had panic attacks and it was very, very emotionally draining. I went to see a counsellor because of my dad and a lot of stuff came up then about the dispute. It was sort of part and parcel with that. The relationship with my mum is not great either, so I went to the counsellor for that, but a lot of the stuff about the dispute came out. The counsellor was really, really supportive, not supportive as in for the strike – obviously she didn't give me any views about that at all – but I was able to talk to her quite openly about it.
(Melanie)

Larissa, also from Worldwide, reflected on the price paid by trade union comrades and the abuse cabin crew received from an antagonistic media. When interviewed in 2012, she used the fuel tanker drivers, who had been involved in a recent industrial dispute, as a point of reference. In her view, the tanker drivers had not encountered the levels of hostility that she and her colleagues had experienced:

It was just so all-consuming and stressful. It was like a destruction of what you believed in, in a way. Because we were very publicly vilified and it was very personal I felt – nobody is saying that fuel truck drivers are the scum of the earth. And yet the impact of what their strike could have been was massive, but it's almost as if they're allowed to do it, which quite right. They should be able to do if that's what they believe in. The way that we were portrayed in the press was terrible. Even people who knew me didn't get what we were about. And you just were tired of trying to explain the story.

I do wonder what the wider impacts of the industrial action and the dispute were on the crew workforce, and not just in terms of the massive stress. It's not just my own case. A good friend of mine had a breakdown, we've had a suicide and we've had more deaths among crew than I've ever known. And you can't categorically say that it was directly caused by the dispute, but there is no question that that level of stress has had a huge impact on people. And I wish that there could be some kind of research to look at the statistics that could prove that the pressure people were put under was the cause of people becoming ill. The main thing that has changed, obviously, since the dispute, is how we are valued as a workforce. That was just destroyed and that has a big impact I think. And that will take a long time to rebuild, all the loyalty.

(Larissa)

BASSA reps, along with those who were suspended or sacked during the dispute, made particular sacrifices. Tom, a CSD on Worldwide, had been a rep for ten years:

Thirty-two years of being with a company I loved. I loved flying. I thought I did a good job and then, suddenly the company accused me of doing something which I didn't do, and then sacked me under some jumped up charge. I was completely and utterly devastated. I'd given 32 years to the company. I've worked Christmases, missed birthdays, missed anniversaries, missed parties. My mum died when I was away on a trip in Abu Dhabi and my dad didn't call British Airways because he didn't want to disrupt my work because he knew I was so committed.

And during the negotiations and during the actual strike, I was working 24/7 because not only was I turning up every day, I don't think there wasn't one day during the industrial problem, that I didn't turn up. I turned up every day, first thing in the morning I was there, last thing at night I was there. And of course, come the evening, you've then got to deal with all the organisation for the next day. So during that period I was an absent father, but I was giving everything to the union.

(Tom)

Stephen, a BASSA Committee member and CSD on Worldwide, conveyed the consequences of the company's hostility for individual BASSA members:

The dispute is one of the biggest things that's ever happened in my life, apart from my kids being born and getting married. It was one of the biggest life lessons I have learnt about how ruthless people could be and how dishonest people could be and that people would go to any ends to achieve their goal. And we were just being treated as a commodity, we're not valued as people. My nephew was sacked through the dispute, he's got two little boys. He posted on the Crew Forum. They got Asset Protection to seek him out, to identify him through his postings, checking his roster, breaching data protection and they caught him when he announced on the Crew Forum that his son was born.

(Stephen)

Louise was married to BASSA's branch secretary, Duncan, who was summarily sacked during the strike. She was put under enormous pressure at home and at work:

Well it was pretty nasty for me and for my family, because of what happened to Duncan. It was very hard for me because I'd have to go into work and do my job and pretend that nothing was happening really. Emotionally it was really hard. I remember we were told by the company we mustn't talk to any passengers and the dispute was not to be discussed. So it was quite a lot of added pressure on me because I'd get people asking me about Duncan. It was hard, probably much more than either of us would like to admit really. I think the emotional pressure was damaging, it was never ending. When I was at home it didn't stop, the phone never stopped ringing, people would come to the door, journalists and all that kind of stuff. The kids were affected too. My two were both at secondary school then and we even had some kids say to them, 'Your parents are very selfish, we can't go on our ski holiday', which was a reference to the proposed twelve days of Christmas, which was horrific. Then, on the other hand, I had a group of teachers sending me emails wishing me good luck and stuff like that. There was good and bad, but I think our family life was put on hold massively. I think the kids must have got so fed up with the phone constantly ringing and us going 'Shush shush, Dad's on the phone', all that business. And then I'd get upset; oh we rowed, oh so much, we had so many rows about it. We were on the same side but you know what I mean? It was intense, it was totally exhausting, totally exhausting. I admit, I got to a stage, I think maybe after the strike, I remember thinking I can't do this anymore, I don't even want to talk about it anymore, I'm sick to death of you asking me questions about it. I really kind of shut down from it for a while because it was so intense, especially in our family, it was so encompassing. Every day there was something happening to do with the dispute and it kept on happening even afterwards, obviously because we had the tribunal and all of that kind of stuff as well.

(Louise)

Sally, a BASSA rep, revealed the damaging effects that dedication to the union had on her personal relationship:

It has affected my life catastrophically. My marriage was on the rocks anyway. My husband actually tried, which is a joke because he's so Tory, he tried to make one last bid to save things by driving a picket van, but that wasn't enough. And then he was so horrible to me, was so abusive about my involvement and that was the final straw. I can't possibly tell you that my marriage demised over the battle with the company, although it certainly didn't help. It had been difficult for a very long time. He didn't agree with it at first, then I think he saw a different side when he drove the vans. I think he was completely blown away by the camaraderie and by the dedication. And then although he would never admit it, I think he came round to some understanding. He's known me for so many decades and he's always known the way I am. But he said to me that ever since I got involved with BASSA that I became completely mental and that I'm addicted. He didn't like it at all. So that was the straw that broke the camel's back I suppose. I found the dispute completely exhausting because as I say, I went every single day, I didn't have a day off, 12 hours a day. It had huge highs, huge lows, and it is very upsetting when you see people suffer.

(Sally)

Sarah also reflected on how the dispute became inextricably linked with her personal life and suggested that the union could have provided counselling for those who had been badly affected:

Personally, I was having a very traumatic time anyway which I wasn't able to devote my whole attention to because I got distracted by the dispute. And it's something I've never got over. My personal issues were inter-twined with the industrial dispute and it was really, really difficult to not keep an eye on what was going on with the dispute. But it did absorb a hell of a lot of my time. My ex worked for the same company, we did the same job. But I think if we hadn't had so many external pressures then we might have been able to sort our own personal issues. It was just unfortunate that the timing wasn't good. I'm seeking counselling now because of the dispute. The effect was magnified because there was nobody to go and talk to about it. Everything just seems to have been covered up, you can't express what you really want to say. I'm a bit disappointed with Unite with that to be honest because I think even though they were able to help with the strike fund and BASSA set up a hardship fund for the people who were sacked and suspended, for all the people involved in the dispute who might have been traumatised by it, I think they should have provided something. There are a lot of people who are still affected by it. You couldn't go to the company to talk to anyone. So you were on your own really and while there were people who would try to talk about things on the forums, they couldn't really talk openly because they knew they were being spied on. So, it was like you didn't have anywhere to go, especially if you didn't have family. It was like a whirlwind really. Every time you picked up and thought you could get to grips and assess what had happened at that point, something else would be thrown at you.

(Sarah)

The impact of the dispute: commitment to and pride in collective action

Despite all the hardships, the psychological damage to individuals, the sickness and ill-health and the corrosion of relationships and family life caused by involvement in this all-consuming conflict, the crew interviewed, to a person, had no regrets regarding their participation:

It defined who I am, definitely. I am very proud that I did what I did. I wish it hadn't been so shitty and nasty, but then that's life as well I suppose. The knowledge that I've now got as well is nice. I can have a chat with you about it, do you know what I mean? We'd never have met, we'd never have had a conversation. I've never really been a clever person and it brought that out a little bit in me. It was like wow I can do this, I can make a difference. It's only me but I am an important thing and it's quite hard to let that go.

(Melanie)

Many posed the rhetorical question as to whether they would do the same all over again and they answered in the affirmative, expressing a sense of pride in the stand they had taken and restating their belief in the importance of collective action:

British Airways just didn't relent, there was no breathing space to get yourself back on your feet and think, 'Oh that's a bit of a shock, we'll get over that, and we'll sort that out.' Just as you're able to comprehend the awful news that they had told you, they would throw something else at you. It was like they were just beating you down all the time really. Did we do the right thing? Yes, I'd do it all again.

(Sarah)

The strike was something I could have done without! But I wouldn't have changed anything for the world, I'd do it all again. I feel very proud of what we did as a community, I feel proud of what we did as a family and my family were great, Duncan's family were great, everybody was very supportive. So I'm proud of it, I would never be embarrassed about it, I'd always openly talk about it. I'd certainly do it again, I'd definitely do it again. I think a lot of people have got great strength from it and didn't realise quite how much, how strong they were, what strong people they were. I think it's certainly made me stronger, definitely.

(Elizabeth)

Rhys, a rep and a CSD on Eurofleet, was another who was adamant that the action he and his colleagues had taken was legitimate and that he would do the same again without hesitation:

I suppose that apart from lack of sleep, stress, loss of money, and the uncertainty of it all, in a really weird sick way I would choose to do it all over again. I would say actually it made me stronger. I think as things happened, it made me more determined to fight for what I believe is right and wrong and what was happening was completely unfair. I think all of us had the moment where we just thought 'Do you know what, I just want to give up, roll over', but I think that's when we relied on each other to give us a lift. We would say to each other, 'Don't be so stupid, come on, we've got to fight this.'

(Rhys)

Nathan, a rep and purser on World-wide, also described his action as 'right', the word most often chosen by crew members to convey their moral certainty, in contrast to the perceived 'wrong' of British Airways' actions:

You've got to make a stand between what's right and what's wrong. I imagine it must be hard if you have a difference of opinion with your partner, because people's families were split as a result of this. But even so you have to – this is the first time in your life when you've had to make a major decision. And you look at yourself in the mirror and you can say *'Yes, I did right'*; I can stand on my own and feel happy with what I did. I haven't met a person yet who went on strike and has regretted it. But I've met many people who haven't been on strike who apologise profusely for what they've done.

(Nathan)

Impact of the dispute: politics and political views

When political implications of the dispute were considered, crew members, firstly, conveyed disenchantment with the Labour Party, both as the party of government and a party from whom cabin crew had expectations of support. Second, there was a wider disillusionment with the political and legal institutions of civil society and with the media. At the same time, a number of cabin crew questioned whether BASSA's action should itself be regarded as political and, linked to this, challenged definitions of both militancy and class identity.

Many crew participants were explicit in their disappointment with the Labour Party, the party of government in the early stages of the dispute until the election of May 2010, which brought the Conservative–Liberal Democrat coalition to power:

I mean, I felt let down by the Labour government, considering they're supposedly, well, not on our side, but are more union-friendly – it was a total waste of time. The media, the whole thing, you learn looking back that the media of this country was just totally against us. But yes, I think most of us felt let down with the Labour government, they could have changed some of the laws, anti-union laws and never did.

(Laurent)

Rhys was particularly angry with the stance taken by the Labour government:

I think I lost respect in all political parties. Labour I was fuming with, because I think they came out and were like 'You shouldn't be doing this.' The Conservatives I didn't expect to support anybody. That to me was, it was just a massive kick in the teeth; everything that I always believed about fair democracy, the fact that you can strike in this country, yet we have the most unprotected laws regarding it. I remember writing to my

MP who is Labour, saying that I was just completely demoralised. So for me it was, I think it was betrayal; I didn't think the government would step in and bail us out or do something like come and join us, but I didn't think Gordon Brown would actively stand there and say, 'You are wrong, you shouldn't be doing this.'

(Rhys)

For others, the sense of disillusionment extended more widely to the institutions of society and to government in its totality. Ian, a long-standing rep, contrasted this disenchantment with his advocacy of collective organisation:

Well, for me personally I would never now trust the judicial system again and I've really got no faith in any governments any more when it comes to any work-related issue. You fight for what you can get on your own ground, you stand your own ground because they're not going to do anything for you. What we've learnt from it is that you want to promote the trade union now and get anyone to come into it, to join up, because it's only by the power of the group effort you will get anywhere. And if you're isolated you will just get trampled on, you have no chance. It's as simple as that and that's what I think Walsh underestimated and I hope it keeps him awake at night that we're still here. We just wouldn't go away and I think that was what built up with us, every day when we came here, we wouldn't go away.

(Ian)

One notable aspect of the dispute was the involvement of European cabin crew, with different histories, understandings of workers' rights and political instincts. Richard, a CSD on Worldwide and a BASSA rep, commented:

I was really surprised by the amount of young European people that I was driving around in the minibuses. Firstly, because I thought that a lot of them, as a direct result of losing their staff travel, would probably not have taken part in the dispute. But they were very vocal and I can only suppose it's because in the countries they come from if your union calls you to strike, you strike. And it's ingrained in them. But I took my hat off to all of them, and especially to the ones who were relying on commuting to go to work, knowing that by going on strike they were going to lose that privilege, which we said we would get back for them eventually, but we certainly had no guarantee that that would ever come back.

(Richard)

Similarly, for Adam, a long-standing BASSA rep:

> The Europeans, not all of them, but the Spanish and the Portuguese and the Italians and the French, oh they stood tall in the dispute, they stood so tall, because in one sense they gave the most.
>
> (Adam)

It is not the intention here to discuss in detail the concept of worker consciousness as analysed in industrial relations literature. However, a brief summary helps to frame the reflections of cabin crew. One main distinction in this literature is that between trade union and class consciousness. The former refers to workers whose ideas or world views are bounded largely by the limits of trade unionism and its objectives, and who seek to defend or improve their terms and conditions within the boundaries of existing (capitalist) social relations. In contrast, class consciousness refers to workers who, while being committed to trade unions, have a political frame of reference that aspires to a socialist transformation of society. This essentialist division does not take account of other differences, such as the strength of commitment to trade unionism, the form of trade unionism to which workers might be committed (e.g. moderate, militant, sectional, occupational) or the version of socialist politics which individuals may embrace.[2] Rigid conceptualisations similarly do not take account of the fact that those taking strike action may not have considered that a legitimate defence of their terms and conditions equated to 'militancy'.

BASSA members were aware that popular characterisation of cabin crew clashed with the historical stereotype of trade unionists. Stephen acknowledged this incongruence. For him, cabin crew were driven by a profound sense of fairness rather than by militancy:

> There were quotes about, 'We're getting back to the 70s' and 'cloth caps and whippets', 'All out, brothers, and down the working man's club'. And we were not like that anymore, the human race has evolved and these cabin crew were people who are gentle people. They're not militants, we're not militant, no, we are not militant. We're not militant, we're not radical, we're pragmatic and we're people that want fairness and recognition for what we do. And that is not being a militant.
>
> (Stephen)

Laurent concurred with this reluctance to define cabin crew and their actions as militant. In so doing, arguably, he was rejecting a caricature of who might be a militant or what constituted militancy in terms of social identity (particularly gender). He chose the adjective 'solid' as descriptor of crew's resilience and resolve:

> I wouldn't say militant, I think it was my colleague who said that if you've got the majority as either middle-aged women or guys who are homosexual then it's the most opposite of militant you would ever find. I don't want to use the word, but I think it's quite laughable. OK, if they were all like me, short haircut and big bloke, you could understand. But the people we represent, it couldn't be further from the truth. People were solid. They were very solid, I think most people just thought, 'Well, I've got nothing to lose' and I think that's how it panned out.
>
> (Laurent)

Julianne, a Eurofleet member, also baulked at the idea that they might be thought of as 'militants'. The meaning she brought to the term was different to that of Laurent. Militancy implied an ill-conceived rush into taking strike action regardless of the consequences, which was quite contrary to the approach that BASSA had adopted. Recalling a discussion prior to the first ballot, she made clear the inappropriateness of the term militant as used by one of her managers, particularly when BASSA had offered additional concessions in order to bridge the financial gap between the company demands and the union's previous position. The following passage additionally highlighted the dissimilarities she perceived between the dispute she was involved in and the miners' strike. However, interestingly, in pondering the meaning of the word militant, Julianne ended up suggesting that the descriptor might be used approvingly in relation to BASSA's action:

> What was quite interesting for me was speaking to a manager before we balloted for strike. I said to him, 'You've got to realise that none of us want to go on strike.' He said, 'Well why don't you tell your reps that?' This was just at the time that BASSA had gone back to British Airways to try and find some more money. And he then said, 'We are not going to accept anything that BASSA puts on the table', so I replied, 'Well if I was on the fence and I didn't know who was telling the truth here, you've just confirmed to me that BASSA are telling me the truth about you.' He then said, 'We are going to sack the first 500 militants' and I said 'How dare you call us militants, but I will be on that picket line.' So that made me absolutely furious. So when Duncan came on the BASSA website and

said 'I'm sorry, we have tried all we can', people went on there saying 'Well we know you have'.

I would say that in some ways we are upper working class, a lot of crew are involved with people who are in the city. The husbands were absolutely appalled about British Airways, but we couldn't really get that message out there, that was the sad thing. I think that British Airways tried very much to try and make it look like we were the miners. Bill Francis said our dispute reminded him of the miners' strike. Well how could it? We were laughing and joking with the police, they put on music for us to dance to. So we were not like that. I don't know what militancy is, I think it is standing up for what you believe is right.

(Julianne)

It is clear from these testimonies that the crew members' understanding of militancy[3] is multi-faceted and complex, ranging from crew's outright rejection of the term to a certain acceptance of it, while ironically recognising that the term was thrust upon them rather than being a matter of their free choice. Sana, a Eurofleet rep, objected to the stereotyping and considered how the crew were defined as militants for standing up to injustice:

Well, we were all turned into militants weren't we? And I usually laugh but I think – I don't even think I'm militant now. People say to me you have to be stroppy and angry to be a rep, no you don't, you just have to believe in justice. But then they made that look – I remember there was one article and it was all about, she's a mother and she's 'this'. But it made that into something bad as well, even though they tried to profile us as real people, they still made us like middle class and live in Surrey or whatever. I was like 'OK, fine. Well, fair enough, you have to see yourself the way you want to.'

(Sana)

Catherine, a BASSA rep of eight years' standing, was more forthright in her rejection of the term's applicability:

The cabin crew is a very diverse community. I wouldn't class us as predominantly militant at all. To my mind this goes against the grain of why you are recruited by British Airways which is because you want to please people. You don't want to disappoint people, you want to offer a good customer service. Yet, we were forever having to apologise for the planes, the poor quality, the lack of food, people were getting frustrated, they couldn't actually deliver what they wanted to deliver as well. Although obviously, as the *Daily Mail* seemed to portray it, the majority of people didn't like us for taking action, there was a lot of support out there as well.

(Catherine)

Along with the uncertainty about militancy was a questioning of the term 'activism'. As with the testimonies of Kevin in Chapter 3 and Melanie in Chapter 4, Louise was unsure of whether she could call herself as an activist:

I can't bear injustice so maybe I am an activist, but not really, no I don't think so. I just felt that I was trying to protect my job and protect other people. I'm sure other crew have said this to you as well, I did talk to passengers, obviously I can't keep my mouth shut, I ended up being in floods of tears with passengers and they likewise, and I sat talking to first class passengers regularly and they were absolutely shocked and horrified this was going on, because obviously they didn't know. So I suppose in that respect yes I was an activist because I wanted people to know, I wasn't going to keep my mouth shut, I wanted the passengers to know, not that it did any good to be honest really because British Airways put profit before people and that includes passengers. There are some good managers left who care, but the good ones don't last long.

(Louise)

In an older debate it was argued that, since trade unions are class-British based organisations, trade unionists will have a class identity, but that this is not the same as a politicised class consciousness. Workers might actively defend their livelihoods and working conditions, but such activity will not necessarily involve challenging the class basis of capitalist society.[4] Interestingly, at the beginning of the dispute and before strike action there was debate among cabin crew as to their class position and identity. In an online poll on the Crew Forum over half of participants (58 per cent) said that they were working class and just over one quarter (27 per cent) middle class. A discussion followed as to whether class should be defined by occupation or by background or lifestyle as, for example, where you shop. Elizabeth, from Worldwide, was one of the majority who considered themselves to be working class. It is interesting that her reflections on her class position were juxtaposed to her perception of the common experience and underlying collectivism of the cabin crew.

22–24.   Grounded aircraft at Heathrow on the first day of strike action, 20 March 2010. BA proclaimed that the numbers of cabin crew reporting for work were 'above the levels' needed 'to operate our published schedule'.

25–28.   BASSA members in action on 20 March 2010. Clockwise from top left: picket at Nene roundabout; inside Bedfont; Hatton Cross roundabout; outside Bedfont FC.

29–33.   Large numbers of BASSA members participated enthusiastically in picketing. Organised into rotas, they observed the appropriate guidelines. Top left and right: Pickets at Hatton Cross. Middle left: At Nene roundabout with Len McCluskey. Middle right: Pickets at Waterside. Bottom: Picket shift change over.

34–39. At and around Bedfont during the first days of the strike. Top left: a 'flying picket'. Top right: Willie Walsh in a urinal at Bedfont. Middle left centre: Tea and solidarity. Middle right: Steve Turner, Len McCluskey and Tony Woodley. Bottom: Greeting returning pickets at Bedfont.

40–42.   Top left: 22 March 2010. Media coverage was considerable at the beginning of the strike.

Top right: 9 June 2010. A single French camera crew was the sole media presence on the last day of strike action.

Middle: 12 May 2011. The media returned in force to report Len McCluskey's announcement of BASSA members' decision to put the final settlement to ballot.

43.   There was general agreement among the strikers that much of the media coverage was hostile.

44.   With a departing glance across the hedge towards their comrades at Bedfont, strikers prepare to tour the picket lines from the top of the BASSA bus.

45.   John McDonnell, Labour MP for Hayes and Hillington, a frequent visitor to the picket lines, offering hugely valued solidarity.

46. The touring bus was a potent symbol of the strikers' humour, vitality and determination.

47. Plane spotters noted the accumulation of grounded of BA aircraft.

48.   BASSA members travelled from Bedfont to TUC Congress House in Central London to lobby negotiations on 30 March 2010.

49–50.   Making some noise at Congress House in central London.

51–54.   On strike, 3 June 2010. Top left: Hatton Cross picket. Top right: Mark Steel, comedian and columnist, addresses strikers at Bedfont. Middle right: Nicky Marcus protesting at Bedfont. Bottom: Scottish strikers travelled down from Glasgow to ride the bus at Bedfont.

55. Billy Bragg brings solidarity to strikers at Bedfont.

56. A picnic at Bedfont.

57-58. Bedfont resembled a festival.

59–60. A group of BASSA members travelled to Parliament on 8 June 2010 to meet with MPs in a committee room. At the photo call on the green, attention was drawn to management's silencing of crew on their return to work on non-strike days.

61–62.   BASSA members with XXXX on their shirts march down the A4 to BA's headquarters at Waterside on the last day of strike action on 9 June 2010.

63–64.   Open top buses with strikers' flags flying and whistles blowing extended the picket line to the roads surrounding Heathrow.

65. BASSA members rally at Bedfont, 9 June 2010, the last day of strike action.

66–67. Members vote to put the settlement to a ballot, 12 May 2011.

68.   12 May 2011. Eighteen months after the announcement of the first ballot, the bonds of solidarity were stronger than ever before.

69. Touring Heathrow on the last strike day.

I think people just thought hang on this is not right. Even though we are very much a remote workforce we don't necessarily know each other and I've made some fantastic friends because of this – so I will say thank you very much British Airways. Again, because you have got that underlying, common denominator, you are all cabin crew, you've all experienced the job. I work for a living therefore I am working class. People fall into this idea that they have become middle class but they haven't. Working class: now, if you hear that term used in the press it's usually to do with council estates, why? You can be working class, but they try and put it negatively. And that's what impacts, so yes I am working class through and through even though my job title suggests I might not be.

(Elizabeth)

Richard agreed with the stereotype of cabin crew as middle-class, Middle England and Conservative voting, and, like others, reiterated the belief that it was a sense of fairness that motivated and mobilised the workforce to resist, rather than class identity:

I think the cabin crew, if anything, tend to be middle-class, Middle Englandy sort of people with a sense of fairness about us and I think it was this sense of unfairness from our employer that really struck a chord with a lot of people that you would not normally associate with any militant actions. It was just this complete way that British Airways were trying to do it – the Willie Walsh way or no way – that turned people that had probably always voted Conservative their entire lives to vote to go out on strike. Oh yes, a lot of our members will be staunch Conservative and they might be married to pilots and bankers and this, that and the other. But it was the complete sense of unfairness and unjustness that led people to taking the action that they did.

(Richard)

Lane and Roberts's study, discussed in Chapter 1, of the unofficial strike at Pilkingtons in 1971 found that very few strikers were political activists or saw their strike in terms that could be described as political, believing that work and politics were separate. For Sally, while the dispute was an event of huge importance to her and her colleagues, it did not mean that BASSA's actions were necessarily political:

I have to say, as I said to you when we spoke about activities that I've been involved in, that I don't find this movement particularly political. And

I don't think it is political particularly, I think it's a case of BASSA has fought for what it believes in, but it isn't a particularly political movement.

(Sally)

Others, including Kate, agreed that the dispute was not political. For her the action was centred on pay and conditions and the loss of them, but she was ferocious in her defence of the justness of BASSA's cause, being prepared to oppose her friends and dismiss their appeals to accept British Airways' position. So, while she did not see her involvement as political, she was unrepentant in her commitment to strike action and located it in a history of struggle for worker's rights:

The dispute was not political, it was about getting paid the right wage for doing your job. At the end of the day all our forefathers fought for unions and bloody toilets, didn't they, they had secret meetings. People went to jail for being in a union and you just think here we are now, supposedly the middle-class mothers, why wouldn't we want a decent salary? I don't think the general public actually put two and two together – that Middle England people, say like me, with two children, married, would be in a union and would act upon being in a union. I've got friends who were just horrified, completely, absolutely horrified. 'How can you go on strike? Everybody's got to tow the line, to tow any line.' They are managers, it was the ones that were actual managers, who were saying, 'You need to tow the line, oh you should take a pay cut then!' I would come back at them, 'Would you take your expenses being cut? Would you take your hours being higher for less money?' They would say, 'Well no', so I would reply, 'Well why would I?' People were saying, 'You've always been overpaid at British Airways' and I would say back at them, 'Do you know exactly what we do then?' Most people don't know what we do. When you say to people, 'Do you know that I missed my children's birthdays, I miss Christmas, I'm not here at New Year, not here on a British Airways holiday. I've missed all that sometimes. And even when you put in to get leave, you don't get it.' People don't understand, they go, 'Yeah, you took that on board when you took the job.' Well yeah, I did take that on board with the job, but I also took the pay that went with it to compensate for those things. If I had to go out on strike tomorrow, for the same reasons, I'd do it again all over again, I would do it.

(Kate)

Duncan reported that the stance adopted by the leadership was to avoid political questions, focusing instead on what might be termed industrial issues, that is, those defined as being of concern to members. This leadership position certainly influenced the ways in which crew spoke of BASSA and their involvement. Nevertheless, this avoidance became increasingly unsustainable as battle lines hardened and some crew drew political conclusions. The actions of the employer, the judgements taken by the courts and the opposition of the Labour Party, much more than the position adopted by BASSA, contributed to making the dispute political. Duncan summarised: 'We tried not to mix politics into the dispute because the crews weren't political, you couldn't afford it, but it was political in the end.'

A careful reading of the interviews suggests that the overall distinction between trade union and political consciousness has some validity. The view and beliefs of a sizable majority of the crew did correspond broadly to a trade union consciousness since their aspirations were expressed almost exclusively in terms of their occupational community and their union, BASSA. However, a minority did see their dispute in wider political terms, as part of a more general class struggle with many of the political implications associated with that worldview and, as discussed below, the ideas of crew did change in the course of their struggle. It is important to emphasise that consciousness is not fixed or unchanging. As many crew revealed, their ideas shifted under the impact of British Airways' punitive actions, media and political hostility, the deepening sense of the fairness of their cause, BASSA's resilience and crucially, the solidarity of their colleagues. This theme of change and transformation is developed in the next section.

Impact of the dispute: transformed individuals and identities

To the extent that the voices of workers involved in strikes or disputes have been documented, participants have frequently described how engaging in struggle changed their ideas. Melanie was far from alone when she said the dispute 'defined' her. Such self-reflection brings to mind some philosophical observations first made by the early Marx,[5] that in the process of acting on the world to change it, people change themselves.

Louise, in contrast to many, was self-consciously political, a lapsed member of the Labour Party and someone who thought of themselves as a fighter for the 'underdog'. She felt that although her colleagues understood the politics of the workplace they did not necessarily see things in explicitly political terms, or 'more globally', as she put it. However, she reported how in the course of the dispute many crew members' values and views did change, an observation that was affirmed by others. For Louise, this shift in ideas opened up new horizons and friendships:

> My politics are definitely left of centre, left of left at the minute. I was a member of the Labour Party, but in recent years I've definitely fallen out with them and I don't really know who I would support now. I'm one of these people that I don't know who on earth to support. I've always been the sort of person who fights for the underdog. Everything that you believed in in your life had suddenly been turned upside down. I think ideas did change. I think suddenly people started to pay an interest in what the newspapers were saying, whereas a lot of crew weren't previously that interested in newspapers unless it was about a celebrity or something. Of course that is a total generalisation and there are an awful lot of crew members who are graduates who have got that sense, but it was unusual for politics to be discussed. It has now become the norm, it's really interesting. And, only because of the strike I've become friendly with a lot of crew who are as political as myself and our friendship is based on that really, not because we're cabin crew, because we've suddenly found a link outside of flying which is lovely. I think a lot of them became politicised during the dispute, definitely.
>
> (Louise)

Such ideas are illustrated in the testimonies of many crew, including BASSA rep Sally, who focused on the significance of self-education:

> As the dispute went on, it was staggeringly obvious how much people were educating themselves and that was great actually. Well they were reading everything, they were on Sky News, people that obviously had lost staff travel and were setting up home on people's sofas. They were coming back the next day, telling you that all the lap tops were on, the telly was on, everyone was watching and reading everything. Everyone was talking to each other. They were so into it, they knew everything that was going on and it became so vital to everybody that they were extremely educated about it. But the underlying hatred then became very strong; we were so isolated, we weren't allowed to talk, we weren't allowed to put our point across and we were vilified by the public.
>
> (Sally)

For a number of those interviewed, the changes in the ways that the strikers thought of themselves were mirrored by changes in how they were perceived from the outside, as the stereotypical caricature of cabin crew was challenged and confounded. For Sally, 'now people think differently of us and I am glad, yes'. Similarly, for Uwe, a BASSA rep on Worldwide, the shock of being involved in such a dramatic and unprecedented event as the strike brought to the surface aspects of his personality and self of which he had previously been unaware:

> How has the dispute changed me? It has made me fight more for what I believe is right, because that's what we did for two years, and we got it, we won. Nobody can come and say we lost it because, we didn't. Of course, you're not going to get everything you want, but we've got the assurance of the main things we wanted. Willie Walsh wanted to destroy the union, we are still here. For me this dispute means a lot, it's the first time ever when I was in something like this – on strike. And I did discover something of myself that I really didn't know I had in me when I was shouting out, calling 'scabs' to the people that went to work. And I was shouting against Willie Walsh. I didn't know I had that in me.
>
> (Uwe)

Nicky regarded her crew colleagues as innately non-political, but revealed that a good number did become politicised during the course of the dispute. She described the participation of a delegation of 'ordinary' crew members at the 2011 anti-cuts protest, the March for the Alternative, organised by the TUC:

> What I've always said about cabin crew whenever I've ended up making speeches is that they don't have that sort of political framework. They live all over the world, and they don't know each other. They don't have a shop floor, they don't come from a dock community or a mining community or whatever. And so what they achieved through their solidarity was actually quite extraordinary. For many of them this was the first political action they had ever taken, but it wasn't to be the last. So you see, suddenly they were on the 26 March demonstration with the BASSA banner.
>
> (Nicky)

The diversity of cabin crew in terms of gender, sexuality, race and ethnicity raises questions about what types of interests were expressed during the strike and whether these identities were changed through struggle. Kat celebrated the role of women in the dispute but, at the same time, suggested the way gender, sexuality and race coalesced into an overriding trade union identity:

> I think we did a fantastic job for women in Britain. I think we showed them that you can go out and have beliefs. I think we changed a lot of people's views. We obviously frightened a lot of people by the rubbish they were printing. They didn't print an awful lot of truth so we must have been scaring them somewhere. You didn't see gay, white, black, anything, you just saw a trade union member or a non-trade union member – a belief in a sense of injustice.
>
> (Kat)

In this sense, conflict can be seen to strengthen group consciousness, shared values and identity with the union.[6] Felipe, a rep who was openly gay, made a similar observation to Kat: that you could not necessarily predict an individual cabin crew member's involvement in the strike from their identity and proposed a more diverse and inclusive conception of class than that which defined the miners' strike of 1984–5:

> What you've got to remember is that our community is made up of so many different people from so many different backgrounds. But usually you get the sort of middle-class white person, mother of children, who is not necessarily involved in politics or union activities and wouldn't know anything about it, who would bury their head in the sand thinking, 'If I close my eyes it will go away'. Now I'm not saying that everybody is like that, but the majority were. If you look at the population, the cabin crew population, we're all made up of foreigners and different cultures, different colours, but mainly you will find there are middle-class white woman. We weren't the miners, we were not the typical stereotype. When we went on the picket lines, I remember, you would see all these glamorous girls on the picket lines and people would stop and comment on that; 'Oh you don't look like the usual militant lot, you don't look that'. Yes, there was an element of that, people have stereotypes, so they think of strikers and they think, in this country they go back to the miners' strike, and they think of you as that. I think the strikers and non-strikers came from all over the mixture, so you had gay men who did strike, gay men who didn't; you had middle-class women who did strike and middle-class women who didn't strike. You had black people who did strike and black people who didn't, because it's such a huge community.
>
> (Felipe)

Yet, for others, the relationship between identity and commitment to action may have been more nuanced than that expressed by Felipe. Asad, a CSD on Worldwide and a rep of 14 years standing, suggested that women, and particularly gay workers, may have been more responsive to attacks on their working conditions because of the historic denial of their rights:

> Well, I think it is a lot less of a stereotypical workforce, because you have got a lot of people who are openly gay and a lot of women. But then, sometimes those type of people will surprise you in being more attuned to their rights. So if you're gay and you've just gone through the whole of the 80s where you had no rights, you are now thinking well, no, I'm not going to go through that again. So it does make you stronger.
>
> (Asad)

Louise wanted female cabin crew to be seen as workers or trade unionists and while she defined herself as a feminist she did not want cabin crew to be seen as 'mothers' or 'women' on strike:

> Definitely, definitely I consider myself a feminist. I don't know if there's that many feminists who fly. I think gender wise, obviously the general public always think cabin crew are very glamorous and all that business and they haven't got a brain, but that's not true. There are a lot of very bright people there, women in particular. We're mainly made up of women anyway and a lot of very strong women actually, amazingly strong women. I know it was mentioned quite a lot in the press that we were – well in fact the union tried to bring out that generally we're mothers – funny enough that used to anger me. I didn't want to be thought of as just a mother, I didn't want it to be just because we're poor women, that sort of thing. I didn't want it to be a gender related strike really, to me, it didn't seem to be that – even though it was mainly women, of course it was mainly women.
>
> (Louise)

While the central role of women in the dispute might suggest some form of feminist consciousness, the interviews indicated that women cabin crew saw themselves foremost as trade unionists, reinforcing studies that suggest women may draw upon feminist ideas without defining themselves as feminists.[7]

This chapter closes with an emblematic reflection by a long-serving crew member. Alex highlighted in a few sentences many of the principal themes that emerged from the crew interviews in words and language that were commonly used. These themes included, particularly, the profound sense of justice that inspired them to take action, the powerful sense of pride they had in the community, their deep attachment to BASSA and the key role it played in countering British Airways' deliberate campaign of misinformation. Above all, though, Alex, in common with all of the participants, placed greatest store by what he considered to be their most important achievement, that they had kept their union alive. As crew have demonstrated over and again in this chapter their successful fight to defend BASSA came at a price of personal sacrifice and hardship but it also changed them as individuals and as a community, enriching their lives in innumerable ways:

If you were to ask me what we've achieved, I think we've helped keep our union. And I think that's very important. Having the opportunity to actually counter any propaganda that the company had and anything that I would see is not right and undermines our union, we're always there to put a stop to it. And if there's any rumours that we believe are not true, we correct it. So I think it got the dispute going. It supported that whole dispute and it supported the whole cabin crew community. Politically, I think I've always been like that – as I said my sense of justice has always been very strong. Even my personal pride and my professional pride has always been there and I think that's what kept me going. And even as cabin crew and I think I'm a very good cabin crew, because of my pride. So did it change me? It made me realise that you really have to speak your mind. So yes, you must speak your mind.

(Alex)

7
Conclusion

Reflections on contrasts with the miners' strike

The BA–BASSA dispute lasted more than two years, prompting labour lawyer Keith Ewing to comment that it was longer than the miners' strike of 1984–5 and that, 'unlike the miners' strike … the union also recovered much of what it had lost during the dispute'.[1] These concluding observations that take Ewing's comment as a point of departure are stimulated also by the fact that many cabin crew participants themselves drew parallels with and contrasts between their own actions and the miners' strike. The iconic conflict had imprinted itself on the memories of cabin crew who had lived through it, while its legacy resonated with younger activists.

Similarities between the conflicts should not be overdrawn. They differed in their political-economic contexts, the industries, the role played by the state and in the scale, scope and dynamics of struggle. The following reflections on contrasts and commonalities do help to throw into sharp relief some of the distinctive features of the cabin crew's action.

The miners' strike, to recall, was the outcome of government policy to reconfigure the country's energy supply in the context of a publicly owned (nationalised) coal industry, to close pits, to break the National Union of Mineworkers and, in so doing, to render impotent the power of organised labour and to recast fundamentally employment relations in the UK.[2] It was a premeditated and set-piece confrontation, reflecting the Thatcher government's determination to achieve a decisive settling of accounts with the strongest section of the British working class, following the miners' defeat of the Heath government in 1974.[3] Further, it involved the mobilisation of the physical force of the British state against the NUM and entire working-class communities leading to the criminalisation of many thousands of miners.[4] Widespread counter-subversion exercises were conducted against the NUM.[5]

In contrast, the British Airways dispute was the result of a strategic decision, taken at corporate level by senior management of the UK's flagship airline, to restructure the terms and conditions of its cabin crew workforce and to reshape employment relations (Chapter 1) through the unilateral imposition of new contracts. Although the dispute would have wider implications for UK employment relations and beyond, not least in terms of employment law (Chapter 4) and the methods and tactics of union organisation (Chapter 5), the provenance was company-specific, in contrast to the broader political-economic and societal significance of the miners' strike. Though, as noted, authoritarian measures were directed against leading BASSA members and intimidation of striking crew, and this is not to diminish them, but the scale of repression directed towards the miners was of a different (and state-directed) order.

While it is true that the BASSA dispute lasted longer than the miners' strike, this fact is of limited comparative significance. As many as 142,000 NUM members were involved in all-out strike action, while BASSA members were engaged in intermittent episodes of strike action. At the heart of the miners' strike was daily picketing, with union members often taking part in mass action, of their own or other pits or of strategic choke points, notably at British Steel's coking plant, Orgreave, where the state mobilised physical force on a massive scale. As is made clear in Chapter 5, cabin crew enthusiastically embraced picketing on strike days, but one legacy of the miners' strike was that secondary trade union action and mass picketing had been outlawed. Ensuring the high visibility and effectiveness of collective action was important for BASSA, but the scale of picketing in the miners' strike, its continuous occurrence over such an extended time frame and the criminalisation of thousands make it incomparable.[6] Milne's verdict is the miners' strike of 1984–5 has no real parallel – in size, duration and impact – anywhere in the world.[7]

At the same time, the intensity of the conflict cannot be gauged simply by reference to the number of strike days taken. As crew made abundantly clear, the conflict in the periods *between* strike days remained acute. Hostilities between British Airways and BASSA and between pro-strike crew and anti-strike crew, pilots and management did not cease when work routines resumed. Indeed, for cabin crew who were committed to their union's action, subjecting themselves to managerial discipline in the face of frequent provocation and having to contain their emotions while working 'normally', was extraordinarily stressful. These interludes, then, were not temporary truces but represented a continuation of conflict. What emerges forcefully and movingly from the testimonies is the all-encompassing nature of the dispute, how it so completely consumed the emotions and the mental resources of the crew over two years. Some graphically referred to their involvement as an obsession or even an addiction.

Contrasts exist between the miners' and cabin crew strikes in their respective relationships to community. The miners' strike involved the mobilisation and collective struggle of entire geographical and historical communities[8] in conditions of acute privation, while these characteristics were evidently not present in the BASSA dispute. This dissimilarity is not to diminish the importance of community for cabin crew because, as we have seen (Chapters 3 and 5), they articulated such powerful notions of community based on their occupation, shared experience, sense of extended family and moral code. Nor is it to trivialise the hardships many faced. Finally, the question of outcome needs to be considered. Ewing emphasises the fact that, 'unlike the miners', cabin crew were able to recover much of what they had lost in the dispute.'[9] Great care, though, should be taken in drawing comparisons. Facing a resolute government, which had mobilised the repressive powers of the state to break the miners in order to implement its programme of pit closures, the NUM was unable to wrest concessions. For all the company's spin to the contrary, British Airways was a highly profitable organisation, operating in an expanding, although competitively intensifying, market, and its workforce was central to its continuing profit. Thus, the product market contexts differ markedly. In the BASSA case, cabin crew possessed greater underlying bargaining power.

Having acknowledged this contrast in the balance of forces, the determination of British Airways, and the support they received from the government and judicial system, in seeking to break their union should not be underestimated. The use of disciplinary measures and internal security to victimise both reps and union members lays bare the darker side of UK industrial relations for which British Airways had previous.

It is not a purpose of this book to deliver a definitive judgement on whether BASSA 'won' or 'lost' the dispute with British Airways. Nevertheless, some evaluation of the facts is necessary. An objective appraisal points to a two-sidedness to the outcome. On the positive side, British Airways' sustained attempt to break the union and to fragment the collective organisation of one of the strongest sections of organised labour in the UK was a failure. The vigilance and determined resistance of cabin crew over years halted an extremely aggressive offensive by one of the UK's flagship employers. They ensured that BASSA remained intact and this achievement in highly adverse circumstances was understood by the trade union movement as a whole. It is also true, to return to Ewing's remark, that BASSA did succeed in recovering much of what had been lost during the dispute, including a matter of great importance for the cabin crew, staff travel allowances.

On the debit side, British Airways succeeded in adding another tier of cabin crew on inferior terms and conditions to its already tiered workforce that had been its objective, and won further concessions on working practices and labour flexibilities. These were negative consequences of some importance, but they were far from the end of the matter. If British Airways had hoped that the mixed fleet would become a compliant workforce, willing to accept vastly inferior terms and conditions and punishing schedules then they were to be disappointed. Unite the Union began successfully to organise the new crew into a branch, distinct from BASSA.

Mixed fleet resistance

The dramatic postscript to this book is the astonishing 85 days of industrial action taken by mixed fleet (who constitute 15% percent of the British Airways cabin crew workforce) at Heathrow between December 2016 and August 2017 in a challenge to the markedly inferior' terms and conditions introduced after the 2009–11 dispute. In December 2016 over 2,000 Unite mixed fleet crew overwhelmingly voted for strike action over low pay, rejecting a 2 per cent pay offer, which the union calculated as representing 6 pence per hour. British Airways informed cabin crew they could receive the original pay deal if they declared they were not a member of a trade union. British Airways were reprising the divisive and malicious tactics that had been so prominent in previous disputes. In response, Unite reported that over 800 cabin crew from British Airways' 'mixed fleet' had joined Unite since the start of the dispute, taking the overall membership to over 2,900 as of January 2017. Mixed crew were then almost continuously on strike in July and August 2017, when they were offered £250 not to take industrial action.[10]

Unlike the 2009–11 dispute, British Airways could no longer use 'the spurious excuse of a tough trading environment'[11] given the parent company IAG's recent declaration[12] of £2 billion pre-tax profit, an increase of one-third on the previous year, with the CEO's remuneration package soaring to £4 million in 2017, a 60 per cent increase from the previous year.[13] Unite reported that basic pay for mixed crew started at £12,192, with £3 an hour flying pay, and that, on average, they annually earned £16,000, including allowances. They had effectively endured a six-year pay freeze and a union survey found that half reported having taken second jobs to make ends meet. More than two-thirds were going to work 'unfit to fly' because they could not afford to be off sick. More than eight out of ten (84 per cent) reported experiencing stress and depression since joining British Airways because of their impoverished financial circumstances. Once again the company refused to negotiate through ACAS, and removed bonuses and staff travel concessions for striking workers. Unite pursued legal action on behalf of mixed fleet cabin crew who were sanctioned in this way which, it argued, effectively amounted to blacklisting. British Airways borrowed Qatar Airways aircraft,[14] to cover for operational disruption on strike days prompting Unite to launch a legal challenge against the government's decision to permit British Airways to 'wet lease' nine Airbus aircraft. The union argued that the lease of aircraft and cabin crew from Qatar Airways breached European regulations for 'wet leasing' aircraft from outside the European Union.

The dispute was settled in October 2017 with 84 per cent voting on an 80 per cent turnout in favour of a pay settlement of at least £1,404, rising to £2,908 by March 2018 depending on experience and subject to inflation – a 11 per cent increase on basic pay with an additional 4 per cent on the hourly rate and the introduction of a new £10 daily overseas allowance.[15] Travel concessions and entitlement to fully participate in the airline's 2017 bonus scheme were returned to cabin crew.

If British Airways had believed that the creation of the mixed fleet post-2011 would mean a docile cabin crew workforce who would willingly accept inferior terms and conditions, they were mistaken. Rather, the mixed fleet dispute should be seen as representing a further episode in the unfolding history of conflictual industrial relations at British Airways, driven by senior management's preoccupation with cost cutting. Without lapsing into unfounded speculation, it is difficult to see how British Airways underlying antagonism to trade unions will not provoke further significant disputes in the future.

Civil aviation in Europe: continuing union action

A broader review of industrial relations in European civil aviation after 2016, reveals several major disputes between airlines and employees. In May 2016 a dispute between Unite and Thomas Cook saw 74 per cent of cabin crew members vote to strike over changes to rest breaks where the company proposed to reduce 20-minute breaks from every six hours to every twelve hours.[16] In April 2017 widespread strikes were taken by workers employed by Alitalia in disputes on pay and conditions. Lufthansa recorded a lengthy struggle with the main German pilots' union, Vereinigung Cockpit (VC), over attempts to reduce costs to compete with low-cost rivals. In March 2017, the company signed an agreement to reduce pilot staffing costs through cuts in pension benefits, a move from defined benefits to defined contributions, increasing pilots' retirement age. It also agreed to hire 700 junior pilots in Lufthansa, its cargo divisions and subsidiary Eurowings which would ensure industrial peace until 2022. Pilots at Lufthansa and its subsidiaries received staggered pay increases of up to 10.3 per cent and a one-off payment of up to 1.8 monthly salaries for the period of May 2012 until June 2022.[17]

In September 2017, Thomas Cook pilots staged one 12-hour and one 24-hour strike over pay and cuts to terms and conditions and threatened further strike action. The company had previously sought a High Court injunction to prevent members from striking, but the judge rejected their case, ordered BALPA's costs to be paid and declined permission for Thomas Cook to appeal. This was the first pilots' strike in the UK for 40 years and resulted in binding arbitration.

Autumn 2017 also saw the escalation of a dispute between pilots and Ryanair, a company resolutely opposed to dealing with trade unions since its establishment 32 years previously. Pilots rejected an offer of up to £12,000 to keep flying during their scheduled leave, many of them putting their names to a letter demanding full employment contracts instead. Chief executive Michael O'Leary had threatened to cancel pilots' time off which prompted an exodus of pilots to competitors and cancelled flights.[18] The dispute centred on Ryanair pilots' desire to negotiate terms via the collective European Employee Representative Council – which encompasses staff at all bases – rather than each of the company's 87 bases agreeing terms separately. In December 2017 Dublin-based Ryanair pilots suspended a 24-hour strike over the absence of union representation when the company agreed to recognise trade unions in Ireland, Germany, Portugal and Italy. Pilots in Italy and Portugal also voted in favour of industrial action and, subsequently, German Ryanair pilots took four hour strike action in December when the company delayed collective bargaining on the issue.[19] In January 2018, UK BALPA signed an agreement recognising it as the sole trade union representing all of Ryanair's 600 UK-based pilots. In the same month the Dutch FNV union called a 24-hour strike at Franco-Dutch airline Air France-KLM among KLM cabin crew in protest at a reduction in staff complements on long-haul flights.[20] Dutch pilots were concerned about Air France plans to change its pension plan and adapt regulations for part-time work. In April 2018, several strikes by Air France (KLM) pilots, cabin crew and ground staff took place in support of a 6 per cent pay rise rejected by the airline in the context of increased operating profits.[21]

In sum, tough inter-firm and inter-alliance competition in the increasingly deregulated global civil aviation industry continues to drive restructuring and cost reduction which, in turn, continues to provoke union resistance. The conclusion drawn by Oxenbridge and colleagues, that the 'strength of union organisation and a willingness to deploy industrial action accounts for limits on unilateral management action in civil aviation', remains valid.[22] What can be added to this encouraging verdict is the emergence of union organisation, collectivism and a determination to improve working conditions in either initially non-union entities (British Airways 'mixed fleet') or in industrial relations environments that have long been unremittingly hostile to trade unions (Ryanair). It is not hyperbolic to suggest that had BASSA been crushed in 2011, a legacy of defeat might have undermined the confidence of workers in the airline industry to take the successful actions described. Further, action by the 'mixed fleet' cabin crew can be seen as a small but significance surge of union activity taken by young workers resisting work characterised by flexibility and non-standard employment contracts. Dubbed #McStrike, strike action was taken in 2018 by the so-called 'self-employed' Deliveroo and Uber Eats delivery workers and staff employed in Wetherspoons pubs, and in TGI Fridays and McDonalds restaurants, with a view to ending poverty pay and insecure work.

A final observation

As demonstrated in Chapter 5, many cabin crew did make reference to the miners' strike that had occurred a quarter of a century previously. Some openly commented on how their struggle was distinct from a strike based upon a section of the male industrial working class, a distinction based on identity. One notable characteristic of the dispute is the diverse composition of the workforce and the way that trade union identity embraced gender, race and sexuality to produce an inclusive conception of cabin crew collectivity and ultimately of class. The final contribution comes from Stephen, a CSD and a union rep who sums up crew members' reflections on the question of identity and their critiques of the dominant caricature of cabin crew and the assumptions that follow from such stereotyping:

I don't like to be stereotyped but people do that anyway. So the stereotypical cabin crew member would be middle class, gay and the woman would be married to a pilot. They have got the disposable income. There won't be some hairy-arsed bloke from northeast London like me, but there we are, we have people like me. We are a myriad of different people. So we are multifaceted as far as class is concerned, but that is ignored because of stereotyping and identity.

(Stephen)

Yet if similarities can be overdrawn, so too can contrasts. Of course, gender, race and sexuality were important dimensions of the wider political solidarity that sustained the miners' strike,[23] but they were integral to the British Airways' dispute. In other respects, though, cabin crew positioned themselves, their struggle and the meaning of their actions explicitly against the historical background of the miners' strike as a signal event in UK working-class history. BASSA members understood the importance of the miners' strike and recognised commonalities between their struggle and of those of their predecessors, but crew also articulated the distinctiveness of their own actions, a different struggle in a different period. However, what they most shared with the miners was the profound sense that the struggle they were involved in was a hugely important event in their lives, if not the single defining experience, which simultaneously transformed the way they viewed the world and their understanding of themselves. Things would never be the same again. Their actions and those of the miners are part of the history of struggle in Britain, part of the collective consciousness of the working class that in definable and indefinable ways contributes to an enduring legacy of strikes that continually reignite – as in the stunning case of the mixed fleet.

Afterword

John Hendy QC

The BA Cabin Crew dispute gave rise to no less than four significant legal cases in which, as Standing Counsel to Unite the Union, I had the honour to represent the union and the cabin crew. Together the cases illustrate the way in which the law and the courts are used as a means of enforcing the hierarchy of power exercised by those who own the means of production over those who actually produce the goods (services in this case). Wrapped in the ostensibly neutral flag of 'the rule of law', the decisions of the courts, governed by laws which embed managerial prerogative, are expected to be obeyed, no matter how unjust their impact. Only where the scale of the perceived injustice inflicted by the law is seen by those who administer it to risk the law being brought into such disrepute that the workers might simply disregard it, does the law, on occasion, retreat. All these features are demonstrated in the four cases thrown up by this dispute.

Malone v. British Airways

The first case in point of time was a challenge brought by Unite the Union against British Airways. It will be recalled that one point of dispute leading to the strike action was BA's announcement that it was going to reduce the crew quota on long haul flights. Those quotas had been set by long-standing and detailed collective agreements reached between management and unions for each route and for each aircraft type. In *Malone v. British Airways*[1] the union sought an injunction to prevent the admitted breaches of the collective agreements. In English law collective agreements are not normally enforceable as between the union and the employer.[2] Instead, provisions in collective agreements setting terms and conditions of employment are normally incorporated into the contracts of employment of the relevant workers. They can therefore sue on a breach of the collective agreement as a breach of their contract. The argument we put forward on behalf of Liz Malone and members representing, in effect, all the cabin crew, was that the number and grades of cabin crew for particular flights set out in the collective agreements was a term of their employment and enforceable as such. We argued that, just as it might be said that if an electrician was employed on the basis that she would have a mate with her to assist, the staffing level was an important term of a contract of employment. The case was launched on 30 October 2009 and, on 19 February 2010, the High Court refused to grant an injunction against BA. So the law refused to help the workers in the face of BA's unilateral breach of agreement. Industrial action was therefore the only alternative.

The case was appealed to the Court of Appeal and judgement handed down on 3 November 2010 whilst the industrial dispute still raged. The judgement is a significant one. It accepted that failure to provide full crew complements in accordance with the collective agreement would have an impact on the working conditions of the remainder of the crew and that 'an undertaking as to the size of the team of workers who will undertake a task may, in some circumstances, be enforceable by individual [workers]'. However, since if the crew complements were contractually binding it would mean that individual members of crew faced with an insufficient crew could refuse to work a flight so causing the flight to be cancelled, the Court concluded that such 'disastrous consequences' cannot have been intended and so the crew complements cannot have been intended to have been contractually binding.

The tortured reasoning amounts to this: that an agreement will be held not to be intended to be legally enforceable if an innocent party refuses to accept a breach by the other party which causes the latter sufficiently disastrous consequences. Were this doctrine to apply in commercial law, the result would be anarchy. It is perhaps not surprising that the cabin crew felt short changed by the law.

British Airways v. Unite

The second case features in some detail in the book. It concerned an injunction brought by BA against the union, *British Airways v. Unite the Union*.[3] Here the High Court was asked to apply the UK statutory law on industrial action which, repeatedly amended in the 1980s and 1990s, is highly restrictive of the right to strike. The judgement records that in the (legally required) strike ballot ending on 14 December 2009, in a turnout of 80 per cent of the BA cabin crew membership of Unite, 10,286 had voted (with an additional two spoilt ballot papers), of which 9,514 were in favour of strike action, representing 92.49 per cent of the votes. As part of BA's cost cutting it had made 1003 cabin crew redundant between the end of October and 15 December. Unite did not know who they were though it knew there were redundancies. It could not identify them so as to prevent ballot papers being sent to them, though it could have issued a warning that those who were leaving should not vote. The court held that the ballot was therefore invalidated and the injunction against the strike granted.

This was on the basis that the legislation required that only those whom the union reasonably believed would be called on to strike were entitled to vote. Those taking redundancy would not be called on to strike. So they should not have been given ballot papers. There is an exemption for small accidental failures which do not affect the result of the ballot but it did not apply to this provision. In any event, the judge held that this was not a small failure. So the union had failed to comply with a requirement of the legislation necessary to establish statutory protection from the law. But the injustice from the union and the members' perspective is self-evident. Apart from the fact that the union did not know who had been made redundant, and BA declined to identify them, the fact remained that even if all 1003 had been members of the union and even if all of them had voted (which obviously many did not on cutting their ties to BA), and even if all of them had voted against the strike, their votes could not have made any difference to the outcome of the ballot. The cabin crew blamed the judge but the real culprit was the legislation introduced by the Conservative governments of Mrs Thatcher and preserved by the Labour governments which followed.

British Airways v. Unite No.2

The third case arose in consequence of the refusal of the union and its cabin crew members not to be deterred by the legal defeat of their overwhelming democratic mandate. They re-balloted in February 2010. This time the turnout was only a few tenths of a percent less than before: 79.39 per cent representing 9,281 voters. There were eleven spoilt ballot papers. There were 7,482 votes (i.e. 80.6 per cent) in favour of strike action and 1,789 against. This, again, was an overwhelming mandate.

Strike action took place in consequence on 20–22 March and 27–30 March. On 10 May the union notified BA of further action from 18 May. On 17 May BA sought and obtained in the High Court (McCombe J) an injunction against the further strike action based on the claim that the union had failed properly to inform its members of the full result of the ballot. The statute required the union to inform members of the number of votes cast, votes in favour, votes against, and spoilt ballots in order for the strike action to be lawful. In particular, it was shown that some union publications contained only the percentages for and against though other publications put the voting figures for and against but had failed to specify that eleven ballots were spoiled. The union had used its website, notices in crew rooms, press conferences and the outcome was broadcast by all the news media. In the UK only someone who did not wish to know could have avoided learning that there was a huge majority for strike action.

The union appealed to the Court of Appeal and the seriousness with which the union viewed this second interference with the membership's unambiguous decision was underlined by the presence of demonstrations outside court and large numbers of cabin crew and both Joint General Secretaries sitting in court. In *British Airways v. Unite the union (No.2)*,[4] on 20 May, the Court of Appeal overturned the High Court but only by a majority of 2:1. Two of the three Lords Justices held that though the union could have done more, it had done what was 'reasonably necessary' to inform its members of the ballot result as the statute required. Hence the strike could lawfully proceed. In passing the Lord Chief Justice noted:[5]

> What I do, however, question is whether as a matter of principle it can be appropriate that even a complete failure to inform the union members – not the employers – of the fact that an infinitesimal proportion of spoilt ballots were returned which could have had no possible bearing on the outcome of the ballot could leave the union liable in tort for calling a strike which had the support of the vast preponderance of its members. At the risk of repetition, it does indeed seem curious to me that the employers can rely on a provision designed to protect the interests of members of the union in order to circumvent their wishes.

The consequence for the rule of law had the injunction been upheld on this flimsy and unjust basis was apparent to all.

Roffey v. United Kingdom

The fourth case is *Roffey v. United Kingdom*.[6] It will be recalled that strikes by cabin crew were intermittent from 20 March to 9 June 2010. From the outset British Airways had penalised all those who took part in any of the single days of official, lawful, strike action by removing their (valuable) travel benefits. Their entitlement to those benefits was not restored until the dispute was ultimately settled on 1 July 2011 after months of protracted negotiations. Proceedings to challenge this sanction were commenced by four representative members of cabin crew and the union in October 2010 (with little hope of success).[7] They were withdrawn as part of the settlement of the dispute in the summer of 2011.

But a claim against the UK for breach of the European Convention on Human Rights was also lodged in the European Court of Human Rights (ECtHR) by four representative members of cabin crew and the union. The basis of the claim was founded on the fact that the ECtHR has held in many judgements that Article 11 of the Convention (which protects trade union rights) requires the State to provide protection to workers against penalisation for participation in strike action.[8]

Applications to the Strasbourg Court must be lodged within six months of the alleged violation. The Application was lodged on 17 December 2010. The Court took the cut-off date from which the six-month period ran as the last date on which written threats to withdraw the benefits were made. The threats were made on 13 April 2010 and 10 May 2010.[9] This enabled the ECtHR to rule the application out of time. That decision was unequivocally unsustainable for a number of reasons.

Firstly, the complaint was not against the *threat* but against the *imposition* of the penalty. That could not be earlier than the date a particular cabin crew member participated in a strike day which triggered the removal of her benefits. Until that moment a crew member continued to enjoy travel benefits. She would not be 'directly affected' by the threat unless and until, by taking strike action, the sanction impacted on her. The industrial action consisted of several separate days of strike action. Crew members not rostered to work on a strike day could not therefore take part in that day's strike. So there were some members who did not join a strike day until the last such day, 9 June 2010, less than six months before the Application was lodged. Such a member would only have lost her entitlement from that date. For her, the application was therefore in time.

Secondly, the sanction did not 'directly affect' a crew member until she claimed and was denied a travel benefit, when the sanction was activated, (whether or not the prior threat to deny was also a violation).

Thirdly, once a crew member had taken strike action, the sanction continued to have effect by barring any subsequent use of the travel benefits until ultimately the benefits were restored on settlement of the dispute more than six months after the Application was lodged. This case was therefore a paradigm example of a continuing violation of Convention rights, a state of affairs which subsisted when the application was lodged. In many previous cases the ECtHR had held that where a violation is continuing, the six-month limitation does not apply at all.[10]

The injustice of the Court's clear error of law in this case was magnified by it denying the Applicants the opportunity of dealing with the point. Neither the government nor the court raised any question about the timing of the application.[11] The Applicants knew nothing of it in advance of the handing down of the decision. In the result, the Applicants were denied any opportunity to respond to what was the crucial argument against them. There is no appeal from a decision on admissibility and the Court refused (as is normal) to reply to correspondence about the case.

It seems likely that the court was influenced by factors other than the merits of the case or the application of relevant legal principles. Professor Ewing and I have suggested that the court, in this and other applications against the UK, was influenced by a desire not to promulgate judgments adverse to the UK which might fuel the government's declared policy to repeal the Human Rights Act and cease to consider itself bound by the Convention.[12]

Whatever the rationale, the cabin crew were entitled to feel bitterly aggrieved by such a perverse and contemptuous refusal to hear their case.

Conclusion

Together, these cases give an insight into the workings of law in the conflict of interest between capital and labour. It is a depressing commentary on the rule of law which extends far beyond the historic industrial dispute which gave rise to the cases.

Appendix
The participants

Abbreviations: CSD, cabin service director; EF, Eurofleet; WW, Worldwide. The first seven rows are people whose real names have been used (with permission) throughout the text; the names in the rest of the table are pseudonyms.

Name	Gender	Race	Age	Job role	Union role
Kevin Cook	Male	White British	40s	Cabin crew WW	Member – sacked during dispute
Duncan Holley	Male	White British	50s	CSD WW until 1990 CSD EF to 2010	Branch secretary; dismissed during dispute
Louise Holley	Female	White British	30s	Cabin crew WW	Member
Lizanne Malone	Female	White British	50s	CSD WW	Chair and Unite NEC member
Nicky Marcus	Female	White British	40s	Cabin crew WW	Rep sacked during dispute
Oliver Richardson	Male	White British	30s	Unite national officer	National officer
Steve Turner	Male	White British	40s	Unite national officer	National officer
Sally	Female	White British	50s	CSD EF	Rep
Rhys	Male	White British	40s	CSD EF	Rep
Adam	Male	White British	50s	Purser WW	Rep suspended during dispute
Alex	Male	Asian British	30s	Cabin crew WW	Member
Carrie	Female	White British	30s	Cabin crew WW	Member
Jade	Female	White British	30s	Purser EF	Rep
Felipe	Male	White Italian	40s	Cabin crew WW	Rep
James	Male	White British	50s	CSD WW	Rep
Stephen	Male	White British	40s	CSD WW	Rep
Laurent	Male	White British	40s	CSD EF	Rep
Max	Male	White British	30s	Purser WW	Rep
Will	Male	White British	50s	CSD EF	Rep

Name	Gender	Race	Age	Job role	Union role
Nathan	Male	White British	50s	Purser WW	Rep
Asad	Male	Asian British	40s	CSD WW	Rep
Richard	Male	White British	40s	CSD WW	Rep
Uwe	Male	Asian European	30s	Cabin crew WW	Rep
Ian	Male	White British	50s	CSD EF	Rep
Sana	Female	White European	40s	Cabin crew EF	Rep
Catherine	Female	White British	40s	CSD EF	Rep
Andrew	Male	White British	60s	CSD EF	Rep
Kat	Female	White British	50s	Cabin crew EF	Member
Tom	Male	White British	50s	CSD WW	Rep
Virginie	Female	White European	40s	Cabin crew WW	Member
Jack	Male	White British	60s	Cabin crew WW	Member
Rose	Female	White British	60s	Cabin crew WW	Member
Elizabeth	Female	White British	40s	Cabin crew WW	Member sacked during dispute
Kate	Female	White British	50s	Purser WW	Member
Sarah	Female	White British	50s	CSD WW	Member
Larissa	Female	White British	40s	Cabin crew WW	Member
Julianne	Female	White British	50s	CSD EF	Member
Amy	Female	White British	50s	Cabin crew EF	Member
Finn	Male	White Irish	40s	Cabin crew WW	Member
Patrick	Male	White British	40s	CSD WW	Member
Gemma	Female	White Australasian	40s	CSD EF	Member
Lara	Female	Black French	40s	Cabin crew EF	Member
Rabea	Female	Black British	50s	CSD demoted in strike to Purser WW	Member demoted during dispute
Savi	Female	Asian British	40s	Cabin crew WW	Member suspended during dispute
Guy	Male	White British	40s	Purser EF	Member
Annie	Female	White British	50s	Purser WW	Member
Melanie	Female	White British	40s	Cabin crew WW	Member
Stephanie	Female	White British	50s	CSD WW	Member suspended in dispute
Ben	Male	White British	50s	Purser WW	Member suspended during dispute
Camille	Female	White European	40s	Purser – single fleet	Member, Gatwick

Notes

Preface

1. The term purser derives from passenger ships where it denoted a senior officer. Airlines, including British Airways, adopted the term to denote a chief flight attendant with responsibility for cabin crew and safety procedures. A purser is subordinate to the Cabin Service Director (CSD) who should be regarded as the on-board manager with overall responsibility for the cabin and crew.

1. Introduction

1. R. Wray (2011) 'British Airways cabin crew reject pay offer', *Guardian*, 22 June, www.theguardian.com/business/2010/jul/20/british-airways-crew-reject-pay-offer (accessed April 2014).
2. J. Eldridge (1968) *Industrial Disputes – Essays in the Sociology of Industrial Relations*, London: Routledge and Kegan Paul; R. Hyman (1997) *Strikes*, 2nd edn, Glasgow: Fontana Collins; R. Hyman (1989) *The Political Economy of Industrial Relations: Theory and Practice in a Cold Climate*, London: Macmillan; E. Shorter and C. Tilly (1974) *Strikes in France, 1830–1968*, Cambridge: Cambridge University Press; E. Batstone, I. Boraston and S. Frenkel (1978) *The Social Organisation of Strikes*, Oxford: Blackwell; R. Franzosi (1995) *The Puzzle of Strikes: Class and State Strategies in Postwar Italy*, Cambridge: Cambridge University Press; J. Kelly (1998) *Rethinking Industrial Relations: Mobilization, Collectivism and Long Waves*, London: Routledge.
3. J. Godard (2017) *Industrial Relations, Economy and Society*, 5th edn, Toronto: Captus Press.
4. S. Williams (2014) *Introducing Employment Relations: A Critical Approach*, 4th edn, Oxford: Oxford University Press; P. Blyton and P. Turnbull (2004) *The Dynamics of Employee Relations*, 3rd edn, Basingstoke: Palgrave.
5. Office for National Statistics (2017) 'Labour disputes in the UK: 2017', www.ons.gov.uk/employmentandlabourmarket/peopleinwork/workplace disputesandworkingconditions/articles/labourdisputes/2017#cause-of-disputes (accessed November 2018).
6. Studies show that strike waves tend to correspond to the onset of downturns in long-term economic cycles, when workers' expectations are rising but employers are facing a crisis of profitability: Franzosi, *The Puzzle of Strikes*. See also Blyton and Turnbull, *The Dynamics of Employee Relations*, pp. 317–60.
7. Blyton and Turnbull, *The Dynamics of Employee Relations*, p. 305.

8. C. Kerr and A. Siegel (1954) 'The interindustry propensity to strike – an international comparison', in A. Kornhauser, R. Dubin and A.M. Ross (eds), *Industrial Conflict*, New York: McGraw Hill.

9. Shorter and Tilly, *Strikes in France*.

10. P. Taylor and S. Moore (2015) 'Cabin crew collectivism: labour process and the roots of mobilisation in the British Airways dispute 2009–11', *Work, Employment and Society*, 29(1), pp. 79–98.

11. D. Lyddon, X. Cao, Q. Meng and J. Lu (2015) 'A strike of "unorganised workers" in a Chinese car factory: the Nanhai Honda events of 2010', *Industrial Relations Journal*, 46(2), pp. 134–52.

12. E.T. Hiller (1928) *The Strike: A Study in Collective Action*, Chicago, IL: University of Chicago Press.

13. J. Hartley, J. Kelly and N. Nicholson (1983) *Steel Strike: A Case Study in Industrial Relations*, London: Batsford, pp. 11–12.

14. These separate processes invoke the stages that Kelly articulates as core to mobilisation theory in *Rethinking Industrial Relations*.

15. Hiller, *The Strike*, p. ix.

16. A. Gouldner (1954) *Wildcat Strike: A Study in Worker–Management Relationships*, New York: Harper.

17. J.E.T. Eldridge (1973) 'Industrial conflict: some problems of theory and method', in J. Child (ed.), *Man and Organization: the Search for Explanation and Social Relevance*, London: George Allen and Unwin, pp. 158–64.

18. See also R.D. Benford and D.A. Snow (2000) 'Reframing processes and social movements: an overview and assessment', *Annual Review of Sociology*, 26, pp. 611–39.

19. Of course, the BA-BASSA dispute of 2009–11 was a broader and more protracted *episode* of industrial *conflict*, but the 22 strike days represented the high point of the struggle.

20. B. Kars (1958) *Diary of a Strike*, Urbana, IL: University of Illinois Press.

21. Ibid., p. 137. Kars makes the additional point that informs the present work of 'the need to find uncomplicated language which would be meaningful to non-sociologists and yet explain complex concepts without doing violence towards them' (ibid., p. 168).

22. T. Lane and K. Roberts (1971) *Strike at Pilkingtons*, London: Fontana.

23. Ibid., p. 12. Previous studies had fallen into one of two groups, either those broader country level surveys intended to show which parts of a labour force are most strike-prone and then sought to identify the social, economic and political conditions connected to high levels, or examinations of specific strikes or strike-prone industries, which usually attempt to reconstruct events post-strike.

24. E.O. Wright (2000) 'Working-class power, capitalist-class interests and class compromise', *American Journal of Sociology*, 105(4), pp. 957–1002.

25. Lane and Roberts, *Strike at Pilkingtons*, pp. 15–16.

26. Ibid., p. 16.

27. Ibid., p. 16.

28. In addition to 25 lengthy post-strike interviews, they surveyed 187 workers during the dispute.

29. Lane and Roberts, *Strike at Pilkingtons*, p. 103.

30. Ibid., p. 105.

31. Ibid.

32. Ibid.

33. Fantasia, *Cultures of Solidarity*.

34. C. Woolfson and J. Foster (1988) *Track Record: The Story of the Caterpillar Occupation*, London: Verso.

35. J. Foster and J. Woolfson (1986) *The Politics of the UCS Work-In*, London: Lawrence and Wishart.

36. J. Lang and G. Dodkins (2011) *Bad News: The Wapping Dispute*, Nottingham: Spokesman Books.

37. A. Sundari and R. Pearson (2018) *Striking Women*, Chadwell Heath: Lawrence and Wishart.

38. Ibid., p. 16.

39. S. Moore, T. Wright and P. Taylor (2018) *Fighting Fire: A History of the Fire Brigades Union*, London: New Internationalist. An earlier book on the strike was by R. Siefert and T. Sibley (2005) *United they Stand: The Story of the UK Firefighters Dispute, 2002–4*, London: Lawrence and Wishart. This latter work did draw upon extensive quotes, but from a narrower range of participants, preponderantly full-time officers.

40. Hartley, Kelly and Nicholson, *Steel Strike*.

41. H. Beynon (ed.) (1985) *Digging Deeper: Issues in the Miners' Strike*, London: Verso; A. Callinicos and M. Simons (1985) *The Great Strike: Miners' Strike of 1984–5 and the Lessons*, London: Bookmarks; J. Winterton and R. Winterton (1993) *Coal, Crisis and Conflict: 1984–5 Miners' Strike in Yorkshire*, Manchester: Manchester University Press; S. Milne (2014) *The Enemy Within: The Secret War Against the Miners*, 4th edn, London: Verso. An additional, utterly compelling and authentic account of the strike is a retrospectively published diary written by a rank-and-file miner at Westoe Colliery, in South Shields. N. Strike (2009) *Strike by Name*, London: Bookmarks.

42. M. Lavalette and J. Kennedy (1996) *Solidarity on the Waterfront: Liverpool Lock Out of 1995–6*, Liverpool: Liver Press.

43. Two articles on contrasting disputes and locations may be cited which do represent workers' voices; Lyddon et al., 'A strike of "unorganised" workers'; and B. Marren (2016) 'The Liverpool Dock Strike, 1995–8: a resurgence of solidarity in the age of globalisation', *Labor History*, 57(4), pp. 463–81.

44. R. Darlingon and D. Lyddon (2001) *Glorious Summer: Class Struggle in Britain, 1972*, London: Bookmarks.

45. G. Gall (2003) *The Meaning of Militancy? Postal Workers and Industrial Relations*, Aldershot: Ashgate.

46. Taylor and Moore, 'Cabin crew collectivism'.

47. Figures from BASSA.

48. Kelly, *Rethinking Industrial Relations*.

49. See for example V. Yow (2016) 'Interviewing techniques and strategies', in R. Perks and A. Thomson (eds) *The Oral History Reader*, 3rd edn, London: Routledge, pp. 153–79.

50. A. Portelli (1991) *The Death of Luigi Trastulli and Other Stories: Form and Meaning in Oral History*, New York: State University of New York Press, p. 50.

51. L. Shopes (2015) 'After the interview ends: moving oral history out of the archives and into publication', *The Oral History Review*, 42(2), pp. 300–310.

52. M. Simons (1984) *Striking Back: Photographs of the Great Miners' Strike, 1984-5*, London: Bookmarks. This stunning book contains images from the front line of the struggle by John Sturrock, John Harris and Martin Shakeshaft.

53. S. Rowbotham (1973) *Hidden from History: 300 Years of Women's Oppression and the Fight Against It*, London: Pluto Press.

54. M. Burawoy (2005) 'For public sociology', *American Sociological Review*, 70(1), pp. 4–28.

55. P. Bourdieu (1999) *Acts of Resistance: Against the New Myths Of Our Time*, London: Polity Press. Bourdieu, P. (1999) *The Weight of the World*, London: Polity Press.

56. P. Brook and R. Darlington (2013) 'Partisan, scholarly and active: arguments for an organic public sociology of work', *Work, Employment and Society*, 27(2), pp. 232–43.

2. Cabin crew collectivism

1. R. Wray (2011) 'British Airways cabin crew reject pay offer', *Guardian*, 22 June, www.theguardian.com/business/2010/jul/20/british-airways-crew-reject-pay-offer (accessed April 2014).

2. J. Kelly (1998) *Rethinking Industrial Relations: Mobilization, Collectivism and Long Waves*, London: Routledge, p. 1.

3. P. Bassett (1986) *Strike Free: New Industrial Relations in Britain*, London: Macmillan.

4. Kelly, *Rethinking Industrial Relations*, p. 1.

5. D. Harvey (2005) *A Brief History of Neo-liberalism*, Oxford: Oxford University Press.

6. G.J. Bamber, J.H. Gittell, T.A. Kochan and A. von Nordenflycht (2009) *Up in the Air: How Airlines Can Improve Performance by Engaging Their Employees*, Ithaca, NY: ILR Press.

7. M. Roberts (2016) *The Long Depression: Marxism and the Global Crisis of Capitalism*, Chicago, IL: Haymarket Books.

8. M. Phillips (2010) 'What's turned the kindly British Airways cabin crew who cured my fear of flying into suicidal strikers', *Daily Mail*, 19 May, www.dailymail.co.uk/debate/article-1279501/BRITISH AIRWAYS-strikes-Whats-turned-kindly-cabin-crew-suicidal-strikers.html. (accessed March 2014). Such characterisations might even find an echo among some cabin crew

themselves. One recalled that they were popularly seen as 'just a bunch of girls or a bunch of gays' (interview with Carrie).

9. R. Dukes (2011) 'The right to strike under UK law: something more than a slogan', *Industrial Law Journal*, 40(3), pp. 302–11.

10. D. Lyddon (2015) 'The changing pattern of UK strikes, 1964–2014', *Employee Relations*, 37(6), pp. 733–45.

11. D. Hale (2012) *Labour Disputes – Annual Article, 2010*, London: Office for National Statistics.

12. S. Bach (2016) 'De-privileging the public sector workforce: austerity, fragmentation and service withdrawal in Britain', *The Economic and Labour Relations Review*, 27(1), pp. 11–28. See p. 21 for a chart plotting public sector strikes against other sectors.

13. J. Kelly (2015) 'Conflict: trends and forms of collective action', *Employee Relations*, 37(6), pp. 720–32.

14. 1996, 2002, 2007 and 2011.

15. Kelly, 'Conflict'; Office for National Statistics (2013) *Labour Disputes – Annual Article*, London: ONS.

16. In an interesting overlap with the BASSA dispute, these stoppages were marked by the high participation of women. The 2002 strike of one million local government workers over pay has been described as the largest strike of women in UK history.

17. For an extended discussion of the meaning of militancy, see G. Gall (2003) *The Meaning of Militancy? Postal Workers and Industrial Relations*, Aldershot: Ashgate.

18. Lyddon, 'The changing pattern of UK strikes'.

19. P. Edwards (ed.) (2003) *Industrial Relations: Theory and Practice (Industrial Relations in Context)*, 2nd edn, Oxford: Wiley-Blackwell. The first edition had contained a discrete chapter on strikes, but this second edition had only a short section within a chapter on trade unions.

20. T. Colling and M. Terry (eds) (2010) *Industrial Relations: Theory and Practice*, 3rd edn, Oxford: Wiley-Blackwell.

21. J. Godard (2017) *Industrial Relations, Economy and Society*, 5th edn, Toronto: Captus Press, p. 300.

22. P. Blyton, N. Bacon, J. Fiorito and E. Heery (eds) (2008) *The Sage Handbook of Industrial Relations*, Los Angeles, CA: Sage.

23. M. Shalev (1992) 'The resurgence of labour quiescence', in M. Regini (ed.), *The Future of Labour Movements*, London: Sage, pp. 102–32.

24. Kelly, 'Conflict', p. 721.

25. Lyddon, 'The changing pattern of UK strikes', p. 735 provides a further telling example of the neglect of the strike in mainstream academia and its ideological reframing by commentators. The first three Workplace Industrial Relations Surveys contained individual chapters on strikes but the fourth contained only two pages. In Lyddon's critique of N. Millward, A. Bryson and J. Forth (2000), *All Change at Work?*, London: Routledge, on their conclusion to the summaries of these surveys, he quotes the latter's assertion that 'unions

with strong negotiating power should never have to resort to industrial action' (ibid., p. 177). This comment, as Lyddon comments, 'abandons more than a century of industrial relations thinking'.

26. R. Darlington (2006) 'The agitator "theory" of strikes re-evaluated strikes re-evaluated', *Labor History*, 47(4), pp. 485–509.

27. R. Hyman (1997) *Strikes*, 2nd edn, Glasgow: Fontana Collins; R. Hyman (1989) *The Political Economy of Industrial Relations: Theory and Practice in a Cold Climate*, London: Macmillan.

28. See S. Williams and D. Adam-Smith (2000) *Contemporary Employment Relations: A Critical Introduction*, 2nd edn, Oxford: Oxford University Press for a succinct summary.

29. Of course, the validity of such observations does not gainsay the mobilisations of workers in wildcat strikes. See A. Gouldner (1954) *Wildcat Strike: A Study in Worker–Management Relationships*, New York: Harper on strike action for union recognition in hitherto unorganised workplaces.

30. Godard, *Industrial Relations, Economy and Society*.

31. Certification Officer of Trade Unions and Employers' Associations, cited in P. Blyton and P. Turnbull (2004) *The Dynamics of Employee Relations*, 3rd edn, Basingstoke: Palgrave, p. 112.

32. J. Achur (2010) *Trade Union Membership 2010*, London: Department for Business Innovation and Skills, A National Statistics Publication.

33. By 2016, overall union density had fallen to 23.5 per cent, with female density at 25.9 per cent. In the private sector, union density for men was now 14.8 per cent compared with 11.6 per cent for women. Department of Business, Innovation and Skills (2017) *Trade Union Membership: Statistical Bulletin*, London: Department for Business, Energy and Industrial Strategy.

34. P. Marginson (2015) 'The changing nature of collective employment relations', *Employee Relations*, 37(6), pp. 645–57.

35. B. Van Wanrooy, H. Bewley, A. Bryson, J. Forth, S. Freeth, L. Stokes and S. Wood (2013) *Employment Relations in the Shadow of the Recession: Findings from the 2011 Workplace Employment Relations Study*, London: Macmillan International Higher Education, p. 80.

36. W. Brown, A. Bryson and J. Forth (2008) *Competition and the Retreat from Collective Bargaining*, Discussion Paper no. 318, London: National Institute of Economic and Social Research.

37. Department of Business, Innovation and Skills (2013) *Trade Union Membership 2012 Statistical Bulletin*, London: Department of Business, Innovation and Skills.

38. Van Wanrooy et al., *Employment Relations in the Shadow of the Recession*.

39. M. Simms and A. Charlwood (2010) 'Trade unions: power and influence in a changed context', in T. Colling and M. Terry (eds), *Industrial Relations: Theory and Practice*, 3rd edn, Chichester: Wiley, pp. 125–48.

40. K. Ewing and J. Hendy (2013) *Reconstruction After the Crisis: A Manifesto for Collective Bargaining*, London: Institute of Employment Rights.

41. S. Williams (2014) *Introducing Employment Relations: A Critical Approach*, 4th edn, Oxford: Oxford University Press.

42. Godard, *Industrial Relations, Economy and Society*.

43. S. Groves and V. Merritt (2018) *A Victory to Remember: The 1976 Equal Pay Trico Strike at Folberth, Brentford*, London: Lawrence and Wishart.

44. R. Pearson, A. Sundari and L. McDowell (2010) 'Striking issues: from labour process to industrial dispute at Grunwick and Gate Gourmet', *Industrial Relations Journal*, 41(5), pp. 408–28.

45. S. Virdee (2014) *Racism, Class and the Racialized Outsider*, Basingstoke: Palgrave Macmillan.

46. C. Thornley and C. Thornqvist (2009) 'Where's the enemy? A comparison of the local government workers' strike of July 2002 in the UK and the municipal workers' strike of spring 2003 in Sweden', paper presented to BJIR Conference in honour of Richard Hyman, London, 28–9 May.

47. A. Cumbers, D. Featherstone, D. MacKinnon, A. Ince and K. Strauss (2015) 'Intervening in globalisation: the spatial possibilities and institutional barriers to labour's collective agency', *Journal of Economic Geography*, 16(1), pp. 93–108.

48. A. Sundari and R. Pearson (2018) *Striking Women*, Chadwell Heath: Lawrence and Wishart.

49. Bilaterals have taken two forms, the more liberal 'Bermuda' agreements, which permit inter-airline pooling and revenue sharing, and more restrictive 'predetermination' agreements.

50. K. Button, K. Haynes and R. Stough (1998) *Flying into the Future: Air Transport Policy in the European Union*, Cheltenham: Edward Elgar.

51. M. Peteraf and R. Reed (2007) 'Managerial discretion and internal alignment under regulatory constraints and change', *Strategic Management Journal*, 28(11), pp. 1089–1112.

52. R. Doganis (2006) *The Airline Business*, 2nd edn, London: Routledge, p. 9.

53. S. Calder (2003) *No Frills: The Truth Behind the Low-Cost Revolution in the Skies*, London: Virgin.

54. K. Lange, M. Geppert, A. Saka-Helmhout and F. Becker-Ritterspach (2015) 'Changing business models and employee representation in the airline industry: a comparison of British Airways and Deutsche Lufthansa', *British Journal of Management*, 26(3), pp. 388–407. It is beyond the scope of the book to discuss fully the significance of such findings, except to indicate the importance of the national institutional regulatory regimes in which the respective companies are embedded and specifically the influence of the mechanisms of employee representation.

55. Qantas is a member of British Airways' Oneworld alliance.

56. T. Sarina and R.D. Lansbury (2013) 'Flying high and low? Strategic choice and employment relations in Qantas and Jetstar', *Asia Pacific Journal of Human Resources*, 51(4), pp. 437–53.

57. Civil Aviation Authority (2006) *No Frills Carriers: Revolution or Evolution*, London: CAA.

58. S. Barrett (2006) *Deregulation and the Airline Business in Europe*, London: Routledge.

59. G. Harvey (2007) *Management in the Airline Industry*, London: Routledge, pp. 13–14.

60. Doganis, *The Airline Business*; P. Turnbull, P. Blyton and G. Harvey (2004) 'Cleared for take-off? Management-labour partnership in the European civil aviation industry', *European Journal of Industrial Relations*, 18(3), pp. 287–307.

61. Doganis, *The Airline Business*, pp. 112.

62. Ibid., pp. 117. Bamber et al., *Up in the Air*, p. 58.

63. P. Taylor and S. Moore (2015) 'Cabin crew collectivism: labour process and the roots of mobilisation in the British Airways dispute 2009–11', *Work, Employment and Society*, 29(1), pp. 79–98.

64. International Labour Organisation (2001) Think Tank on the Impact of the 11 September Events on Civil Aviation, Geneva, 29–30 October.

65. Bamber et al., *Up in the Air*.

66. C. Curley and T. Royle (2013) 'The degradation of work and the end of the skilled emotion worker at Aer Lingus: is it all trolley dollies now?', *Work, Employment and Society*, 27(1), pp. 105–21.

67. Instone, Handley Page, Daimler Airways and British Air Marine Navigation Company.

68. 'The Edwards Report – Principal Recommendations' (1969) *Flight International*, 745, 8 May.

69. J. McGurk (2000) 'The deregulation of airline employment in the USA and Europe: an emerging comparison', PhD thesis, Glasgow: University of Glasgow.

70. Harvey, *A Brief History of Neo-liberalism*.

71. D. Campbell-Smith (1986) *Struggle for Take-Off: The British Airways Story*, London: Coronet.

72. Ibid., p. 24.

73. M. Gregory (2000) *Dirty Tricks – The Inside Story of British Airways' Secret War Against Richard Branson's Virgin Atlantic*, London: Little Brown and Company.

74. D. Parker (2009) *The Official History of Privatisation, Volume 1, The Formative Years (1970–1987)*, London: Routledge.

75. D.J. Thaxter (2011) *The History of British Caledonian Airways, 1928–1988*, David J. Thaxter.

76. Latterly, during the course of the 2009–11 dispute, British Airways took over what was then the largest domestic full-service carrier, British Midland.

77. Gregory, *Dirty Tricks*.

78. Ibid., p. 134.

79. In the 1970s David Burnside had been press officer of the Vanguard Progressive Unionist Party, a breakaway from the Ulster Unionist Party, which had close connections with several loyalist paramilitary groups. Indeed, Vanguard had its own paramilitary organisation; see A. Guelke and

J. Smythe (2000) 'The Ballot bomb: terrorism and the electoral process in Northern Ireland', in L. Weiberg (ed.), *Political Parties and Terrorist Groups*, London: Cass, pp. 103–24. Burnside was recruited by Lord King in 1984 to head British Airways public relations.

80. It is not just the confluence of political and company/business interest in a general sense that is significant. What is striking is the extent to which this mutual interest is embodied in key personnel. Lord King was secretary of state for employment, 1983–5. Sir Robert Ayling, later British Airways Group MD and CEO, was appointed company secretary in 1987 having been an under-secretary at the Department of Trade and was the British government's special adviser in the battle against Laker's anti-trust suite.

81. Gregory, *Dirty Tricks*, p. 230ff.

82. Ibid., p. 358.

83. Ibid.

84. David Hyde, then Director of Safety, Security and the Environment, retired his full-time position in 2002 after 34 years employed with British Airways, but continued thereafter in a part-time consulting capacity.

85. K. Ewing (2011) *Fighting Back: Resisting Union Busting and Strike-Breaking in the British Airways Dispute*, London: Institute of Employment Rights, pp. 33–4.

86. Bamber et al., *Up in the Air*.

87. McGurk, 'The deregulation of airline employment in the USA and Europe', p. 54.

88. Doganis, *The Airline Business*, p. 214.

89. The GO venture was short-lived.

90. McGurk, 'The deregulation of airline employment in the USA and Europe', p. 164.

91. Emotional labour was a concept first developed by the sociologist Arlie Hochschild (1983) in her influential book *The Managed Heart: Commercialisation of Human Feeling*, Oakland, CA: University of California Press. Her focus was on female flight attendants and made important analytical distinctions between surface and deep acting in the ways that FA's engaged with customers. It stimulated and continues to stimulate debates in academic literature on gendered work and employment; see e.g. S. Bolton and C. Boyd (2003) 'Trolley-dolley or skilled emotion manager? Moving on from Hochschild's Managed Heart', *Work, Employment and Society*, 23(3), pp. 548–60. Much work on women's work in call centres has evaluated its applicability. At British Airways' Dr Nick Georgiades, director of human resources, explicitly called on customer facing staff, particularly cabin crew, to engage in what we call 'emotional labour'; cited in A. Corke (1986) *British Airways: The Path to Profitability*, London: Pinter.

92. H. Hopfl, S. Smith and S. Spencer (1992) 'Values and valuations: the conflicts between cultural change and job cuts', *Personnel Review*, 21(2), pp. 24–38.

93. A. Corke (1986) *British Airways: the Path to Profitability*, London: Pinter; Campbell-Smith, *Struggle for Take-Off*, p. 135.

94. Ibid.
95. See Blyton and Turnbull, *The Dynamics of Employee Relations*.
96. McGurk, 'The deregulation of airline employment in the USA and Europe', p. 57.
97. I. Grugulis and A. Wilkinson (2002) 'Managing culture at British Airways', *Long Range Planning*, 35(2), pp. 179–94.
98. Blyton and Turnbull, *The Dynamics of Employee Relations*, p.74.
99. T. Colling (1995) 'Experiencing turbulence: competition, strategic choice and the management of human resources in British Airways', *Human Resource Management Journal*, 5(5), pp. 18–32.
100. A general observation of industrial relations at British Airways is that crisis conditions have provided opportunities to implement restructuring measures that otherwise might have been unacceptable to unions. Examples include the proposed sell-off of the Highland Division to Logan Air in 1988, the threat to British Airways Regional from Mersk in 1991 and the chaos at Gatwick following the bankruptcy of Dan Air in 1993. On the latter, British Airways took advantage to develop a low-cost network out of Gatwick that would stand as a rival to and would expose operations at Heathrow. This fault line has had legacy effects up to and including the 2009–11 dispute, for union density and activism were significantly lower at Gatwick. In all these cases of adversity, unions (including BASSA) believed they have little choice other than to submit to restructuring.
101. Hopfl et al., 'Values and valuations'.
102. British Airways transcript, Monday 20 May 2002 at 09:00 (UK time), available at http://media.corporate-ir.net/media_files/irol/24/240949/BAPres/Q40102transcript.pdf.
103. Bamber et al., *Up in the Air*, p. 36.
104. BBC (2010) 'BA strike: The three men trying to find a solution', 22 March, http://news.bbc.co.uk/1/hi/business/8579778.stm (accessed 26 February 2018).
105. McGurk, 'The deregulation of airline employment in the USA and Europe', p. 50.
106. A.J.N. Blain (1972) *Pilots and Management: Industrial Relations in the UK Airlines*, London: George Allen and Unwin.
107. J.T. Dunlop (1958) *Industrial Relations Systems*, Carbondale, IL: Southern Illinois University Press.
108. R. Dubin (1954) 'Constructive aspects of industrial conflict', in A. Kornhauser, R. Dubin and N. Ross (eds), *Industrial Conflict*, New York: McGraw Hill, pp. 37–47.
109. McGurk, 'The deregulation of airline employment in the USA and Europe', p. 90.
110. Ibid., pp. 106–7.
111. This section draws on an unpublished manuscript by Duncan Holley, elected in 2000 as BASSA Branch Secretary and remaining in that role during the

course of 2009–11, although dismissed by British Airways in 2010. Hereafter referred to as 'Holley manuscript'.

112. A. Callinicos and M. Simons (1985) *The Great Strike: Miners' Strike of 1984–5 and the Lessons*, London: Bookmarks.

113. Holley manuscript.

114. BASSA (2012) *Membership Statistics*, London: BASSA/Unite the Union.

115. British Airways (1997) *British Airways: Flying into the Future: Restructuring Policies for Cabin Crew*, London: British Airways.

116. The figures were not publicly disclosed.

117. Harvey, *Management in the Airline Industry*, pp. 8–9.

118. Blyton and Turnbull, *The Dynamics of Employee Relations*, p. 74.

119. See McGurk, 'The deregulation of airline employment in the USA and Europe', p. 174.

120. Civil Aviation Authority (2004) *Effect of Liberalisation on Aviation Employment*, CAP749, London: CAA.

121. Holley manuscript.

122. Bamber et al., *Up in the Air*, p. 36.

123. Blyton and Turnbull, *The Dynamics of Employee Relations*.

124. Holley manuscript, p. 13.

125. Ibid., p. 12.

126. After the TGWU's merger with Amicus, BASSA became the biggest branch in Unite the Union.

127. When negotiations require the participation and presence of the BASSA officers, the collective agreement states that they are rostered off, a practice that was, as we have seen, a source of conflict with BASSA as British Airways suspended this right.

128. Manifest tensions existed between BASSA and the Unite the Union leadership in the early stages of the 2009–11.

129. See www.bassa.co.uk.

130. Holley manuscript.

131. B. Clement, *The Independent*, 26 January 2007: 'The T&G is in a difficult position. Cabin crew are threatening to set up a rebel organisation if their leaders "cave in", as they see it. The T&G is also understood to have been threatened with legal action by British Airways managers if the strikes go ahead. The airline has argued that the walkouts by T&G baggage handlers in support of Gate Gourmet workers sacked in 2005 were unlawful. If the industrial action goes ahead, management will begin litigation over the Gate Gourmet dispute, it is said.'

132. It should be noted that British Airways registered a record operating profit of £887 million in 2007–8. British Airways (2008) *British Airways Annual Report and Accounts, 2007–8*, London: British Airways.

133. The CC89 project, always questionable, was now unsustainable. It was no longer possible for CC89 to present a case that its moderate, management friendly, company interest brand of unionism offered greater protection for cabin crew than did BASSA. British Airways' offensive on the crew's

conditions of work and employment over almost two decades undercut the material conditions for such an appeal, especially given the supine nature of CC89 leadership and the sustained campaign by BASSA to win over its members.

134. Ewing, *Fighting Back*; Unite the Union (2008) *Emergency Announcement*, 20 June, London: Unite the Union.

135. British Airways (2008) *Project Columbus Factsheet*, London: British Airways, 2008.

136. Ibid.

137. An important point is the fact that, as previously indicated, a two-tier cabin crew workforce already existed as an outcome of the 1997 dispute so this would mean a third-tier on vastly inferior terms and conditions. The divisive and unpalatable experience of the two-tiered workforce was a deep well-spring of discontent that helps explain the depth and extent of cabin crew response in the 2009–11 dispute.

138. British Airways (2008) *2007–08 Annual Report and Accounts*, London: British Airways, available at www.britishairways.com/cms/global/microsites/ba_reports/index.html.

139. Within as little as £7,000.

140. Airline Personnel Costs (UK and Overseas) 2008 accessed on 20 February 2017 at www.caa.co.uk/docs/80/airline_data/2008annual/Table_1_14_Airline_Personnel_Cost_UK_and_Overseas_2008.pdf (unfortunately this URL is no longer live and no alternative URL for the same source could be located when this book went to press).

141. Ewing, *Fighting Back*.

142. In the subsequent hearing on the issue, delayed to in February 2010, the court supported the company's right to reduce the crew complement, as the terms of the collective agreement were not legally enforceable. An appeal against this decision was rejected by the High Court in November 2010.

143. Holley manuscript.

144. J. Prassl (2011) 'To strike to serve? Industrial action at British Airways', *Industrial Law Journal*, 40(1), pp. 82–91.

145. Ewing, *Fighting Back*, pp. 25–6.

146. Ibid.

147. *British Airways v. Unite the Union* [2009] EWHC 3541 (QB), [2010] IRLR 423, paras 80–84 – judgement quoted in Ewing, *Fighting Back*.

148. G. Gall (2017) 'Injunctions as a legal weapon in collective industrial disputes', *British Journal of Industrial Relations*, 55(1), pp. 187–214; Dukes, 'The right to strike under UK law: something more than a slogan'; B. Simpson (2013) 'The labour injunction and industrial action ballots', *Industrial Law Journal*, 42(1), pp. 54–60.

149. 'Reprieve for British Airways passengers as court rules strike action invalid', *Financial Times*, 17 December 2009, p. 18.

150. *British Airways v. Unite the Union* [2009].

151. Dukes, 'The right to strike under UK law: something more than a slogan'.

152. Ewing, *Fighting Back* provides an excellent account of the legal proceedings and implications.
153. It is remarkable, although perhaps unsurprising that given the size of the majority of these ballot results, British Airways claimed that BASSA 'failed to represent the views of the majority of cabin crew'. British Airways (2010) *British Airways Annual Report and Accounts, 2009–10*, London: British Airways.
154. The term 'counter-mobilisation' comes from Kelly, *Rethinking Industrial Relations*. The utility of the term is that it conveniently designates those diverse actions taken by an employer in response to and with the aim of undermining or preventing the mobilisation of the union and its members.
155. Ewing, *Fighting Back*, p. 20.
156. *The Guardian*, 27 March 2010.
157. *The Guardian*, 2–3 April 2010.
158. *The Guardian*, 27 March 2010.
159. Ewing, *Fighting Back*, pp. 22–3.
160. BBC (2011) 'Q&A: What's the BA dispute about?', 12 May, www.bbc.co.uk/news/business-11868081, cited in Ewing, *Fighing Back*, p. 32.
161. M. Upchurch (2010) *Creating a Sustainable Work Environment in British Airways*, London: Middlesex Business School, p.5.
162. Holley manuscript.
163. *The Independent*, 27 February 2015. Asset Protection was a department responsible for matters pertaining to aircraft security, including theft, fraud and activities where employees might have broken British Airways' disciplinary code. AP's ranks included former members of Metropolitan and Heathrow Police Forces, one of whom is mentioned in Graeme McLagen's (2003) *Bent Coppers: The Inside Story of Scotland Yard's Battle Against Police Corruption*, London: Orion.
164. *The Times*, 17 November 2009. Also see Ewing, *Fighting Back*, p. 33.
165. M. Upchurch and R. Grassman (2016) 'Striking with social media: the contested (online) terrain of workplace conflict', *Organization*, 23(5), pp. 639–56; Taylor and Moore, 'Cabin crew collectivism'.
166. Holley manuscript.
167. BASSA (2010) 'Leaked reports and photographs, taken with long range telephoto lenses, signed by asset-protection staff', *BASSA Newsletter*, p. 5, quoted in Ewing, *Fighting Back*, p. 33.
168. *The Independent*, 27 February 2015.
169. J. Logan (2006) 'The union avoidance industry in the United States', *British Journal of Industrial Relations*, 44(4), pp. 657–75.
170. S. Moore (2004) 'Union mobilisation and employer counter-mobilisation in the statutory recognition process', in J. Kelly and P. Willman (eds), *Union Organisation and Activity*, London: Routledge.
171. *Birmingham Mail*, 14 December 2006.
172. BASSA (2011) 'Leiden for beginners', *BASSA Newsletter*, March.

173. Employment tribunal cases subsequent to the dispute confirmed the existence of 'the Leiden Room' at British Airways headquarters, in which dispute-related 'disciplinary cases' were investigated and administered outside established disciplinary procedure, and which the tribunal deemed to have been illegitimate.

174. R. Martin (1992) *Bargaining Power*, Oxford: Clarendon Press.

175. *The Guardian*, 25 March 2010.

176. See www.mypccc.co.uk/home (accessed 12 February 2019).

177. BBC (2010) 'Gordon Brown says BA strike deplorable and unjustified', 15 March, http://news.bbc.co.uk/1/hi/8567409.stm (accessed 26 February 2018).

178. BBC (2002) 'Blair takes on public service "wreckers"', 3 February, http://news.bbc.co.uk/1/hi/uk_politics/1798234.stm (accessed 26 February 2018).

179. S. Moore, T. Wright and P. Taylor (2018) *Fighting Fire: A History of the Fire Brigades Union*, London: New Internationalist.

180. Campbell, A. (2013) *The Burden of Power: Countdown to Iraq; The Alistair Campbell Diaries, vol. 4*, London: Arrow.

181. *Daily Mail*, 17 December 2009.

182. *Daily Mail*, 17 December 2009; *Daily Mail*, 17 May 2010.

183. Ewing, *Fighting Back*, pp. 33–4.

184. Limited exceptions were *Guardian* reports by transport correspondent Dan Milmo, and *The Independent*.

185. P. Taylor et al. (2010) 'British Airways strike letter: "Macho Walsh wants to break the union"', *The Guardian*, 25 March, www.theguardian.com/business/2010/mar/25/ba-strike-letter-academics-walsh (accessed 26 February 2018).

186. M. Upchurch (2013) 'The internet, social media and the workplace', *International Socialism Journal*, 14(1), pp. 119–38.

187. A.-M. Greene, J. Hogan and M. Grieco (2003) 'E-collectivism and distributed discourse; new opportunities for trade union democracy', *Industrial Relations Journal*, 34(2), pp. 282–89; J. Hogan, P. Nolan and M. Grieco (2010) 'Unions, technologies of coordination, and the changing contours of globally distributed power', *Labor History*, 51(1), pp. 29–40; S. Little and M. Grieco (2010) 'Big Pharma, social movements, international labor, and the Internet: critical perspectives on coordination', *Labor History*, 51(1), pp. 71–86.

188. Upchurch, 'The internet, social media and the workplace'.

189. BASSA's revised demands were: the immediate restoration of staff travel concessions; binding arbitration through ACAS of all disciplinary cases related to the dispute; restoration of deducted pay to crew members who had been off sick on strike days; full discussion of the trade union facilities agreement with the removal of all the threats made by the company against it; non-acceptance of the introduction of the Mixed Fleet, as the new fleet was now known, without BASSA's agreement.

190. British Airways, 'Letter to cabin crew', December 2010, reproduced as Appendix 2 in Ewing, *Fighting Back*.

191. Ewing, *Fighting Back*, p. 38.

192. Ibid.
193. Unite the Union, 'Statement on British Airways ballot', 8 February 2011, cited in Ewing, *Fighting Back*, p. 38.
194. ACAS stands for the Advisory, Conciliation and Arbitration Service. It is funded largely by the Department of Business, Innovation and Skills (BIS), but is a non-governmental body whose independent council is responsible for strategic direction.
195. Ewing, *Fighting Back*.
196. 'British Airways cabin crew in landslide vote to peace deal', *Financial Times*, 22 June 2011, p. 2.

3. Project Columbus

1. Taylor and Moore have provided a detailed analysis of the roots of cabin crew collectivism: P. Taylor and S. Moore (2015) 'Cabin crew collectivism: labour process and the roots of mobilisation in the British Airways dispute 2009–11', *Work, Employment and Society*, 29(1), pp. 79–98.
2. In academic language, the CEO is a 'strategic actor', albeit that his actions are constrained by the influence of intrinsic and extrinsic factors and by other actors.
3. A. Hochschild (1983) *The Managed Heart: Commercialisation of Human Feeling*, Oakland, CA: University of California Press.
4. See P. Taylor, I. Cunningham, K. Newsome and D. Scholarios (2010) '"Too scared to go sick": reformulating the research agenda on sickness absence', *Industrial Relations Journal*, 41(4), pp. 270–88, for a critique of the increasingly harsh sickness absence management policies that were now becoming the norm across diverse sectors of the economy in conditions of austerity and wholesale cost cutting.
5. K. Ewing (2011) *Fighting Back: Resisting Union Busting and Strike-Breaking in the British Airways Dispute*, London: Institute of Employment Rights.

4. Balloting, the right to strike and British Airways counter-mobilisation

1. References to these figures in the testimonies tend to vary slightly.
2. K. Ewing (2011) *Fighting Back: Resisting Union Busting and Strike-Breaking in the British Airways Dispute*, London: Institute of Employment Rights.
3. See R. Dukes (2010) 'The right to strike under UK law: not much more than a slogan? *Metrobus v. Unite the Union*', *Industrial Law Journal*, 39(1), pp. 82–91. An injunction was upheld on the grounds that Unite had not provided the 'explanation' required by TULRCA 1992 as to how it had arrived at the figures it provided for the numbers, categories and workplaces of its members set out in its notices of ballot and of industrial action.
4. As noted, the mandate was higher at 93 per cent.
5. This comment recalls Roderick Martin's observation regarding power being ghost at the negotiating table the way that BASSA regarded its ability

to exercise power: R. Martin (1992) *Bargaining Power*, Oxford: Clarendon Press.

6. J. Logan (2006) 'The union avoidance industry in the United States', *British Journal of Industrial Relations*, 44(4), pp. 657–75.

7. Where crew report in before flights.

8. *K. Cook v. British Airways plc.* (2011) employment tribunal, case no. 3304081/10.

9. Ibid. The ET report quotes a number of examples of humour from *Scabbin Crew News*, including that pilots are described as in receipt of 'scab pay of £160 per hour' (p. 120). The suggestion is made that 'Some pilots can't see an a**e without feeling the urge to shove their heads up it' (p. 121). There is also the suggestion that British Airways will pay for the use of prostitutes by volunteering pilots (p. 121).

10. Ibid.

11. *The Independent*, 27 February 2015.

6. Outcomes: worlds turned upside down

1. K. Ewing (2011) *Fighting Back: Resisting Union Busting and Strike-Breaking in the British Airways Dispute*, London: Institute of Employment Rights.

2. The principal distinction in terms of socialist politics is essentially that between reform and revolution, between a belief that societal change can be brought about through Parliament and the existing institutions of society and a critical perspective that emphasises thoroughgoing, bottom-up, worker-led transformation of society.

3. The most comprehensive, recent treatment of militancy is G. Gall (2003) *The Meaning of Militancy? Postal Workers and Industrial Relations*, Aldershot: Ashgate. Gall refers to the loose way in which the concept has been used. Reviewing the relevant literature, he concludes that the terms militant and militant action have been directly or implicitly equated with a high propensity to take strike action. There are some notable exceptions. Two are V.L. Allen (1966) *Militancy of British Miners*, Shipley: Moor Press; and J. Kelly (1996) 'Union militancy and social partnership', in P. Ackers, C. Smith and P. Smith (eds), *The New Workplace and Trade Unions*, London: Routledge. If academic definitions of militancy are imprecise, then the popular, mainstream media uses of the term are wholly negative, conjuring up images of aggressive, intimidating worker behaviour in pursuit of unrealistic and unattainable demands.

4. P. Anderson (1977) 'The limits and possibilities of trade union action', in T. Clarke and L. Clements (eds), *Trade Unions under Capitalism*, Glasgow: Fontana; R. Hyman (1971) *Marxism and the Sociology of Trade Unions*, London: Pluto Press.

5. For an accessible account see, for example, T. Eagleton (1997) *Marx*, London: Routledge.

6. B. Kars (1958) *Diary of a Strike*, Urbana, IL: University of Illinois Press.
7. B. Skeggs (1997) *Formations of Class and Gender*, London: Sage.

7. Conclusion

1. K. Ewing (2011) *Fighting Back: Resisting Union Busting and Strike-Breaking in the British Airways Dispute*, London: Institute of Employment Rights, p. 43.
2. A. Callinicos and M. Simons (1985) *The Great Strike: Miners' Strike of 1984–5 and the Lessons*, London: Bookmarks; S. Milne (2014) *The Enemy Within: The Secret War Against the Miners*, 4th edn, London: Verso.
3. The hard evidence that supports this contention is the so-called Ridley Report (or Plan) that was leaked to the *Economist* in May 1978. A facsimile of *The Final Report of the Nationalised Industries Policy Group*, the report's full title, can be found in the archive of the Margaret Thatcher Foundation, www.margaretthatcher.org/archive/displaydocument.asp?docid=110795 (accessed 12 February 2019).
4. It has been estimated that 11,291 people were arrested, 8,239 charged with breach of the peace and at least 9,000 miners were dismissed while picketing even though no charges were brought. S. Van der Velden, H. Dribbusch, D. Lyddon and K. Vandale (2001) *Strikes around the World: Case Studies of 15 Countries*, Amsterdam; Aksant Academic Publishers.
5. Milne, *The Enemy Within*; S. Rimmington (2001) *Open Secret: The Autobiography of the Former Director General of MI5*, London: Hutchinson.
6. One other contrast is in legal context. The miners' strike of 1984–5 followed the initial anti-union legislation of the Conservative government, and it was declared illegal in September 1984. However, it preceded the legislation on balloting (1993) with which unions have been legally bound to comply. By 2009, unions faced far greater restrictions in instituting 'lawful' industrial action.
7. Milne, *The Enemy Within*, p. ix.
8. J. Winterton and R. Winterton (1993) *Coal, Crisis and Conflict: 1984–5 Miners' Strike in Yorkshire*, Manchester: Manchester University Press.
9. Ewing, *Fighting Back*, p. 43.
10. *The Independent*, 30 August 2017.
11. A second letter from academics was published in *The Guardian* on 13 March 2017.
12. BBC (2017) 'BA owner IAG's profits hit by weak pound', 24 February, www.bbc.co.uk/news/business-39074813.
13. J. Salmon (2018) 'Bumper pay rises for British Airways bosses after company shrinks legroom and scraps perks for passengers', *Daily Mail*, 2 March, www.dailymail.co.uk/news/article-5452505/Bumper-pay-rises-British-Airways-bosses.html.
14. Qatar Airways owns one-fifth of British Airways' parent company IAG.

15. See www.itfaviation.org/british-airways-mixed-fleet-cabin-crew-over whelmingly-back-pay-deal-and-end-long-running-dispute-unitetheunion-org.
16. Press Association (2016) 'Thomas Cook cabin crew vote to strike', *The Guardian*, 25 May, www.theguardian.com/business/2016/may/25/thomas-cook-cabin-crew-vote-to-strike (accessed 4 March 2019).
17. DW (2017) 'Lufthansa strikes major labor deal with pilots', 11 October, www.dw.com/en/lufthansa-strikes-major-labor-deal-with-pilots/a-40901286 (accessed 12 February 2019).
18. DW (2017) 'Ryanair cancels thousands of flights due to pilot shortage', 27 September, www.dw.com/en/ryanair-cancels-thousands-of-flights-due-to-pilot-shortage/a-40709859 (accessed 12 February 2019).
19. BBC (2017) 'Ryanair's German pilots to strike on Friday', 21 December, www.bbc.co.uk/news/business-42447475 (accessed 12 February 2019).
20. DutchNews (2018) 'Strikes planned at both KLM and Air France next week: FD', 5 January, www.dutchnews.nl/news/archives/2018/01/strikes-planned-at-both-klm-and-air-france-next-week-fd (accessed 12 February 2019).
21. S. Calder (2018) 'Air France strikes: when are they and how will they impact UK travellers?', *The Independent*, 14 April, www.independent.co.uk/travel/news-and-advice/air-france-strikes-explained-pilots-cabin-crew-ground-staff-qa-a8304901.html (accessed 12 February 2019).
22. S. Oxenbridge, J. Wallace, L. White, S. Tiernan and L. Lansbury (2010) 'A comparative analysis of restructuring employment relationships in Qantas and Aer Lingus: different routes, similar destinations', *The International Journal of Human Resource Management*, 21(2), p. 193.
23. Women Against Pit Closures and Lesbian and Gay and Black community support groups.

Afterword

1. [2010] EWCA Civ 1225; [2011] IRLR 32; [2011] ICR 125; discussed in R. Russell, '*Malone and others v. British Airways plc*: protection of managerial prerogative?' [2011] *ILJ* 40(2), 207–13; and F. Reynold and J. Hendy, 'Reserving the right to change terms and conditions: how far can the employer go?' [2012] *ILJ* 41(1), 79–92.
2. Except in the circumstances of s.179 Trade Union and Labour Relations (Consolidation) Act 1992.
3. *British Airways Plc v. Unite the Union* [2009] EWHC 3541 (QB); [2010] IRLR 423; discussed in N. Countouris and M. Freedland, 'Injunctions, Cyanamid, and the corrosion of the right to strike in the UK', [2010] *ELLJ* 1(4), 489–507; J Prassl. 'To strike, to serve? Industrial action at British Airways. *British Airways plc v. Unite the Union (Nos 1 and 2)*', [2011] *ILJ* 40(1), 82–91.
4. [2010] EWCA Civ 669; [2010] ICR 1316; IRLR 809; discussed in J. Prassl, 'Industrial action at British Airways: a case study', (2011) CIL, 11(2), 117–38;

J. Prassl. 'To strike, to serve? Industrial action at British Airways. *British Airways plc v. Unite the Union (Nos 1 and 2)*', [2011] *ILJ* 40(1), 82–91.

5. [62].
6. *Roffey and ors v. United Kingdom* (1278/11) [2013] 5 WLUK 535; (2013) 57 E.H.R.R. SE14, discussed in K.D. Ewing and J. Hendy, 'Article 11(3) of the European Convention on Human Rights' [2017] *EHRLR* 4, 356–75.
7. *McCallum v. British Airways* unrep. Proceedings were also commenced by other cabin crew in Reading employment tribunal on the ground that the sanctions discriminated against overseas members. That case was dismissed: *Russo v. British Airways* unrep. 25 July 2012.
8. E.g. *Danilenkov v. Russia* (2014) 58 *EHRR* 19.
9. The Court described the latter date as 'the date of the interference complained of' and 'the date on which the act complained of occurred' (at [43] and [36]).
10. E.g. *Dudgeon v. United Kingdom* (1982) 4 *EHRR* 149.
11. The suggestion that the Application was made out of time was not raised by the UK government in its lengthy written Observations; nor by the Court in its Statement of Facts which identified five questions for the parties to answer. Nor indeed was the point raised in the Government's Response. All this was effectively acknowledged by the Court at [33].
12. K.D. Ewing and J. Hendy, 'Article 11(3) of the European Convention on Human Rights' [2017] *EHRLR* 4, 356–75.

Bibliography

Achur, J. (2010) *Trade Union Membership 2010*. London: Department for Business Innovation and Skills, A National Statistics Publication.

Allen, V.L. (1966) *Militancy of British Miners*. Shipley: Moor Press.

Anderson, P. (1977) 'The limits and possibilities of trade union action'. In T. Clarke and L. Clements (eds), *Trade Unions under Capitalism*. Glasgow: Fontana.

Bach, S. (2016) 'De-privileging the public sector workforce: austerity, fragmentation and service withdrawal in Britain'. *The Economic and Labour Relations Review*, 27(1), pp. 11–28.

Bamber, G.J., Gittell, J.H., Kochan, T.A. and von Nordenflycht, A. (2009) *Up in the Air: How Airlines Can Improve Performance by Engaging Their Employees*. Ithaca, NY: ILR Press.

Barrett, S. (2006) *Deregulation and the Airline Business in Europe*. London: Routledge.

Bassett, P. (1986) *Strike Free – New Industrial Relations in Britain*. London: Macmillan.

Batstone, E., Boraston, I. and Frenkel, S. (1978) *The Social Organisation of Strikes*. Oxford: Blackwell.

Benford, R.D. and Snow, D.A. (2000) 'Reframing processes and social movements: an overview and assessment'. *Annual Review of Sociology*, 26, pp. 611–39.

Beynon, H. (1985) (ed.) *Digging Deeper: Issues in the Miners' Strike*. London: Verso.

Blain, A.J.N. (1972) *Pilots and Management: Industrial Relations in the UK Airlines*. London: George Allen and Unwin.

Blyton, P., Bacon, N., Fiorito, J. and Heery, E. (eds) (2008) *The Sage Handbook of Industrial Relations*. Los Angeles: Sage.

Blyton, P. and Turnbull, P. (2004) *The Dynamics of Employee Relations*. 3rd edn. Basingstoke: Palgrave.

Bolton, S. and Boyd, C. (2003) 'Trolley-dolley or skilled emotion manager? Moving on from Hochschild's *Managed Heart*'. *Work, Employment and Society*, 23(3), pp. 548–60.

Bourdieu, P. (1999) *Acts of Resistance: Against the New Myths of Our Time*. London: Polity Press.

Bourdieu, P. (1999) *The Weight of the World*. London: Polity Press.

British Airways (1997) *British Airways: Flying into the Future: Restructuring Policies for Cabin Crew*. London: British Airways.

British Airways (2008) *British Airways Annual Report and Accounts, 2007–8*. London: British Airways.

Brook, P. and Darlington, R. (2013) 'Partisan, scholarly and active: arguments for an organic public sociology of work'. *Work, Employment and Society*, 27(2), pp. 232–43.

Burawoy, M. (2005) 'For public sociology'. *American Sociological Review*, 70(1), pp. 4–28.

Button, K., Haynes, K. and Stough, R. (1998) *Flying into the Future: Air Transport Policy in the European Union*. Cheltenham: Edward Elgar.

Calder, S. (2003) *No Frills: The Truth Behind the Low-Cost Revolution in the Skies*. London: Virgin.

Callinicos, A. and Simons, M. (1985) *The Great Strike: Miners' Strike of 1984–5 and the Lessons*, London: Bookmarks.

Campbell, A. (2013) *The Burden of Power: Countdown to Iraq. The Alistair Campbell Diaries vol. 4*. London: Arrow.

Campbell-Smith, D. (1986) *Struggle for Take-Off: The British Airways Story*. London: Coronet.

Civil Aviation Authority (2004) *Effect of Liberalisation on Aviation Employment*. CAP749. London: CAA.

Civil Aviation Authority (2006) *No Frills Carriers: Revolution or Evolution*. London: CAA.

Colling, T. (1995) 'Experiencing turbulence: competition, strategic choice and the management of human resources in British Airways'. *Human Resource Management Journal*, 5(5), pp.18–32.

Colling, T. and Terry, M. (eds) (2010) *Industrial Relations: Theory and Practice*, 3rd edn. Oxford: Wiley-Blackwell.

Corke, A. (1986) *British Airways: the Path to Profitability*. London: Pinter.

Cumbers, A., Featherstone, D., MacKinnon, D., Ince, A. and Strauss, K. (2015) 'Intervening in globalisation: the spatial possibilities and institutional barriers to labour's collective agency'. *Journal of Economic Geography*, 16(1), pp. 93–108.

Curley, C. and Royle, T. (2013) 'The degradation of work and the end of the skilled emotion worker at Aer Lingus: is it all trolley dollies now?'. *Work, Employment and Society*, 27(1), pp. 105–21.

Darlington, R. (2006) 'The agitator "theory" of strikes re-evaluated strikes re-evaluated'. *Labor History*, 47(4), pp. 485–509.

Darlingon, R. and Lyddon, D. (2001) *Glorious Summer: Class Struggle in Britain, 1972*. London: Bookmarks.

Department of Business, Innovation and Skills (2013) *Trade Union Membership 2012 Statistical Bulletin*. London: Department for Business, Energy and Industrial Strategy.

Department of Business, Innovation and Skills (2017) *Trade Union Membership – Statistical Bulletin*. London: Department for Business, Energy and Industrial Strategy.

Doganis, R. (2006) *The Airline Business*, 2nd edn. London: Routledge.

Dubin, R. (1954) 'Constructive aspects of industrial conflict'. In A. Kornhauser, R. Dubin and N. Ross (eds), *Industrial Conflict*, pp. 37–47. New York: McGraw Hill.

Dukes, R. (2010) 'The right to strike under UK law: not much more than a slogan? Metrobus v Unite the Union'. *Industrial Law Journal*, 39(1), pp. 82–91.

Dukes, R. (2011) 'The Right to Strike under UK Law: Something More than a Slogan'. *Industrial Law Journal*, 40(3), pp. 302–11.

Dunlop, J.T. (1958) *Industrial Relations Systems*. Carbondale, IL: Southern Illinois University Press.

Eagleton, T. (1997) *Marx*. London: Routledge.

Edwards, P. (ed.) (2003) *Industrial Relations: Theory and Practice (Industrial Relations in Context)*, 2nd edn. Oxford: Wiley-Blackwell.

'The Edwards Report – Principal Recommendations' (1969) *Flight International*, 745, 8 May.

Eldridge, J. (1968) *Industrial Disputes – Essays in the Sociology of Industrial Relations*. London: Routledge and Kegan Paul.

Eldridge, J.E.T. (1973) 'Industrial conflict: some problems of theory and method'. In J. Child (ed.), *Man and Organization: the Search for Explanation and Social Relevance*, pp. 158–64. London: George Allen and Unwin.

Ewing, K. (2011) *Fighting Back: Resisting Union Busting and Strike-Breaking in the British Airways Dispute*. London: Institute of Employment Rights.

Ewing, K. and Hendy, J. (2013) *Reconstruction after the crisis: a manifesto for collective Bargaining*. London: Institute of Employment Rights.

Foster, J. and Woolfson, J. (1986) *The Politics of the UCS Work-In*. London: Lawrence and Wishart.

Franzosi, R. (1995) *The Puzzle of Strikes: Class and State Strategies in Postwar Italy*. Cambridge: Cambridge University Press.

Gall, G. (2003) *The Meaning of Militancy? Postal Workers and Industrial Relations*. Aldershot: Ashgate.

Gall, G. (2017) 'Injunctions as a legal weapon in collective industrial disputes'. *British Journal of Industrial Relations*, 55(1), pp 187–214.

Godard, J. (2017) *Industrial Relations, Economy and Society*, 5th edn. Toronto: Captus Press.

Godard, J. (2011) 'What has happened to strikes?'. *British Journal of Industrial Relations*, 49(2), pp. 282–305.

Gouldner, A. (1954) *Wildcat Strike: A Study in Worker-Management Relationships*. New York: Harper.

Greene, A-M., Hogan, J. and Grieco, M. (2003) 'E-collectivism and distributed discourse; new opportunities for trade union democracy'. *Industrial Relations Journal*, 34(2), pp. 282–89.

Gregory, M. (2000) *Dirty Tricks – The Inside Story of British Airways' Secret War Against Richard Branson's Virgin Atlantic*. London: Little Brown and Company.

Groves, S. and Merritt, V. (2018) *A Victory to Remember – The 1976 Equal Pay Strike at Trico Folberth, Brentford*. London: Lawrence and Wishart.

Grugulis, I. and Wilkinson, A. (2002) 'Managing culture at British Airways'. *Long Range Planning*, 35(2), pp. 179–94.

Guelke, A. and Smythe, J. (2000) 'The Ballot bomb: terrorism and the electoral process in Northern Ireland'. In L. Weiberg (ed.), *Political Parties and Terrorist Groups*, pp. 103–24. London: Cass.

Hale, D. (2012) *Labour Disputes – Annual Article, 2010.* London: Office for National Statistics.

Hartley, J., Kelly, J. and Nicholson, N. (1983) *Steel Strike: A Case Study in Industrial Relations.* London: Batsford.

Harvey, D. (2005) *A Brief History of Neo-liberalism.* Oxford: Oxford University Press.

Harvey, G. (2007) *Management in the Airline Industry.* London: Routledge.

Hiller, E.T. (1928) *The Strike: A Study in Collective Action.* Chicago, IL: University of Chicago Press.

Hochschild, A. (1983) *The Managed Heart: Commercialisation of Human Feeling.* Oakland, CA: University of California Press.

Hogan, J., Nolan, P. and Grieco, M. (2010) 'Unions, technologies of coordination and the changing contours of globally distributed power'. *Labor History*, 51(1), pp.29–40.

Hopfl, H., Smith, S. and Spencer, S. (1992) 'Values and valuations: the conflicts between cultural change and job cuts'. *Personnel Review*, 21(2), pp. 24–38.

Hyman, R. (1971) *Marxism and the Sociology of Trade Unions.* London: Pluto Press.

Hyman, R. (1989) *The Political Economy of Industrial Relations: Theory and Practice in a Cold Climate.* London: Macmillan.

Hyman, R. (1997) *Strikes*, 2nd edn. Glasgow: Fontana Collins.

International Labour Organization (2001) *Think Tank on the Impact of the 11 September Events on Civil Aviation*, Geneva, 29–30 October.

Kars, B. (1958) *Diary of a Strike.* Urbana, IL: University of Illinois Press.

Kelly, J. (1996) 'Union militancy and social partnership'. In P. Ackers, C. Smith and P. Smith (eds), *The New Workplace and Trade Unions.* London: Routledge.

Kelly, J. (1998) *Rethinking Industrial Relations.* London: Routledge.

Kelly, J. (2015) 'Conflict: trends and forms of collective action'. *Employee Relations*, 37(6), pp. 720–32.

Kerr, C. and Siegel, A. (1954) 'The interindustry propensity to strike – an international comparison'. In A. Kornhauser, R. Dubin and A.M. Ross (eds), *Industrial Conflict.* New York: McGraw Hill.

Lane, T. and Roberts, K. (1971) *Strike at Pilkingtons.* London: Fontana.

Lang, J. and Dodkins, G. (2011) *Bad News: The Wapping Dispute.* Nottingham: Spokesman Books.

Lange, K., Geppert, M., Saka-Helmhout, A. and Becker-Ritterspach, F. (2015) 'Changing business models and employee representation in the airline industry: a comparison of British Airways and Deutsche Lufthansa'. *British Journal of Management*, 26(3), pp. 388–407.

Lavalette, M. and Kennedy, J. (1996) *Solidarity on the Waterfront: Liverpool Lock Out of 1995–6.* Liverpool: Liver Press.

Little, S. and Grieco, M. (2010) 'Big Pharma, social movements, international labor and the Internet: critical perspectives on coordination'. *Labor History*, 51(1), pp. 71–86.

Logan, J. (2006) 'The Union Avoidance Industry in the United States'. *British Journal of Industrial Relations*, 44(4), pp. 657–75.

Lyddon, D. (2015) 'The changing pattern of UK strikes, 1964–2014'. *Employee Relations*, 37(6), pp. 733–45.

Lyddon, D., Cao, X., Meng, Q. and Lu, J. (2015) 'A strike of "unorganised workers" in a Chinese car factory: the Nanhai Honda events of 2010'. *Industrial Relations Journal*, 46(2), pp. 134–52.

Marginson, P. (2015) 'The changing nature of collective employment relations'. *Employee Relations*, 37(6), pp. 645–57.

Marren, B. (2016) 'The Liverpool Dock Strike, 1995-8: a resurgence of solidarity in the age of globalisation'. *Labor History*, 57(4), pp. 463–81.

Martin, R. (1992) *Bargaining Power*. Oxford: Clarendon Press.

McGurk, J. (2000) 'The deregulation of airline employment in the USA and Europe: an emerging comparison'. PhD thesis. Glasgow: University of Glasgow.

McLagen, G. (2003) *Bent Coppers: The Inside Story of Scotland Yard's Battle Against Police Corruption*. London: Orion.

Millward, N., Bryson, A. and Forth, J. (2000), *All Change at Work?* London: Routledge.

Milne, S. (2014) *The Enemy Within: The Secret War Against the Miners*, 4th edn. London: Verso.

Moore, S. (2004) 'Union mobilisation and employer counter-mobilisation in the statutory recognition process'. In J. Kelly and P. Willman (eds), *Union Organisation and Activity*. London: Routledge.

Moore, S. (2011) *New Trade Union Activists: Class Consciousness or Social Identity?* Basingstoke: Palgrave Macmillan.

Moore, S., Wright, T. and Taylor, P. (2018) *Fighting Fire: A History of the Fire Brigades Union*. London: New Internationalist.

Office for National Statistics (2013) *Labour Disputes – Annual Article*. London: ONS.

Office for National Statistics (2017) *Labour Disputes in the UK: 2017*. London: ONS. Available at www.ons.gov.uk/employmentandlabourmarket/peopleinwork/workplacedisputesandworkingconditions/articles/labourdisputes/2017#cause-of-disputes.

Oxenbridge, S., Wallace, J., White, L., Tiernan, S. and Lansbury, L. (2010) 'A comparative analysis of restructuring employment relationships in Qantas and Aer Lingus: different routes, similar destinations'. *The International Journal of Human Resource Management*, 21(2), pp. 180–96.

Parker, D. (2009) *The Official History of Privatisation, Volume 1, The Formative Years (1970–1987)*. London: Routledge.

Pearson, R., Sundari, A. and McDowell, L. (2010) 'Striking issues: from labour process to industrial dispute at Grunwick and Gate Gourmet'. *Industrial Relations Journal*, 41(5), pp. 408–28.

Peteraf, M. and Reed, R. (2007) 'Managerial discretion and internal alignment under regulatory constraints and change'. *Strategic Management Journal*, 28(11), pp. 1089–1112.

Portelli, A. (1991) *The Death of Luigi Trastulli and Other Stories: Form and Meaning in Oral History*. New York: State University of New York Press.

Prassl, J. (2011) 'To strike to serve? Industrial action at British Airways'. *Industrial Law Journal*, 40(1), pp. 82–91.

Rimmington, S. (2001) *Open Secret: The Autobiography of the Former Director General of MI5*. London: Hutchinson.

Roberts, M. (2016) *The Long Depression: Marxism and the Global Crisis of Capitalism*. Chicago, IL: Haymarket Books.

Rowbotham, S. (1973) *Hidden from History: 300 Years of Women's Oppression and the Fight Against It*. London: Pluto Press.

Sarina, T. and Lansbury, R.D. (2013) 'Flying high and low? Strategic choice and employment relations in Qantas and Jetstar'. *Asia Pacific Journal of Human Resources*, 51(4), pp. 437–53.

Shalev, M. (1992) 'The resurgence of labour quiescence'. In M. Regini (ed.), *The Future of Labour Movements*, pp. 102–32. London: Sage.

Shopes, L. (2016) 'Editing oral history for publication'. In R. Perks and A. Thomson (eds), *The Oral History Reader*, 3rd edn, pp. 470–90. London: Routledge.

Shorter, E. and Tilly, C. (1974) *Strikes in France, 1830–1968*. Cambridge: Cambridge University Press.

Siefert, R. and Sibley, T. (2005) *United they Stand: The Story of the UK Firefighters Dispute, 2002–4*. London: Lawrence and Wishart.

Simms, M. and Charlwood, A. (2010) 'Trade unions: power and influence in a changed context'. In T. Colling and M. Terry (eds), *Industrial Relations: Theory and Practice*, 3rd edn. Chichester: Wiley.

Simons, M. (1984) *Striking Back: Photographs of the Great Miners' Strike, 1984–5*. London: Bookmarks.

Simpson, B. (2013) 'The labour injunction and industrial action ballots'. *Industrial Law Journal*, 42(1), pp. 54–60.

Skeggs, B. (1997) *Formations of Class and Gender*. London: Sage.

Strike, N. (2009) *Strike By Name*. London: Bookmarks.

Sundari, A. and Pearson, R. (2018) *Striking women*. Chadwell Heath: Lawrence and Wishart.

Taylor, P. (2013) *Performance Management and the New Workplace Tyranny*, Report for Scottish Trades Union Congress, Glasgow, www.stuc.org.uk/files/Document%20download/Workplace%20tyranny/STUC%20Performance%20Management%20Executive%20Summary%20final.pdf.

Taylor, P., Cunningham, I., Newsome, K. and Scholarios, D. (2010) '"Too scared to go sick": reformulating the research agenda on sickness absence'. *Industrial Relations Journal*, 41(4), pp. 270–88.

Taylor, P. and Moore, S. (2015) 'Cabin crew collectivism: labour process and the roots of mobilisation in the British Airways dispute 2009–11'. *Work, Employment and Society*, 29(1), pp. 79–98.

Thaxter, D.J. (2009) *The History of British Caledonian Airways, 1928–1988*, 2nd edn. David J. Thaxter (4 Jan. 2011).

Thornley, C. and Thornqvist, C. (2009) 'Where's the enemy? A comparison of the local government workers' strike of July 2002 in the UK and the municipal workers' strike of spring 2003 in Sweden'. Paper presented to BJIR Conference in honour of Richard Human, London, 28–9 May.

Turnbull, P., Blyton, P. and Harvey, G. (2004) 'Cleared for take-off? Management-labour partnership in the European civil aviation industry'. *European Journal of Industrial Relations*, 18(3), pp. 287–307.

Upchurch, M. (2010) *Creating a Sustainable Work Environment in British Airways*. London: Middlesex Business School.

Upchurch, M. (2013) 'The internet, social media and the workplace'. *International Socialism Journal*, 14(1), pp. 119–38.

Upchurch, M. and Grassman, R. (2016) 'Striking with social media: the contested (online) terrain of workplace conflict'. *Organization*, 23(5), pp. 639–56.

Van der Velden, S., Dribbusch, H., Lyddon, D. and Vandale, K. (2001) *Strikes Around the World: Case Studies of 15 Countries*. Amsterdam: Aksant Academic Publishers.

Van Wanrooy, B., Bewley, H., Bryson, A., Forth, J., Freeth, S., Stokes, L. and Wood, S. (2013) *Employment Relations in the Shadow of the Recession: Findings from the 2011 Workplace Employment Relations Study*. London: Macmillan International Higher Education.

Virdee, S. (2014) *Racism, Class and the Racialized Outsider*. Basingstoke: Palgrave Macmillan.

Williams, S. (2014) *Introducing Employment Relations: A Critical Approach*, 4th edn. Oxford: Oxford University Press.

Williams, S. and Adam-Smith, D. (2000) *Contemporary Employment Relations: A Critical Introduction*, 2nd edn. Oxford: Oxford University Press.

Winterton, J. and Winterton, R. (1993) *Coal, Crisis and Conflict: 1984–5 Miners' Strike in Yorkshire*. Manchester: Manchester University Press.

Woolfson, C. and Foster, J. (1988) *Track Record: The Story of the Caterpillar Occupation*. London: Verso.

Wright, E.O. (2000) 'Working-class power, capitalist-class interests and class compromise'. *American Journal of Sociology*, 105(4), pp. 957–1002.

Yow, V. (2016) 'Interviewing Techniques and Strategies'. In R. Perks and A. Thomson (eds), *The Oral History Reader*, 3rd edn, pp. 153–79. London: Routledge.

Index

Parkinson, Cecil 26
pay xvii, 2, 16, 20–1, 23, 32, 34–5, 37–8,
    45, 48, 49, 61, 66, 84, 119, 123, 125,
    142, 144, 152–5, 165, 168–9, 171,
    178, 180–2, 186
pensions 21, 34, 36, 153–4
picket line viii, x, 5, 7, 12, 14, 33, 42,
    91–2, 98–100, 105, 110–16, 128, 138,
    146
Pilkington strikers 5–6, 141, 166–7, 187
pilot forum 86
pilots' union, Vereinigung Cockpit
    (VC) 153
pluralist 3
political consciousness 143
Post Office 63
postal ballot 33, 76
preflight briefing 39, 51–2
Preliminary Investigations (PI) 85, 87
Professional Cabin Crew Council
    (PCCC) 45
Project/Operation Columbus vii, ix,
    xvii, 14, 36–7, 50–1, 53, 55
Promotion 32, 65, 70, 84
public support 46, 118
publicity 33, 102–4
purser xv, 10, 39, 60, 69, 74, 84, 100,
    102, 116, 128, 134, 163–5

Qantas 43, 182, 191, 208, 209
Qatar Airways aircraft 153

Rail Maritime and Transport workers'
    union (RMT) 112
Reagan, President 25
redundancies xvii, 21, 24–5, 34, 39, 61,
    75–6, 158–9
retirement age 154
Richardson, Oliver 122–5, 163
right to strike vii, xvii, 14, 17, 40–1,
    74–5, 82, 158, 169, 176, 179, 182, 185
room parties 53
Royal Mail 9, 40
Ryanair 27, 44, 80, 81, 86, 112, 143,
    154, 174, 175, 202

Safety reps 92–3
Sandown Race Course ix, 39, 46
Scabbin' Crew News 85–7, 180
Scargill, Arthur 111
Second World War 9
secondary industrial action 21, 36
Secret operations ('Operation Covent
    Garden' and 'Operation Barbara') 26
SEP (Safety and Emergency Procedure)
    62, 92
service standards 60, 66
settlement of dispute 14, 118–19,
    124–6, 153, 160–1
sexuality 8, 10, 17, 118, 145–6, 155–6
shareholders 30, 89–90
Short haul 10, 14, 31, 35, 37–8, 44, 57,
    59–60, 64, 68, 80, 100
sickness absence 67, 179, 189
Sky News 144
social identity 138, 188
social media18, 46–8, 84, 177–8, 180,
    190
socialism 137, 178, 180, 190
SOGAT (Society of Graphical and
    Allied Trades) 8
solidarity x, 7, 13–14, 21, 35, 53, 83,
    91, 101, 103, 113, 115, 143, 145, 156,
    167, 187–8
staff travel xiii, xviii, xix, 49, 70, 79, 91,
    99, 111, 119, 136, 144, 151, 153, 178
Stansted Airport 27
Star Alliance 23
Steel strike 8, 186, 207
sticker campaigns 102–3
stress 88, 99, 125–6, 129–30, 134, 150,
    152
strike action viii, ix, x, xvii–xx, 1, 3,
    5, 7, 9, 12, 14–16, 18–19, 21, 33,
    36–7, 39, 41, 47–8, 67, 71, 74–6,
    78–9, 81–2, 88, 98, 100, 102, 118–20,
    137–8, 140, 142, 150, 152, 154–5,
    157–61, 170, 176, 180
strike breaking vii, 41, 48, 80, 82, 88,
    173, 179–81, 186
strike fund 113, 133